PERGAMON INTERNATIONAL LIBRARY
of Science, Technology, Engineering and Social Studies

*The 1000-volume original paperback library in aid of education,
industrial training and the enjoyment of leisure*

Publisher: Robert Maxwell, M.C.

A Career
in Catering

Choosing a Course

THE PERGAMON TEXTBOOK
INSPECTION COPY SERVICE

An inspection copy of any book published in the Pergamon International Library will gladly
be sent to academic staff without obligation for their consideration for course adoption or
recommendation. Copies may be retained for a period of 60 days from receipt and returned if
not suitable. When a particular title is adopted or recommended for adoption for class use and
the recommendation results in a sale of 12 or more copies, the inspection copy may be retained
with our compliments. The publishers will be pleased to receive suggestions for revised
editions and new titles to be published in this important International Library.

INTERNATIONAL SERIES IN HOSPITALITY MANAGEMENT

Editor-in-Chief: JOHN O'CONNOR, Head, Department of Catering
Management
Oxford Polytechnic, England

Editors: EWOUT CASSEE
GERALD LATTIN
DONALD SMITH

This series aims to reinforce and to extend the body of knowledge of the profession of hospitality management, a profession which includes the management of hotels and other forms of accommodation; the management of catering and of food and beverage service establishments; and the management of clubs, and conference and holiday centres. The series will include textbooks, monographs and papers of value in the education, training and development of students and managers beginning their careers. It will also provide material for the continuing education of members of the profession, including managers, teachers and research workers, developing their understanding of and effectiveness within the hospitality industry.

Some Titles in the Series

ATKINSON, D.
Hotel and Catering French
Menu French

NOTICE TO READERS

Dear Reader

An invitation to Publish in and Recommend the Placing of a Standing Order to Volumes Published in this Valuable Series

---

If your library is not already a standing/continuation order customer to this series, may we recommend that you place a standing/continuation order to receive immediately upon publication all new volumes. Should you find that these volumes no longer serve your needs, your order can be cancelled at any time without notice.

The Editors and the Publisher will be glad to receive suggestions or outlines of suitable titles, reviews or symposia for editorial consideration: if found acceptable, rapid publication is guaranteed.

ROBERT MAXWELL

Publisher at Pergamon Press

A Career in Catering
Choosing a Course

by

ROY HAYTER

PERGAMON PRESS
OXFORD · NEW YORK · TORONTO · SYDNEY · PARIS · FRANKFURT

U.K.	Pergamon Press Ltd., Headington Hill Hall, Oxford OX3 0BW, England
U.S.A.	Pergamon Press Inc., Maxwell House, Fairview Park, Elmsford, New York 10523, U.S.A.
CANADA	Pergamon of Canada, Suite 104, 150 Consumers Road, Willowdale, Ontario M2J 1P9, Canada
AUSTRALIA	Pergamon Press (Aust.) Pty. Ltd., P.O. Box 544, Potts Point, N.S.W. 2011, Australia
FRANCE	Pergamon Press SARL, 24 rue des Ecoles, 75240 Paris, Cedex 05, France
FEDERAL REPUBLIC OF GERMANY	Pergamon Press GmbH, 6242 Kronberg-Taunus, Hammerweg 6, Federal Republic of Germany

First edition 1980

British Library Cataloguing in Publication Data

Hayter, Roy
A career in catering. — choosing a course. —
(International series in hospitality management)
(Pergamon international library).
1. Food service — Vocational guidance —
Great Britain
I. Title II Series
642'.47'023   TX911.2   79-41628

ISBN 0-08-024708-3 (Hardcover)
ISBN 0-08-024707-5 (Flexicover)

Printed in Great Britain by A. Wheaton & Co. Ltd., Exeter

A. M. D. G.

Contents

Acknowledgements

MY grateful thanks are due first of all to those who made the writing of such a book possible: John O'Connor at Oxford Polytechnic, editor of the series, Peggy Ducker and Alan Radford of Pergamon Press, Elizabeth Gadsby and Ann Nixon of the HCIMA. To all my colleagues at the HCIMA I owe a great debt of gratitude; Susan Rogers deserves special thanks for her help in correcting all my typing, and Vi Neary for the regular cups of coffee while I typed late at night. Malcolm Allcock put up with my bad temper at home, and undertook much of the proof reading.

Many kind people helped me with my research on the history of catering education: Peter Stevens of the City and Guilds of London Institute not only loaned me his office and back copies of the Institute's Broadsheet, but spent a lot of his valuable time solving subsequent mysteries. The principal of Westminster College, Mr E. A. Bradley, put the College's archives at my disposal, and Miss J. O. Brown, the College Librarian, helped me greatly with my research; the first three photographs between pages 70 and 71 come from these archives. Miss Claudine Morgan, Principal of Queen Margaret College, Edinburgh, loaned valuable historical material; she and Miss Jean Harrison-Prentice helped me with the photograph that appears opposite page 71. Work by Paul Johnson and Roger Norman also helped me with this aspect of the book.

Pat Snell and Anthony Coles of the City of the Guilds of London Institute not only spent a lot of time providing me with information, but then had the patience to check and correct my draft for a large section of Chapter 5. The help and assistance I received from Mr A. G. Bucklitsch of the Guild of Sommeliers regarding the Guild's courses was invaluable. Miss S. Y. Hay, Assistant Chief Officer of SCOTBEC, was most co-operative and helpful too.

Dr Madeline Melia, Advisory Officer of TEC, and Mr J. R. Kennedy, Education Officer of SCOTEC, took a lot of trouble checking over my drafts, providing me with additional information and re-checking. Cecelia Flack of the Joint Committee was most helpful providing copies of National Diploma regulations and lists of colleges.

Professor Philip Nailon helped me at several stages, with the provision of many photographs, one of which appears opposite page 119, with the checking of both the degree entry and the Management Development Programme entry. David Gee kindly loaned me old articles on the Scottish Hotel School, Professor John Beavis checked the degree entry. Mr Len Ambery, Dean of Hollings Faculty and Dr George Wilson, Head of Department at Manchester Polytechnic helped with snippets of useful information and by checking the degree entry. The following people also helped me in this way: Hamish Davidson, Mrs Nancy Blackburn,

Roger Benson and Joan Rushworth, Mary Cobb, John O'Connor, Derek Gladwell and Rab Larmour.

Over forty people helped me with the profiles. Those who agreed to participate must be especially thanked. They devoted a lot of time — providing the information, normally writing it so well that I had very few changes to make, checking drafts, and obtaining suitable photographs. I am no less thankful to those who let me interview them. I would like to express deep gratitude to the kind people who provided the contacts, particularly Victor Ceserani, Bob Kidner, Mary Cobb, June Collis, Les Pennington, Derek Black and Joan Greenfield. Many people at the HCITB helped me: Duncan Rutter and Bill Guthrie particularly.

Mr J. G. Ransom, Head of Department of Tourism, Catering and Hotel Administration at Dorset Institute of Higher Education provided me with the two photographs between pages 118 and 119 that were taken at the Dorset Institute.

Dr Bernard Hawes was one of several people who helped in providing information for the construction of the college lists in Chapter 9.

Mr J. G. Miles, Director of the Brewers' Society Training Centre, provided me with comprehensive material on the courses for the licensed trade described in Chapter 8. Many people helped with the information in Chapter 10, some of whom I have already mentioned. Others include: Mr P. B. Meredith of the BHRCA, Mr R. J. Down of the Civic Catering Association, Mr J. L. Shakeshaft of the Cookery and Food Association, Dr Edwin Kerr and Dr David Billing of the CNAA, Mr R. C. Miller, President of the Association of Marine Catering Superintendents, Mr Stuart Vass of the College Caterers Association, Mr Russell Kett of BAHA, and Mr I. A. M. Harkness of the FBMA.

Roy Hayter BA MHCIMA MBIM

1

A Career in Catering

Introductory chapter outlining the extent of the book, explaining the division
of the material

"OPPORTUNITIES" is a word that occurs frequently in this book. The reason is quite simple: for those who seek a career in catering there are great opportunities and there are many.

Not only is the industry itself extraordinarily diverse, but so are the means of preparing for a career in it and — looking ahead a little — of keeping up to date with new techniques, of keeping in touch with fellow professionals, and of advancing the status of the industry.

Choosing a Course

This book provides information on the different means of preparing for a career in catering. It deals comprehensively with over eighty-five different courses from craft level to degree.

For school leavers suitable courses include those demanding two or three 'A' levels, while others require no formal qualifications whatsoever.

For those who have already commenced a career in the industry there are large numbers of courses, some of which have been designed for particular career paths, whilst others provide a means of achieving a management qualification.

For mature people, including those who are new entrants to the industry, there are a number of intensive short courses. There are also a growing number of opportunities for such people to undertake full-time or part-time study for a management qualification.

Finally there are courses designed for those already working in the industry who want to up-date themselves on new techniques.

Each of these courses is described in detail. The information provided normally includes an outline of the syllabus, the aims of the course, the entry requirements, the length, mode of study, examination arrangements, any industrial experience requirements, and the award-making body responsible.

Value judgements are not made at any point, about any course. Great importance has been attached to providing accurate, factual information. In all cases the principal source of information has been the award-making body responsible for the course. Usually this information has been supplemented by facts gleaned from wide reading and research. Major sections have been checked by senior officers of the organisation concerned.

A Spectrum of Time

Catering education is constantly evolving. Although the first schools of cookery were established in the 1870s, and the first hotel school in 1910, the major developments in catering education have taken place since the end of the Second World War. Hardly a year has passed since then without a new course appearing.

A major aim of this book has therefore been to put all the different courses that are currently available, as well as those that are about to commence, in their context of time. "Nothing is new" is not an accurate expression for describing catering education. Titles of courses frequently change, syllabuses are constantly being reviewed and revised, entry requirements change. The structure of further and higher education itself changes from time to time.

Pattern of Provision

What has not changed is the pattern of provision. Expressed in the simplest possible way, education and training for a career in the catering industry falls into four categories:

*the opportunities for acquiring craft skills
*training for supervisory and management skills
*for the most highly qualified, degree courses in hotel and catering studies
*for mature people entering the industry, and for those already in the industry, the opportunities for catching up.

A chapter is devoted to the courses which fall into each of these categories. Chapter 5 describes in detail the courses provided by the City and Guilds of London Institute, as well as those of the Regional Examining Bodies, the Guild of Sommeliers, the Wine and Spirit Education Trust . . . to name but a few . . . and includes supervisory courses.

Chapter 6 describes all the courses suitable for those aspiring to supervisory and management positions in the industry, except for the degree courses which are described in Chapter 7. The new courses of study of the Technician Education Council and the Scottish Technical Education Council are carefully explained in Chapter 6.

Chapter 8 describes the opportunities for "catching up".

Courses have in fact existed to serve all these needs for many years. One of the most famous schools of cookery held its first class in 1874 — the National Training School of Cookery. The first hotel school to be established in the UK was the London County Council Westminster Technical Institute, in 1910.

In their history, described briefly in Chapter 4, there is much of interest, for these two colleges have played an important, if very different, role in the development of the industry. Scotland, which has often been ahead of developments in the rest of the UK, and certainly never far behind, should not be ignored either. The Edinburgh School of Cookery, opened publicly in 1875, has a colourful history typical of many of the colleges throughout the UK that today offer catering courses.

Whilst craft courses may appear to those in the industry to have changed beyond recognition from the time they were at college, the pattern of provision has not altered significantly. Since the early initiatives of the City and Guilds of London Institute and the Hotel and Catering Institute, there have been courses for food preparation, the service of food and wine, housekeeping, book-keeping and reception, hygiene and nutrition.

Management courses have perhaps changed less frequently than craft courses, and have done so on a ten year cycle. Major changes took place in 1959, 1969 and in 1979/80. The history of these changes, and the role played in them by the professional bodies, is also described in Chapter 4.

1980 will see the introduction of new courses of study leading to Technician Education Council and Scottish Technical Education Council awards — TEC and SCOTEC. These new awards are described in detail in Chapter 6, as are the Ordinary and Higher National Diploma courses which they will shortly replace. The courses of the Hotel, Catering and Institutional Management Association are also described in this chapter.

It is one thing to know precisely how many degree courses in hotel and catering studies are available at a particular point in time, to list them and to describe them. This book does this, in Chapter 7, but it also explains how the degree courses have developed and why and what other postgraduate and post experience higher awards are available.

An Outline of the Industry

In the years since the end of the Second World War, the hotel and catering industry has made great strides in the eyes of the general public and government. The influences that have contributed to this phenomenon include the work of professional, trade and government bodies, changes in the economic structure of Britain, and a growth in both domestic and international tourism.

These influences are explained in Chapter 2. The results of the Hotel and Catering Industry Training Board's Tier I study indicate that the industry employs over two million people. It is however a heterogeneous industry consisting of units of many different types often engaging in a combination of activities. While career progression in the welfare sectors is fairly well defined, elsewhere the picture on salaries and conditions of employment is less clear. By and large it is an industry that rewards for results: there is great opportunity for people with talent to reach high positions.

Career Patterns — At Work in the Industry

No two persons' career paths in the hotel and catering industry are identical. Few are even similar! A description by one person of the industry would fail to do it justice.

Chapter 3, a major section of this book, has therefore been devoted to the profiles of some thirty-five different people, men and women, working in different sectors of the industry, in different jobs, from different courses. Some have come to this industry from another, others have had no formal college education at all. Some are making a start in their careers, a few are managing directors, some have degrees, and even master degrees, others have craft qualifications.

Some are working in large companies, others are running their own businesses.

The sectors of the industry covered include: hotels, restaurants, employee feeding, school meals, clubs, transport catering, the Forces, the licensed trade, hospital catering and domestic services, halls of residence.

Finding a College

As courses change from time to time, so do the names of the colleges offering them. The precise range of courses offered by any particular college varies, sometimes from one term to another. The most accurate source of information on the courses available at a college is the college itself.

Chapter 9, an important section of this book, is devoted to "Finding a College", with basic information on fees and grants, and a list of over 260 colleges with an indication of the level course they offer (craft, diploma, higher diploma, and degree), and the full postal address. The addresses and telephone numbers of Local Education Authorities are provided, for advice regarding grants.

Throughout this book, when the term "college" is used in a general sense, it is meant to include all those establishments in further and higher education offering courses in hotel and catering studies: universities, polytechnics, central institutions, colleges of further education, technical colleges and institutes of higher education.

Agencies

The final section of this book is devoted to a description of the work and role of the different organisations that are encountered both in catering education and in a career in the industry. This section includes the different award-making bodies, as well as trade and professional bodies.

Some thirty-five different organisations are described in Chapter 10.

Addresses

In addition to the comprehensive address list provided in Chapter 9, which was painstakingly constructed from ten different sources, at the end of Chapters 2, 5, 6, 7, 8 and 10 the addresses and telephone numbers of the different organisations mentioned are listed.

The index at the back of the book cross-references all details.

A More Informed Choice

This book aims to provide the depth and extent of information that will make it possible for students, as well as their parents, teachers, careers officers and future employers, to understand better the complex catering education scene.

It can be difficult to choose between one course and another. This book does not make the choice, but it does aim to provide the information necessary for it to be made with full knowledge of all the facts.

A Guide for Employers

With the continually changing scene in catering education, it is difficult for employers to keep up to date with the meaning of qualifications job applicants present them with. It is harder still for them to relate these to qualifications they themselves hold.

The trade press has often been critical of catering education, regretting the need for changes, sometimes failing to see the significance of changes elsewhere in technical education, or to understand the effect they have on catering education. The attitude of employers has been affected by this comment, and by the absence until now of an authoritative account of the total provision, with a description of its development.

2

An Outline of the Industry

The importance of the hotel and catering industry. The influences that have contributed to this phenomenon: growth in consumer expenditure, changes in the economic and social structure of Britain, the rapid development of international tourism, recognition of the value of service industries as employers and the work of professional, trade and government bodies. Conditions of employment. The industry's structure. Useful addresses. Trade publications.

THE hotel and catering industry provides a fascinating range of career opportunities. The next chapter, which is devoted to a description of the careers of thirty-five different people, illustrates the diversity that exists. It is a heterogeneous industry consisting of units of many different types often engaging in a combination of activities.

The profiles in Chapter 3 fall into the following groups, reflecting broadly the component sectors of the industry: hotels, restaurants, the Forces, hospital catering, hospital domestic services, school meals service, residential accommodation, employee feeding, clubs, public houses. The careers of four chefs are described separately. The chapter concludes with the careers of six "specialists" working in the fields of personnel management, sales, consultancy, accountancy and training.

The profiles illustrate not only how rewarding a career in catering can be, but some of the personal attributes demanded. The hours of work can be long. The conditions of employment vary. The pay does not always seem attractive. In what has been described as a "people industry" an important requirement is the ability to please guests, even when they seem utterly unreasonable. It is equally important to be able to work effectively with fellow employees, junior and senior.

The article which appeared in a number of London and regional papers in February 1935 described some of the qualities required of an hotel manager in timeless words. It was describing a new course at the only hotel school of the day (now Westminster College).

"Boys of the public school type who wish to become hotel managers are to have a special two year course at the LCC Hotel and Restaurant School.

"There they will learn some of the thousand things that the hotel manager — the man with a genius for always doing the right thing at the right moment — must know. The '100 per cent' hotel chief must know how to receive a King, or how to teach a waiter his job, or give a little advice to the chef.

"He must be a man who keeps cool and thinks of the right 'way out' whether the hotel catches fire or the two most distinguished guests each complain that they have been given the second best room.

"In fact as everybody who has watched him knows, the chief of a big hotel must be something of a superman and have a 'personality' that makes a duke or a humble bed and breakfast visitor feel equally at home.

"Boys of 17 and over are eligible to do the course. They need not be public school boys — anybody may be admitted — but each student must first pass an examination to see whether he is the right type to come into the industry . . . Languages will be taught. After two years of this full time training will a boy be able to take control of an hotel? Oh! dear no. But he will be able to take an appointment in a big hotel and be very useful there."

Influences on the Development of the Industry

In the years since the end of the Second World War the hotel and catering industry has made great strides in its economic performance and is seen to have done so in the eyes of the general public and government. The provision of hospitality to the weary traveller has of course always been an important service and the beginning of catering and hotel-keeping can be traced back to ancient civilisations. But the industry is not an easy one to define and its value has only recently been quantified in economic terms. Estimates of the manpower employed by the industry still vary widely. There is no accurate figure for the number of hotels in the country. Even the word hotel is subject to differing uses.

In the last forty years recognition of the value of the industry has grown markedly. This growth has been matched by an improvement in the quality and provision of education and training, described in Chapter 4.

The first statutory recognition of hotel and catering services was the Catering Wages Act 1943 which resulted in the setting-up of the Catering Wages Commission and of Wages Boards for the industry. The Commission published several reports on a wide range of aspects of the industry including the 1946 report "Training for the Catering Industry", which summarised the state of catering education and made important recommendations.

The emergence of an identity for the industry was reinforced by its inclusion in the Standard Industrial Classification 1948 and its subsequent successors. Most of the available statistical information about the industry is based on the Standard Industrial Classification. One of the consequences of this is that the data base is stronger for the commercial element of the industry. Thus the wide range of organisations operated with a view to profit are included: hotels, motels, holiday camps, guest houses, boarding houses, hostels, restaurants, cafes, snack bars, milk bars, coffee bars, refreshment rooms, tea shops, function rooms, fish and chip shops, ice cream parlours, public houses, residential and licensed clubs, industrial canteens and school canteens (the last two if operated by catering contractors).

The Classification does not include hotel and catering activities provided as a service to some other main function of the organisation. Non-catering companies operating their own staff restaurants, hospital meals and school meals (unless contracted out), passenger transport catering . . . are examples of activities not included.

Other influences have contributed to the growing importance of the hotel and catering industry: the growth in consumer expenditure, changes in the economic and social structure of Britain, the rapid development of international tourism, recognition of the value of service industries as employers and the work of professional, trade and government bodies.

Growth in Consumer Expenditure on Eating Out

The demand for meals and refreshments outside the home is stimulated by different situations and needs. Firstly travellers away from home usually require refreshment, particularly if their journey involves an overnight stay when accommodation will also be sought. Secondly there is a demand for refreshments and/or meals outside the home as a form of entertainment. Thirdly there is a demand for meals unconnected with travel or entertainment, from patients in hospitals, children in schools, students at college or university and men and women at work.

Before the Second World War eating out was a luxury for most people. In 1941 there were about 110 000 catering establishments of various types, from school canteens to hotels, and about 79 million meals served weekly. Food rationing, the formation of the school meals service and a great increase in the number of industrial canteens were the main influences which brought about a substantial increase by 1946. At the beginning of that year the number of establishments was

Estimate of annual expenditure on catering in the hotel and catering industry (£ million)

	April 1974 — March 1975	April 1975 — March 1976	April 1976 — March 1977
Personal meals (excluding education establishments, cost of alcoholic drink and other drinks taken without food, but including industrial catering, canteens etc.)	1223	1627	1716
Alcoholic drinks (excluding pubs and clubs)	311	375	431
Alcoholic drinks in pubs and clubs	2440	3020	3564
Non-alcoholic drinks without food	38	45	51
Educational establishments:			
School meals service (including milk)	372	497	540
Further and higher education (including universities)	62	70	77
Hospitals and penal institutions	150	170	187
Local authority and residential homes	80	90	95
Overseas tourists	125	150	210
	4801	6044	6871
Other services: cigarettes, tobacco and other goods	774	890	988
TOTAL	5575	6934	7859

Source: *Trends in Catering, Annual Report April 1976–March 1977*, Hotels and Catering EDC

put at 143 200 by the Ministry of Food, and 157 million meals were served per week.

The post-war higher standards of living and more even distribution of incomes transformed the increase into a stable trend. A survey conducted by the Hotels and Catering EDC* put the total expenditure by households on personal meals outside the home in the year to March 1977 at over £1700 million.

The figure below shows how the level of *per capita* spending on meals out varies between the different socio-economic groups, and what the trends in spending were over the three years of the Hotels and Catering EDC survey. In each of the three years, *per capita* spending was highest in the professional and managerial AB group, and lowest for the DE group (unskilled manual workers etc.). During the year 1, the two middle groups spent roughly the same amount, but in years 2 and 3, spending by the C1 group (other office and "white collar" workers) outstripped that of the C2 group (skilled manual workers).

Changes in per capita spending on meals out, by socio-economic group
(total population aged 11 and over)

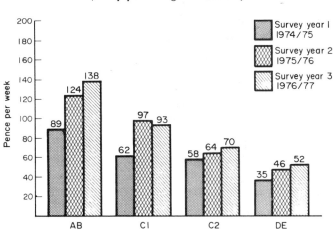

Source: *Trends in Catering, Annual Report April 1976–March 1977*, Hotels and Catering EDC

Demand for Accommodation

Demand for accommodation away from home falls into two categories. Firstly there is the requirement of the holiday-maker away from home; some hotels, notably those in resort towns, owe their existence entirely to this demand. Secondly there is the requirement of the business traveller. These are broad categories for business trips and conferences are sometimes combined with holidays and vice versa.

At the beginning of the 1950s about 3 million people, roughly 45% of the British population, spent their holidays away from home. The figure had risen to 30 million

* *Trends in Catering, A Study of Eating Out, Annual Report April 1976–March 1977*, Hotels and Catering EDC, 1978.

All tourism by British residents to destinations in Britain

Year	Nights (million)				Estimated spending (£ million)			
	Britain	England	Scotland	Wales	Britain	England	Scotland	Wales
1973	590	460	65	65	1450	1150	175	150
1974	535	415	55	65	1800	1375	200	200
1975	550	430	60	60	2150	1700	250	200
1976	545	435	50	60	2400	1925	250	250
1977	545	420	65	65	2625	2000	350	275
1978	530	405	55	65	3100	2400	375	325

Source: *British Home Tourism Survey 1978*

Accommodation used and location for holiday tourism by British residents to destinations in Britain, 1978*

	Britain	England	Scotland	Wales
Number of nights (millions)				
Holidays lasting 1 to 3 nights	55	45	5	5
Holidays lasting 4 or more nights	350	260	35	50
Accommodation used (percentage of total nights) **				
Licensed hotels	10	10	13	5
Unlicensed hotel or guest house	7	7	8	6
Holiday camp	5	5	3	8
Camping	6	5	7	8
Towed caravan	4	4	7	5
Fixed caravan	16	13	15	32
Rented flat	5	6	2	4
Other rented	8	8	7	9
Paying guest	2	2	1	3
With friend or relative	34	37	36	18
Second home	1	1	—	1
Boat	1	1	—	—
Other or in transit	1	1	1	1
Location (percentage of total nights) **				
Seaside	43	45	30	46
Small town	14	16	12	7
Large town (except London)	8	8	13	7
London	4	5	—	—
Countryside	26	22	42	34
Not sufficiently specified	4	4	3	6

*Trips that were partly to visit friends or relatives are included as holidays when the tourist described them as such. Trips that were solely to visit friends or relatives are excluded.
**Columns may add to more than 100% because more than one type of accommodation was used on some trips.
Source: *British Home Tourism Survey 1978*

at the end of the decade, 60% of the population. During the 1960s the growth came in an increase in additional holidays and in holidays spent abroad.

In 1975 about 40 million holidays of four nights or more and 31 million of between one and three nights were taken in Britain by the British population. These accounted for about 550 million nights spent away from home. Since 1975 there has been a slight decline in these figures, although spending has increased.

The hotel and catering industry is a relatively minor provider of accommodation for holidays in Britain; if holiday camp accommodation is added, its share is about one-quarter. There are significant regional and national differences.

No assessment of the business demand for accommodation was made until the late 1960s. In 1975 it was estimated that 17 million business and conference trips were made by British residents, accounting for 45 million nights. Of this figure, over half were spent in hotels and guest houses. The number of trips increased to 19 million by 1977, but then decreased in 1978 to return to the 1975 level. The number of nights also declined in 1978 from 50 million the previous year to 45 million.

Changes in the Economic and Social Structure of Britain

As the standard of living has risen so the facilities and services provided by the hotel and catering industry have become more important. In response to the greater demand the industry has grown in size and in recognition. Not only has the number of people travelling on holiday and on business increased many times over, but as real disposable incomes have grown there has been more money available for leisure activities.

The non-profit making sector of the industry has grown as much in importance as the commercial sector. Medical care and its associated facilities have improved, more employers have become aware of the value of providing catering services for their work force, the school meals service has established itself as a valued part of community life.

More leisure time and greater mobility have meant that more people have been able to enjoy travel, holidays and eating out. It is difficult to recall that in 1951 there were only 2.2 million private cars registered, and that only one per cent of the manual work force enjoyed holidays of three weeks and over.

Transport developments in the nineteenth century made tourism possible, the transport revolution of the twentieth century created tourism as a mass phenomenon. The advent of the packaged holiday has had a profound effect on the growth of tourism. Improvement in communications accompanied by greater use of the mass media for promotional activities has contributed to the development of the hotel and catering industry.

Tourism

The growth of domestic tourism has been an important factor in the health of the hotel and catering industry. It has been the growth of international tourism however that has had the major impact on the government's attitude to the industry.

Before the Second World War the peak year for overseas visitors to Britain was 1937, when about 500 000 visitors came. By 1963 the number of visitors from the US alone reached 500 000, and by 1973, US visitors had tripled in number to 1.5 million.

In 1975 the number of visitors to Britain reached 9.5 million. Examining the demand for accommodation in the same year about 33 million nights were spent in the hotel sector by overseas visitors of which about 7 million were for business trips. About half the total number of bed nights were spent in private homes.

The increase in the number of visitors continued through 1975 to 1978 when over 12.6 million arrivals were recorded and spending reached £2502 million. UK residents going abroad in 1978 spent £1548 million.

These figures emphasise the value of tourism to the country's balance of payments. In 1978 foreign tourists' spending in Britain accounted for nearly 14% of all invisible earnings, and just under 5% of all exports.

The proportion of overseas arrivals at hotels in England and London reached a peak in 1976 at 19% and 64% respectively. In London in 1978 with the average yearly room occupancy running at 75%, overseas arrivals accounted for 58% of the total.

The Henley Centre for Forecasting has recently estimated that 80% of the total number employed in hotels and other residential establishments is due to tourism, both domestic and international.

Manpower

Two studies published in the 1970s estimated the total manpower employed in the hotel and catering industry: the Department of Employment Manpower Studies No 11, *Catering*, published in 1972, and the Hotel and Catering Industry Training Board's report *Manpower in the Hotel and Catering Industry*, published in 1978. The regular estimates of employees in employment published by the Department of Employment only cover those sectors of the industry defined by the Standard Industrial Classification.

Manpower Studies No 11, *Catering*, estimated that nearly 1.4 million persons were employed in the hotel and catering industry in 1969, that is about 5.7% of the total civilian labour force in Great Britain.

The Hotel and Catering Industry Training Board's survey to establish basic data about the total industry work force was undertaken in 1977. The Board's report published in 1978 compared the previous " best estimate" (based on a combination of several sources) and the results of its own Tier I study (the results of Tier II had not been published at the time of going to press; the objectives of this phase of the study include measuring the movement of employees into and out of the industry, between sectors and between occupational groups, and producing profiles of individuals employed in the industry).

Catering staff by sector and main occupational group, 1969 (thousands)

Main occupational group	Sector									Total
	Hotels	Industrial catering	Hospital catering	Restaurants	Public houses	Local authorities	Universities	Other private education	Clubs	
Managerial and clerical	22.4	11.9	2.5	21.7	80.0	3.2	1.3	1.0	5.0	149.0
Reception, front office and hall	38.8									38.8
Housekeeping and linen-room	64.4		0.6							65.0
Kitchen and food preparation	62.8	81.6	24.3	62.2	15.0	134.1	4.4	10.0	15.0	409.4
Restaurant, food and beverage service	64.8	65.6	15.4	90.9	13.0	49.9	5.6	1.0	14.0	320.2
Bar, cellar and lounge	25.9			8.2	104.0		0.3		6.0	144.4
Stores and equipment	1.6			1.2						2.8
Others (including those not classified)	1.3	30.9	3.2	29.2	4.0	21.9	1.7	4.9	10.0	107.1
Staff in hotels and restaurants employing less than 5 or 6 staff	95.0			45.0						140.0
All catering staff	377.0	190.0	46.0	258.4	216.0	209.1	13.3	16.9	50.0	1376.7
Non-catering staff including maintenance	14.0			0.8						14.8
TOTAL	391.0	190.0	46.0	259.2	216.0	209.1	13.3	16.9	50.0	1391.5

Source: Department of Employment Manpower Studies, No 11, *Catering*, HMSO 1972

The number of employees include all persons full-time, part-time, seasonal, temporary and casual:

Category of employer	Tier I		"Best estimates"	
	No of employees (thousands)	Percentage %	No of employees (thousands)	Percentage %
Hotels	485	22.7	285	19
Guest houses	48	2.3	95	6
Restaurants	209	9.8	212	14
Cafes	132	6.2		
Contract and industrial catering	176	8.2	197	13
Public houses	460	21.5	308	20
Clubs	133	6.2	69	4
Hospitals	45	2.1	45	3
Education	430	20.1	297	20
Hostels—Residential	19	0.9	14*	1
TOTAL	2137	100.0	1522	100

*Local Authority (excluding education)

The HCITB manpower study adopted seven broad levels as a basis for subsequent analysis of occupational classification by sector of industry:

I   Senior managers, working proprietors
II   Departmental heads and managers
III Supervisors
IV   Craftsmen and technicians
V   Sub-craft employees
VI   Other catering staff
VII Non catering staff, including accounting, personnel and other specialist staff.

On this basis and using the Tier I figures the picture opposite of the industry's manpower structure emerges.

In percentage terms these indicate that 25% of all full-time employees in the industry are at Level I (senior management and working proprietors), 29% at Level V (sub-craft). The bulk of the part-time employees are at Level VI (25%).

It is possible to compare some of these figures to the 1971 census report data which estimated that about 30% of the men and women employed in the industry were in management positions however two-thirds of these were self-employed. This is regarded as characteristic of small-unit industries with a high proportion of owner-managers.

The second largest occupational group in the industry according to the 1971 census were waiters and counter hands: about 20% of the total.

	Sector	Number of employees by occupational level (thousands)						
		I	II	III	IV	V	VI	VII
Hotels	F/T	36	29	24	45	138	30	18
	P/T	2	1	4	8	112	30	8
Guest houses	F/T	20	—	—	3	1	2	—
	P/T	2	—	—	7	6	7	—
Restaurants	F/T	20	11	5	21	42	13	4
	P/T	1	1	1	5	62	21	2
Cafes	F/T	32	—	—	7	7	18	—
	P/T	3	—	—	6	19	40	—
Industrial	F/T	15	—	18	31	14	80	—
	P/T	1	—	2	10	9	62	—
Pubs & clubs	F/T	117	9	10	7	38	16	4
	P/T	10	1	13	7	251	106	4
Local authority	F/T	2	—	19	25	41	2	6
	F/T	—	—	6	7	133	6	93
TOTAL		261	52	102	189	873	433	139

Note F/T = full-time staff
   P/T = part-time staff
All employees — other than National Health Service and Local Authorities (Scotland)

The Department of Employment quarterly estimates based on the Standard Industrial Classification give an indication of trends in the numbers employed in the sectors covered.

Employees in employment, Great Britain (at June each year)

	Thousands				
	1975	1976	1977	1978	1979
Hotels and other residential establishments	255	264	280	283	289
Restaurants, cafes, snack bars	163	162	166	170	178
Public houses	230	243	250	253	260
Clubs	99	105	108	108	113
Catering contractors	69	66	68	70	69

Source: *Central Statistical Office Annual Abstract of Statistics,* 1979 edition and *Department of Employment Gazette,* October 1979

Professional and Trade Bodies

There is a variety of professional and trade associations in the hotel and catering industry. Common issues and common problems encourage co-operation and federation both between individual caterers and hoteliers and between different firms. That there are so many is a reflection of the diversity of the industry and the often highly individualistic people that work in it.

Many of the corporate bodies are described in Chapter 10. They fall into two groups: government sponsored bodies, and voluntary bodies. The second group can be sub-divided into professional bodies, personnel associations, trade unions and trade associations.

The Cookery and Food Association, which is probably the oldest surviving example from the second group, was established in 1885 with the purpose of promoting the art and science of cookery. One of the Association's earliest activities was the promotion of culinary exhibitions and competitions.

The British Hotels Restaurants and Caterers Association traces its history back to 1907, when a group of hoteliers got together to form the National Hotel Keepers Association. In the previous year the Liberal party had been elected to power and intended to abolish a third of the country's public houses, raising the compensation fund from the remaining licensees. Through the newly formed Association, the hoteliers were able to persuade the chancellor to reduce the compensation levy on bona fide hotels to one-third of the share that the licensees were to pay.

This defensive response to a problem facing a sector of the industry is a characteristic feature of the formation of trade associations in the hotel and catering industry. The British Hotels Restaurants and Caterers Association (BHRCA) has been the principal trade association for the industry since 1972, when the British Hotels and Restaurants Association merged with the Caterers' Association of Great Britain. The latter body included amongst its membership a variety of catering businesses, mainly non-residential.

A year before the formation of the BHRCA the industry's two professional bodies merged. They were the Institutional Management Association, formed in 1938, and the Hotel and Catering Institute formed in 1949. Both had made a valuable contribution in helping to raise the status of their members and thereby improve working conditions, and in stimulating the provision of educational facilities for potential entrants to the industry.

Since 1971 the Hotel Catering and Institutional Management Association has continued and built on the work of its predecessors in the fields of professionalism, education, training and services to its members. As a result of the Association's strict criteria for membership, which are based on a combination of knowledge and experience, its corporate grades of membership are now widely recognised as a qualification for managerial appointments in the industry.

The old-established management personnel associations include the Catering Managers' Association and the Industrial Catering Association with membership drawn from the welfare sector of catering, and the Hospital Caterers' Association.

Trade Unions

In contrast to the well established industries, one form of association has played a relatively minor role in the development of the hotel and catering industry: trade unions. This is largely a result of the nature of the industry and indeed of the people who work in it.

Trade union membership of hotel and catering employees has been put at about 5% of the total. The proportion varies in different sectors of the industry, health service and local authority catering having the highest, restaurants one of the lowest.

It is an industry with a reputation for high labour turnover. Foreign staff have always played an important role in running hotel and catering operations in Britain (the well publicised Garners' dispute is however an example of strong national identity strengthening trade union support). It employs a large proportion of women, and part-time and casual workers.

These factors are examples of those which have held down the growth of trade unionism in the hotel and catering industry. Consequently there is no hotel and catering workers union as such. The principal unions with hotel and catering membership are the General and Municipal Workers' Union (GMWU), the Transport and General Workers' Union (TGWU), the National Union of Railwaymen (NUR) (in British Rail's hotel and catering operations), the Union of Shop, Distributive and Allied Workers (USDAW) and the National Union of Public Employees (NUPE). The other unions represented on the TUC's Hotel and Catering Committee are the Transport Salaried Staffs' Association, the National Association of Theatrical and Kine Employees and the Bakers Union. This TUC committee acts as a co-ordinating body.

Government Bodies

The Wages Boards established in 1944 and 1945 became Wages Councils in 1959 when the Terms and Conditions of Employment Act 1959 repealed the Catering Wages Act. The Wages Councils, like the former Boards, consist of equal numbers of employer and employee representatives plus not more than three independent members including the Chairman. A Wages Council has power to make proposals for the fixing of minimum remuneration and of holidays. Once the proposals have been agreed the Council makes a Wages Order which has legal force but of course an employer is free to employ workers on more favourable terms.

The second governmental body of importance is the National Economic Development Council established in 1962. The Council established a series of Economic Development Committees (EDCs) for particular industries including the Hotel and Catering EDC in 1966. There were eventually two parts to the role of the Hotel and Catering EDC (it was wound-up in October 1979): assessing the economic progress of the industry for purposes of national planning, and examining and evaluating the whole field of activities of the industry with a view to improving its efficiency. During its life the Hotel and Catering EDC influenced the thinking of the government, the industry and the public more than any other agency.

The third governmental body was established after the Carr Committee drew attention to the unsatisfactory state of training for industries in Britain at the beginning of the 1960s. Under the Industrial Training Act 1964 statutory boards were set up to be responsible for all aspects of training in individual industries. Although some training had been carried out within a few companies, notably J. Lyons & Company and Trust Houses, the criticisms of training were felt to be justified for the hotel and catering industry as for most others.

Apart from the schemes established by the National Joint Apprenticeship Council for cooks and waiters and a few company training schemes for management, most training took place on the job informally. For many it was a question of gaining experience by starting at the bottom and working slowly up the ladder. Training was done by departmental heads who may have had neither the time nor the skill to impart knowledge. The learning process was unstructured and haphazard. The primary motive was more often to get the job done — by methods which were not always the best — rather than giving the trainee the opportunity to learn.

In 1966 a high-powered training committee was established by the Hotel and Catering Institute and produced a report and recommendations based on what came to be known as the "brick system". Skills in various occupations were classified into modules or bricks, which could be added, one to the other, or one near by another.

When the Hotel and Catering Industry Training Board (HCITB) was established in the same year, training recommendations were drawn up on similar lines to the brick system. Encouragement of training was on an incentive basis, through a levy and grant system. Employers were required to pay a levy based on a percentage of the total emoluments of their staff and could claim grants for training carried out.

Grants were paid for registered trainees (the HCITB took over the work of the NJAC), for management trainees, for sandwich course students, for training officers and instructors and for courses and seminars and other forms of off-the-job training.

The levy and grant system ran into a number of problems, which were more serious for some training boards than others. By 1969/70 the grants paid out by the HCITB had exceeded levy income (the running expenses of the Board had to be met from the same source), and it was clear that the more successful the Board's staff were in encouraging employers to train, the greater the deficit would be.

The Employment and Training Act 1973, under which the Manpower Services Commission was set up, provided for the administrative expenses, including salaries of the ITBs to be funded from the Treasury. Secondly the concept of exemption from levy was introduced. Employers able to satisfy the HCITB that they are carrying out systematic training are exempt from payment of levy.

The proposals submitted to the Manpower Services Commission in October 1979 by the HCITB, as part of a comprehensive review of its long-term aims and financial structure, argued strongly for the continuation of the Board's activities. The review was part of the MSC's reappraisal of the effectiveness of all the training boards. A change in the method of funding was put forward by the HCITB, so that in the future all the Board's costs would be met by a direct levy upon existing leviable employers (that is those with a wage bill in excess of £90 000).

Conditions of Employment

The hotel and catering industry is a service industry with none of the monotony of a production line, but with none of the regularity either.

The "product" has unique characteristics. The school meals sector has to meet different requirements to the luxury restaurant. The same basic ingredients are used by both in the preparation of meals. Hygiene and nutrition are important to both, good presentation of the food equally so. Good purchasing, accurate costing and strict control are common concerns.

The children will be on holiday and away from school at regular periods during the year. They will not require evening meals unless boarding, and will arrive at about the same time for their lunch. By contrast the luxury city centre restaurant will be open throughout the year for two periods a day, lunch and dinner, possibly remaining closed on Sunday. The city centre hotel will have a third busy period at breakfast, and may offer 24 hour room service of meals and light refreshments. The snack bar in a football stadium will only be open when games are being held, and will be busiest at half time if the match is good. On the other hand an overnight cloudburst may mean the match has to be cancelled at the last minute.

Thus to meet the demand for the industry's services, full-time employees often work irregular hours. Secondly the industry relies on a large part-time and casual work-force. Thirdly many of the busiest times are when other people are enjoying themselves. Fourthly shift-work is a frequent requirement, sometimes split shifts are involved (more and more employers do try to avoid the necessity for split shifts).

In all sectors of the industry the labour cost forms a very significant proportion of the total cost of the product. The pressure to keep costs down is accentuated in the commercial sector by the obvious concern of the employer to make a reasonable profit. Faced with only limited scope for mechanisation, the industry moved out of the Victorian era with a millstone around its neck: a dependence on tips to compensate for inadequate wages. Before the Catering Wages Act there were some jobs where tips were so high that the staff actually paid the management for the jobs. The employers, for their part, had to move from a situation where many of their staff worked a 100 hour week (the alternative was worse) and labour costs were about 11% of turnover, to one in the mid-1960s where the basic week was between 42 and 46 hours and labour costs were about 22% of turnover. If the employers did not keep a close check on all costs, ruin resulted. The same is true today. In the sectors of the industry where demand is variable and sometimes unexpectedly high or low, it is not an easy task to maintain the appropriate staffing level.

The basic hours of work in the hotel and catering industry have been steadily reduced in the life time of the Wages Councils although progress has been somewhat slower than in other industries. In June 1970 the Industrial and Staff Canteen Wages Council reduced weekly hours from forty-one to forty; the other three Councils followed in 1974/75.

The actual hours worked are usually higher than the basic — as in other industries. In 1977 the situation was as follows:

	Total hours	Basic hours	Overtime
Men			
Catering	44.1	40.7	3.4
All other industries and services	45.7	39.9	5.8
Women			
Catering	39.9	38.6	1.4
All other industries and services	39.4	38.5	1.0

Source: *British Hotelier & Restaurateur*, July/August 1978

The forces of supply and demand in the labour market remain a most important factor in the level of wages paid in the hotel and catering industry, rather than the statutory minima prescribed by the Wages Council. Highly skilled and experienced workers are in the strongest position. However, in the parts of the country where alternative sources of employment are scarce, and for unskilled workers as well as those who are expected to supplement their income with tips, the rates determined by the Wages Council are the deciding factor.

The annual round of negotiations on minimum hotel and catering wages takes place in autumn. The increase agreed by the Wages Councils in 1978 was of the order of 17%, and in 1979 of the order of 25%.

The effect of the 1979 increase agreed by the Licensed Residential and Licensed Restaurant Wages Council was to increase the minimum wages from £35.60 a week in London to £45.20, and from £33.20 to £41.20 a week in the provinces. These figures relate to service workers, staff who are expected to receive tips in addition to their basic wage.

The increase for non-service workers in 1979 took the minimum wages up from £42.80 to £54 a week in London and from £40.40 to £50 a week in the provinces. Chambermaids were reclassified as non-service workers with the result that their minimum wage in the provinces was increased from £33.20 to £50 per week.

Other decisions made in the 1979 negotiations by the Licensed Residential and Licensed Restaurant Wages Council included: adult rates would be paid from the age of 20 rather than 21; and the 17 days' statutory holiday after two years' service would be increased to 20 days. The reduction for staff meals was not increased in 1979, but the amount deducted for full board was raised to £13 a week.

The New Earnings Survey published annually by the Department of Employment indicated that in April 1979 the average earnings of all full-time adult employees, aged 18 and over, were £88.40 per week. Within this figure, the average for men aged 21 and over was £101.40, for men aged 18 and over, £99.00, and for women aged 18 and over, £63.00. These averages include payment for overtime work and cover employees in every type of occupation in all sectors of the economy.

Looking in greater detail at the figure for catering the following situation emerges:

	Average gross weekly earnings £	Percentage earning under			Increase in weekly earnings April 1978 — April 1979 including overtime pay %
		£50 %	£75 %	£100 %	
Full-time men *					
Licensed residential establishment and licensed restaurant	63.3	35	75	92	11.9
Licensed non-residential establishment	68.0	18	70	92	22.3
Full-time manual men *					
Hotels and other residential establishments	64.4	36	77	90	15.9
Restaurants, cafes, snack bars	62.9	33	69	91	17.6

	Average gross weekly earnings £	Percentage earning under			Increase in weekly earnings April 1978 — April 1979 including overtime pay %
		£50 %	£75 %	£100 %	
Full-time non-manual men *					
Hotels and other residential establishments	95.0	11	38	65	17.0
Public houses	74.2	12	59	85	19.4
Full-time men * (occupations)					
Hotel, catering, club or public house managers	82.3	11	52	78	16.4
Catering supervisors	85.5	5	45	76	13.0
Chefs/cooks	77.4	17	53	81	12.9
Barmen	70.1	19	69	91	19.7
Kitchen porters/hands	65.7	26	74	87	11.6
Full-time women **					
Licensed residential establishment and licensed restaurant	45.0	36	73	95	13.1
Licensed non-residential establishment	43.2	46	75	94	13.7
Unlicensed place of refreshment	44.9	35	73	98	13.0
Full-time manual women **					
Hotels and other residential establishments	45.1	34	72	94	13.5
Catering contractors	45.6	42	74	92	14.0
Full-time non-manual women **					
Hotels and other residential establishments	54.9	25	52	82	8.3
Full-time women ** (occupations)					
Hotel, catering, club or public house managers	58.0	27	40	69	10.7
Catering supervisors	56.6	7	39	85	10.6
Chefs/cooks	51.4	17	59	91	10.2
Waitresses	45.6	40	72	92	17.0
Barmaids	44.9	37	72	95	14.4
Counter hands	49.3	29	58	91	10.9
Kitchen hands	44.6	47	78	95	7.6

Note: *Aged 21 and over   **Aged 18 and over

Source: *Department of Employment Gazette*, October 1979, Tables 2–9.

At Management Level

In the school meals service salaries are negotiated nationally by the Soulbury Committee. The salary scales are related to those of local government officers. A similarly well defined structure — of salaries, job grading, responsibilities, conditions of employment — applies to the hospital sector, to educational establishments, to civic catering and to the Forces.

The advertisements that appear for positions in these sectors always state clearly the salary scale, plus the value of any special allowances, for example London weighting.

In striking contrast, advertisements for management positions in the hotel sector very rarely state the salary being offered. Favourite expressions are "an above average salary", "an appointment offering great opportunities at a salary really commensurate with experience, accommodation if required", "a good salary will be offered to the right applicant", and the simpler "salary negotiable".

Three factors often predominate: what the company believes it can afford, what the previous going rate has been for the position, how much has to be offered to attract the right applicant. The individuality of each type of operation does make it difficult to rationalise salary structures, even within a group of hotels. There is a big variation in management responsibility between a 12 bedroom hotel with an important bar and restaurant trade, and a 500 bedroom city centre hotel.

Fringe benefits also complicate the hotel industry picture and, because of the taxation position, somewhat brighten it up. Many hotel managers have traditionally received benefits in the form of free accommodation, free food, clothes allowance, liquor allowance and more now receive benefits similar to those of their counterparts in other industries: company car, pensions scheme, free medical insurance and bonus schemes.

The Industry's Structure

The Hotel and Catering EDC report *Hotel Prospects to 1985* estimated that there were about 33 600 *licensed and unlicensed hotels* in Britain at the beginning of 1974. The HCITB report *Manpower in the Hotel and Catering Industry* put the figure at 32 000, compared to what it regards as the previous best estimate of 48 000.

The average British hotel is small — if licensed about twenty bedrooms, if unlicensed about ten bedrooms. Just over 1% of all hotels have more than 100 bedrooms (EDC estimate: 384), and just over 2.5% between 50 and 100 bedrooms (EDC estimate: 880). However, according to the HCITB study, about 48% of the work-force in the hotel sector were employed in hotels with 50 bedrooms and over.

The geographical spread of the hotel industry in 1974 was seaside 55%, small towns (with population of under 100 000) 21%, large towns (with population of over 100 000 including London) 12% and countryside 12%.

The HCITB study estimated that in 1977 there were about 35 000 *restaurants and cafes*, a figure which relates closely to the Hotels and Catering EDC report *The Catering Supply Industry*. Included in this total are fish and chip shops with significant sales for consumption on the premises (about 5000).

The number of *public houses* has been variously quoted in different sources ranging from 59 000 to 73 000. This discrepancy is largely due to the difficulty in classifying units where in addition to substantial liquor sales there are either a number of letting bedrooms or a busy restaurant.

The number of *clubs*, that is establishments providing food, drink and sometimes accommodation to members and their guests, in 1975 was over 30 000. The nature and characteristics of clubs vary considerably from the famous establishments in St James's and exclusive sporting clubs to the different working men's clubs.

So much for those organisations whose main activity is providing food, drink and accommodation. There is also a wide range of organisations whose main activity is in some other field, but where food/drink/accommodation are also provided: for example halls of residence at a university, services catering for army, air force and navy personnel, and catering for the staff and patients in hospitals, as well as providing the domestic services.

It was estimated at the beginning of the 1970s, that there were about 76000 units in *industrial and welfare catering* (M. Koudra in HCIMA Review Volume 1, No 1), of which 48 000 were in the public sector. Schools formed the most significant category with over 36 000 units, industrial catering the second with 25 000 of which about 4500 were operated by catering contractors.

Industrial and welfare catering — number of units (1970-72)

	Public sector	Private sector	Total
Industrial catering	5000	20 000	25 000
Schools	33 281	3067	36 348
Further and Higher Education	1134		1134
Hospitals	2760	150	2910
Homes	5000	5000	10 000
Armed Forces	450		450
NAAFI	338		338
Penal establishments	150		150
Approximate total:	48 000	28 000	76 000

Source: HCIMA Review No 1, M. Koudra *Industrial and Welfare Catering 1970-80*

The Department of Employment Manpower Studies No 11, *Catering*, published in 1972 (statistical data for 1969) provides the most detailed information on these and other sectors of the catering industry. The study found that about 75% of all firms engaged in manufacturing and a considerable proportion of non-manufacturing firms did have canteens. About 80% of the canteens were in manufacturing industries. In 1969 there were about 800 government staff canteens, a further 500 in the Post Office and 200 provided for local authority staff. Women and girls comprised more than 85% of all the staff employed in industrial catering, in the smaller canteens virtually all of the staff were female.

Note

Much of the material in this chapter came from *Profile of the Hotel and Catering Industry* by S. Medlik, 2nd edition, Heinemann, London, 1978. Other references included *Fortune, Fame and Folly: British Hotels and Catering from 1878 to 1978* by Derek Taylor, IPC Business Press, 1977; the Hotel and Catering Industry Training Board's report *Manpower in the Hotel and Catering Industry*, 1978; other sources of up to date information have been specified in the text; extracts from HMSO publications have been reproduced with the permission of the Controller, Her Majesty's Stationery Office.

Useful Addresses

Each year a special careers supplement is published by the weekly journals *Caterer and Hotelkeeper* and *Catering Times*. Amongst other useful information these features include a list of companies offering training schemes and employment opportunities.

Caterer and Hotelkeeper, IPC Consumer Industries Press Ltd, 40 Bowling Green Lane, London EC1R 0NE (Tel 01-837 3636)
Catering Times, 2nd Floor, 20 Soho Square, London W1V 6DT (Tel 01-734 1255)

These journals carry regular situations vacant columns as do:

Hospitality, the monthly journal of the Hotel, Catering and Institutional Management Association (previously called HCIMA Journal), and the HCIMA's *Mid-Month News,* 191 Trinity Road, London SW17 7HN (Tel 01-672 4251)
Staff and Welfare Caterer, monthly, IPC Consumer Industries Press Ltd, 40 Bowling Green Lane, London EC1R 0NE (Tel 01-837 3636)

Other trade journals published in the UK include:

British Hotelier & Restaurateur, monthly journal of the British Hotels Restaurants and Caterers Association, 13 Cork Street, London W1X 2BH (Tel 01-499 6641)
Catering and Hotel Management, monthly, Link House Magazines (Croydon) Ltd, Link House, Dingwall Avenue, Croydon CR9 2TA
Fast Food, published ten times a year by IPC Consumer Industries Press Ltd, 40 Bowling Green Lane, London EC1R 0NE (Tel 01-837 3636)
Food & Cookery Review, published six times a year by the Cookery and Food Association, 1 Victoria Parade, 331 Sandycombe Road, Richmond-upon-Thames, Surrey TW9 3NB (Tel 01-948 3870)
Industrial Catering Association Bulletin, published six times a year, ICA, Victoria Parade, 331 Sandycombe Road, Richmond, Surrey TW9 3NB (Tel 01-940 4464)
Marine and Air Catering, monthly, 213 Tower Building, Water Street, Liverpool L3 1LN (Tel 051 236 4511)
Service, the newspaper of the Hotel and Catering Industry Training Board (published regularly), HCITB, PO Box 18, Wembley HA9 7AP (Tel 01-902 8865)

Other Sources of Information
A list of companies which offer management training schemes is available from the Hotel, Catering and Institutional Management Association. The HCIMA also has available a list of major hotel and catering operators, and a list of employment agencies.
HCIMA, 191 Trinity Road, London SW17 7HN (Tel 01-672 4251)

For information about training in the hospital sector:
DEPARTMENT OF HEALTH AND SOCIAL SECURITY, Hannibal House, Elephant and Castle, London SE1 6TE (Division P4AE for information about training in catering management, Catering and Dietetic branch for information about the trainee cook scheme)

DEPARTMENT OF HEALTH AND SOCIAL SECURITY, Division P4AE, Friars House, 157-168 Blackfriars Road, London SE1 8EU (for information on training for domestic service posts)
MANAGEMENT EDUCATION AND TRAINING DIVISION, COMMON SERVICES AGENCY FOR THE SCOTTISH HEALTH SERVICE, Scottish Health Service Centre, Crewe Road South, Edinburgh EH4 2LF
WELSH OFFICE, HEALTH SERVICES PERSONNEL DIVISION, Health and Social Work Department, Pearl Assurance House, Greyfriars Road, Cardiff CF1 3RT

For information about training in the Forces:

ARMY CATERING CORPS, St Omer Barracks, Aldershot, Hants GU11 2BN
ROYAL AIR FORCE, Officer Careers, London Road, Stanmore, Middlesex HA2 5PZ
ROYAL NAVY Careers Service, Old Admiralty Building, Spring Gardens, London SW1A 2BE

3

At Work in the Industry

Profiles of many different people working in different sectors of the industry, in different jobs, from different courses, men and women. Sectors include: the Forces (Royal Air Force, Royal Navy, the Army Catering Corps), hotels, hospital catering, hospital domestic services, School Meals Service, halls of residence, restaurants, contract catering, employee feeding, clubs, public houses. People include a quartet of chefs, entrepreneurs and specialists: personnel officers, accountants, hotel consultant, sales director and training manager.

Hotels

HCI Inter + Final
1961–65

STUART MAY was appointed Managing Director of Rank Hotels in 1978. He was a student at the School of Hotelkeeping and Catering at Ealing College of Higher Education from 1961 to 1965 on the HCI Intermediate and Final.

Travel

Between completing his course and joining Rank Hotels as an assistant manager in 1966, Stuart travelled and worked in the USA for eight months. In 1967 he travelled abroad again, to work in the Bermudiana Hotel in Bermuda for a year as assistant manager.

Appointed General
Manager 1969

When he returned to England in 1968, Stuart joined the Forte organisation (now part of Trusthouse Forte) as Senior Assistant Manager of the Excelsior Hotel (which then had about 300 rooms) at London's Heathrow Airport. A year later he was given his first appointment as General Manager, at Rank's 190 room Unicorn Hotel in Bristol; subsequently Rank transferred him to the Coylumbridge Hotel. This hotel, which has over 130 rooms, was opened in November 1963 by Prince Philip and was the first major hotel to be built as part of the tourist development at the foot of the Cairngorm mountains in Scotland. The hotel is not far from the Aviemore centre.

Opened
Birmingham
Metropole
complex 1975

In 1971, Stuart was moved to the Royal Lancaster Hotel in London (436 rooms) as General Manager, where he remained for four years before leaving Rank for a period to open the new Birmingham Metropole complex in 1975. The complex, which includes two hotels, one of 500 rooms, one of 200 rooms and a conference centre for 1500 people, is part of the National Exhibition Centre on the outskirts of Birmingham.

In 1977, Stuart May returned to Rank Hotels as Assistant

Managing Director, and was promoted to his present position of Managing Director in November 1978.

Appointed
Managing Director
Rank Hotels
1978

Rank Hotels is part of a huge industrial and leisure group, the Rank Organisation, which in 1977-78 reported a turnover of £485 million. The hotel division, Rank Hotels, own and operate 12 hotels with over 3000 rooms and an annual turnover of over £35 million. The group's London hotels include The Athenaeum, The Royal Garden and The White House (which were acquired from Oddenino's in 1973), The Gloucester and The Royal Lancaster. The two other UK hotels are The Unicorn in Bristol and The Great Danes in Maidstone, and abroad the group has an hotel in Belgium, another in France, two in Italy, and one in the Canary Islands.

General Manager
Hotel Inter-
Continental

GRAHAM JEFFREY is General Manager of the Hotel Inter-Continental at Hyde Park Corner, London, which was opened by the Duke of Wellington in September 1975. The hotel has ten floors, 540 guest rooms and suites, and a conference/banqueting area which totals 14 000 square feet.

Intercontinental Hotels Corporation (which Graham joined in 1968 after holding several management positions in hotels throughout the world) is a worldwide chain with luxury hotels in over 50 countries. Before returning to London, he was General Manager of the company's hotel in Manila for three years, and prior to that, of the Inter-Continental Rawalpindi in Pakistan.

Scottish Hotel
School Diploma

Graham Jeffrey started his career in the hotel industry at the Dorchester Hotel. He studied at the Scottish Hotel School, Glasgow, where in the early 1950s a two year diploma course was available. Later in his career, Graham studied at the School of Business Management at Columbia University in America.

OND + HCIMA
Final

DAVID FRANKLIN NORTHEY MHCIMA passed the HCIMA Final Membership examination in summer 1974. After leaving school with 8 'O' levels he went to Cambridge College of Arts and Technology, to study for an OND in Hotel and Catering Operations (1971-73). He then continued his studies for a management qualification, enrolling on the HCIMA Final Membership one year full-time course at Bournemouth College of Technology.

16 months
trainee manager
Centre Hotels

After leaving college, David joined Centre Hotels as a trainee manager spending 16 months in the following departments: Reception/Advanced Reservations (St James's Hotel, London), Cash/Machine Operations, Accounts (Regent Centre Hotel), Control, Wages, Banqueting, Bars (Liverpool Centre Hotel), Personnel (West Centre Hotel), Assistant to the Administration Manager (Head Office), Purchasing, Statistics, Sales (Head

Office), Food Statistics, Food Purchasing (Centre Restaurants Ltd, Head Office), Kitchen (Bloomsbury Centre, Regent Centre), Restaurant (West Centre).

First post

David then spent 5 months as Group Relief Manager (mainly in London, but for four weeks was based in Dundee) before being given a post as Personnel and Training Manager at the 250 room Ivanhoe Hotel, London.

Promotion

Eighteen months later David was promoted to Front of House Manager at the St James's Hotel in Buckingham Gate (520 rooms) and after another year moved to the West Centre Hotel as Assistant to the Deputy General Manager (510 rooms and function facilities for 2000 people).

Joins Gardner Merchant

To further his catering experience David joined Gardner Merchant Food Services in April 1979 as District Relief Catering Manager where he will learn in more detail the characteristics of employee feeding operations, the many challenges and opportunities as well as the difficulties that sometimes have to be encountered.

Master Innholder

MALCOLM REED MSc FHCIMA was one of the first seven winners of the Master Innholder Award (a scheme launched in 1978 by the HCIMA and Worshipful Company of Innholders).

Area Manager Swallow Hotels

An Area Manager for Swallow Hotels, Malcolm is based at the company's head office in Sunderland, and controls the operation of 13 hotels with a total of 654 guest rooms and turnover of about £4 million p.a.

National Diploma 1963-66

He has always had a keen interest in food and enjoys meeting people. After studying for a National Diploma in Hotel Keeping and Catering at Hollings College (1963-66) Malcolm was accepted by Trust Houses as a management trainee (one of the six that year).

THF 3 year Training Scheme

On completion of the company's three year training scheme (which for Malcolm included 5 months in France) and after a short period training staff for new hotels (including the Excelsior at Glasgow Airport and the Leicester Post House) he was appointed to his first job as manager at the age of 23. He has managed a number of distinctly different operations since, including the Tyneside Post House for two years, and the St George's, Liverpool (as relief manager).

MSc in Business Management

While with THF Malcolm Reed spent a year on a full-time basis studying for an MSc in Business Management at Durham University. He has maintained a close link with catering education, working as an assessor in accommodation studies for several years for the Joint Committee for National Diplomas in Hotel, Catering and Institutional Management, and currently as a Moderator for the HCIMA's new Professional Qualification membership examination.

GILLIAN GRANT FHCIMA is General Manager of Trusthouse Forte's Randolph Hotel in Oxford. She was awarded a National Diploma in Hotel Keeping and Catering at South Devon Technical College in 1961.

National Diploma 1961

Gillian explains she has always had a natural curiosity in people and places — she has travelled extensively. Before her appointment as General Manager of Trust Houses' Hertford Hotel (now the Bayswater Post House) in 1967, she worked in the Caribbean, North America and Europe. She was Resident Manager of a large hotel in East Africa when Trusthouse Forte offered her a general managership of a new resort hotel in Barbados. From there Gillian moved to the Bahamas, opening four hotels in as many years. She returned to England in 1977, and in her position of Management Training Manager was closely involved in the development and conduct of management training schemes for THF. She was appointed Manager of the 4 star Randolph Hotel in 1978. The hotel has 111 rooms and a thriving restaurant and banqueting business.

First appointment as General Manager 1967

Caribbean, Africa and Europe

In an article in the HCI Journal in 1961, Gillian, an Hotelympia Travelling Scholar, described her first job in Nassau:

"After three years of studying hotel management at the hotel and catering department, South Devon Technical College, I decided to travel into the sun, and found it in the Bahamas. I worked there for five months as a receptionist-cashier on the front desk of a resort club in Nassau, owned by the Hotel Corporation of America. Nassau was a paradise after what had been a wonderfully happy routine of college life. Each day was as hot as the previous one, and time off meant such luxuries as swimming, snorkeling, lung diving, water ski-ing or night clubing.

Her first job in Nassau

"Working hours, however, meant working hard. During the slack period, we were allowed one day off per week, but this was cancelled during the high season, and my hours were 8 am to 3 pm or from 3 pm to finish, carrying out general reception and cashier duties. In this millionaire's paradise, guests were fussy and wanted innumerable things. They loved to talk and appreciated being listened to, even though their conversation might have been most uninteresting, and work might well have been piling up. We could not help this, however, and the sum total was that we broadened our knowledge and outlook on life, and perhaps, more important, learnt just a little tolerance and patience in dealing with guests and staff alike.

A millionaire's paradise

"Most guests were pleasant and exceedingly friendly. Generally, they would breeze into Reception with a cheery 'Hi! How are you?' If they did not like the accommodation

Friendliness

they had booked they would simply walk out in a very casual manner.

"One somewhat unexpected arrival was a handsome couple who had a second taxi load of luggage in tow. They swaggered up to Reception and forcefully announced that they were the famous film stars . . . and had reservations at the club. I re-checked the arrivals sheet, saw no such name, so then asked to see their confirmation reservation slip issued by the club. With a tremendous flourish this was produced. I read it. Then I carefully explained that their reservations were made at an hotel of the same name in Florida — many miles from Nassau! Like a burst bubble their vanity vanished. Fortunately, we were able to take care of them and they thoroughly enjoyed their somewhat unexpected holiday in Nassau."

Tact (margin)

Restaurateurs and Entrepreneurs

GEORGE SILVER, Chairman of Banquets of Oxford, joined the army as a Royal Fusilier Territorial in 1938 and subsequently became a founder member of the Army Catering Corps. He left the Corps in 1947 as a senior officer after overseas service in Africa, India and Burma where he was known as Long John.

Long John (margin)

He opened a restaurant of that name in a side street in Oxford, and it became popular with members of the University due largely to George's efforts in trying to serve interesting classical style dishes which he prepared in large quantities. The emphasis was on bulking up the food with lots of sauce and garnish and reducing the quantity of meat or fish — this made it possible for the food to be served at the low prices undergraduates could afford.

Oxford Restaurant (margin)

From that small restaurant George developed a reputation for outside banqueting and catering, notwithstanding the necessity in the first year or two of having to hire all the equipment and transport and employ only part-time staff. During this initial period he successfully undertook extensive public and private functions from mammoth show catering to dinner parties of the most recherché description all over the UK as well as in France.

Outside banqueting (margin)

The main outdoor catering group was sold in 1976 leaving some of the more prestigious contracts plus the "static" businesses of fast food units, pubs, various restaurants and cafes.

George is a Fellow of the Hotel, Catering and Institutional Management Association, as well as several other professional and trade organisations; he also serves as a committee member of the Réunion des Gastronomes and on the Regional Advisory

Work with HCIMA, Réunion des Gastronomes, HCITB (margin)

Committee of the Training Board. He was an original member of the HCI Apprenticeship Council for the training of chefs and was Chairman of the Oxford Catering Advisory Committee for many years.

A huge appetite

He considers himself a gourmet — on one occasion in New Orleans with a party of well-known British hoteliers and restaurateurs he ate 150 large oysters before breakfast. He enjoys cooking, particularly aspic work and decoration, and likes to write his restaurant menus personally.

To acting

A few years ago, he was going berserk at some poor waiter in one of his restaurants, and this must have interested Albert Finney who was having lunch at the time. He subsequently offered George a leading part in the film "Gumshoe" which resulted in George becoming an actor. Since then he has been in many films in England and abroad and considers it highly agreeable to have started a new career at his age, especially when he doesn't have to worry too much about the "bread".

HCI General
Catering Diploma
+ Final
Membership
Examination

JOHN REED MHCIMA left Thanet Technical College in 1969 after completing a two year course leading to the HCI General Catering Diploma and the City and Guilds of London Institute Certificates Nos. 150, 151 and 435. He worked for a year with Trusthouse Forte as a food and beverage trainee in the kitchens of the Excelsior Hotel, Heathrow, before commencing the HCI Final Membership course at Ealing College of Higher Education in 1970.

After leaving Ealing, John worked for two years as an assistant manager at the Richmond Hill Hotel (140 rooms), where he was responsible for banqueting, twelve conference rooms and five bars.

John then continues in his own words:

Swiss hotel
experience

"I left to work in Switzerland at the Mirabeau Hotel, Lausanne, which was a marvellous training ground. I started off in the bar then working in the guéridon service restaurant and once I could speak French well enough I was moved to the office and reception area responsible for the switchboard, reservations and cashiering.

Hotel manager?
Or own business?

"On returning to England I went to the Skyline Hotel, Heathrow as a receptionist, night auditor, then into the accounts office. My ambition was to become an hotel manager in a large hotel and perhaps could have achieved this after working for a few years as an assistant manager etc. I then thought about the advantages of owning my own establishment and realised to do this I would have to start in a small way. So I changed my ideas from hotels to restaurants and at the beginning of 1975 I managed a 60

London restaurant
experience

seater restaurant near Richmond, and then worked for a while in a busy restaurant in Old Brompton Road.

"During this period I had obtained with two friends a shop on Kingston Hill, and had been busy converting the premises for use as a restaurant. In October 1975, Clouds Restaurant opened serving French/English cooking in a relaxed, informal atmosphere and at the same time value for money. It was a huge success and in a year we had extended the building thus doubling the seating capacity.

Ambition
achieved – Clouds
Restaurant opened

"In 1978 I took over another two shops on Kingston Hill and converted these into another restaurant more on the lines of a French cafe, which is also called Clouds and open daily from 11 am to 11 pm; it is so busy that people queue every night for tables. I serve 2500 covers a week and estimated turnover for 1979 is approaching £500 000. I am also opening a wine bar above the restaurant which I hope will be as successful as my previous two ventures."

Success and
expansion

A Family of Entrepreneurs —
Hoteliers

GEORGE BUZASI BA MHCIMA is a director of the Hotel Antoinette in Kingston-upon-Thames with his father, Arpad, and wife Hilary.

With a constantly increasing number of bedrooms (over 100 in August 1979) the hotel plays a key role in attracting tourists to Kingston as well as providing modestly priced accommodation for businessmen, and conference and banqueting facilities. It is Kingston's only large hotel and yet in 1970 all that the Buzasis had was their own home, in which bed and breakfast guests were accommodated.

From B & B in 1970
to a 100 room hotel
in 1979

Refugees in 1956

Arpad Buzasi, his wife and son of eight years were forced to leave their home in Hungary in 1956 and came to England as refugees, unable to speak English, with very little money. Soon, Arpad with the help of a benefactor (with the Christian name of Antoinette) acquired properties in Kingston and with indefatigable energy transformed it into a thriving bed and breakfast business.

As soon as George had completed his schooling he went to Ross Hall in Glasgow to study for a BA degree in Hotel and Catering Management at the University of Strathclyde. His father had been against such a choice but was persuaded by the school careers master — who remains a close friend of the family — that the hotel and catering industry could provide attractive, worthwhile and interesting opportunities. When George graduated in 1970 he did not immediately join his father. He had of course spent every vacation during the course working in

Careers Master's
advice

the hotel and helping his father wherever possible, but, one of the top students of his year, he was attracted to join Watney Mann.

George began to play a greater and more permanent role in the operation of the Hotel Antoinette from 1971. Since then, sound business judgement, as well as courage, luck, the support of a dedicated team of staff, and the local bank manager have totally changed the hotel's image and tripled its size. Hard work, methodical planning and a positive approach to selling the hotel have played no small part in this transformation.

Support of staff and bank manager

Positive approach to sales

In 1971, George mounted his first major overseas drive to sell the hotel to a wider market. With a load of 10000 brochures printed in several languages, George toured Europe contacting hundreds of travel agents. Since then the pressure has been maintained; in 1978/79 over 100000 mailings of brochures were sent to tour operators and travel agents throughout the world. Regular sales efforts are also made to local industry to promote the hotel's function and banqueting facilities. In 1978 some 75% of the hotel's business came from abroad and the hotel was chosen as the venue for the Kingston Chamber of Commerce's celebration of the crowning of Ethelred the Unready at Kingston-upon-Thames in the year 979.

A Quartet of Chefs

JOHN ELLIOTT, Head Chef at the British Embassy in Washington, writes:

"I first became interested in the catering industry through the Scout movement, of which I have been an active member for a long time. I had always enjoyed participating on the catering side of the service crew, which involved simple cooking for the cub scouts.

"My sister was also interested in cooking, and after she took her course at Ealing Technical College, I realised it was a really creative art and followed suit.

"I attended Ealing Technical College in 1974 for two years the course was hard work, fun and very rewarding. I spent the following year at the Capital Hotel in Knightsbridge as a Commis Chef. It was then through Ealing Technical College I received information on a job as Second Chef at the British Embassy in Washington. I was lucky enough to get this position. Six months later the position of Head Chef became vacant and I was offered the job, which I accepted.

"I have greatly enjoyed working in the USA, but I feel I must get back to London soon, for the experience and to take the City and Guilds 706/3 Advanced Cookery certificate, on day release from work. After two or more

Commis Chef at Capital Hotel

Second Chef, now Head Chef at the British Embassy, Washington

years at college, I should like to work in the South of France to improve my French and to gain more experience in the catering industry. I would then like the experience of working throughout Europe. Then to get back to London and run my own establishment, or that of someone else."

Executive Chef, London Hilton, 2000–2500 meals per day

MR OSWALD MAIR is Executive Chef at the London Hilton. He joined the staff of the hotel in December 1962 as a senior Sous Chef, and was put in charge of the kitchens five years later. Today with a brigade of 80–100 (including kitchen and pastry helps and his secretary) he is responsible for eight food operations and banqueting, an average of 2000 to 2500 meals per day ranging from a club sandwich to a ten course meal.

Apprenticeship in Germany

Mr Mair, who speaks fluent French, English, Italian and some Spanish in addition to his native tongue, German, served his apprenticeship in Germany. For the first two years he travelled one day every week to chefs' classes, as well as classes for butchers and bakers. The autumn of 1951, the final three months of the apprenticeship, he spent studying at an hotel school in the old spa town of Bad-Überhingen — midway between Stuttgart and Ulm. He was one of a group of forty-five students, the first to be admitted to the then new school. (The school has since moved from what was the spa hotel to new premises and admits nearly 300 students at one time.)

Experience with Germany's King of Chefs

After successfully completing his apprenticeship, Mr Mair went to work at the Four Seasons Hotel in Hamburg, as 5th commis garde-manger. During the next two years he worked with the chef garde-manger, the chef saucier, the poissonnier, the grill and the boucher, and finally as 2nd chef garde-manger. The hotel had a brigade of thirty-two with eight in the garde-manger. Next he went to Munich to the Hotel Vier Jahreszeiten to work with the King of Chefs in Germany, Alfred Walterspiel. He joined the brigade as a 1st commis garde-manger and when he left after a year was acting garde-manger. When not on duty in the hotel kitchen, he was working in the kitchen of a recently opened Munich nightclub.

An hotel for millionaires in the Swiss Alps

He then worked for a short time, three months, at the Hotel Hessischerhof in Frankfurt. Here was one of Germany's greatest chef garde-mangers, a man who liked all cold buffet displays to be presented in straight lines, not, as Mr Mair had been doing, at an angle. No wonder his efforts were not enthusiastically received! For the summer season, Mr Mair worked in Switzerland at the Hotel Waldhus Vulpera, a hotel for millionaires right at the top of the Alps, as 1st commis garde-manger.

One of his main reasons for going to work in Switzerland was to improve his French, but most of the time the kitchen brigade spoke German. All orders in the kitchen — and he often acted as aboyeur — were of course given in French. For the winter Mr Mair worked in Geneva as chef entremettier in the Restaurant du Globe.

His next job was in England, in 1955, at one of London's most famous restaurants at the time, the Mirabelle (the manager was something of a character having been an English Master Spy in the war). It was a very busy kitchen, and Mr Mair with his expertise and orderly mind was called upon to improve the organisation of the garde-manger.

He was two years at the Mirabelle before moving as chef tournant to the L'Ecu de France, and then in 1957, as senior sous chef to the Talk of the Town, which he helped open. Each day, he recalls, this theatre restaurant served about 800 à la carte meals at 37/6 for three courses. Mr Mair was responsible for the buying and butchery preparation.

Before joining the London Hilton in 1962 Mr Mair worked for one year in the USA, including a period at the Embassy Hotel in Montreal in Canada. He has worked for a time in India as well, and visited many countries of the world. The idea of regular international food festivals at the London Hilton came from these regular trips abroad — watching, observing, finding out about the area's restaurants and hotels. At the London Hilton he is regarded as a hard task master, very fair to his staff, extremely hard working (on duty every morning by 7 am), very professional, very dedicated to the industry, and a tremendous administrator, highly efficient at his job.

MICHAEL ROBERTSON has used his HCITB travelling scholarship to spend a year in the USA where he has been working at the Ritz-Carlton in Boston. Before this he had spent 19 months working as a second commis chef in the Dorchester in Park Lane, gaining experience in different sections of the kitchen, and studying at Westminster College for the first year of the City and Guilds 706/3 Advanced Cookery scheme (which he intends to complete).

Michael was with the Waldorf Hotel before then. When he left school at the age of 16 he entered a four year apprenticeship which included day release at Westminster College (2 years for the City and Guilds 706/1, 2 years for the 706/2). At the beginning of his apprenticeship Michael was placed in the fish section, then to the sauce section, roast, vegetables, larder, pastry and back to fish. After the successful completion of his apprenticeship he was appointed first commis garde-manger.

PETER WALTERS also studied for the City and Guilds 706/1 and 706/2 on a part-time basis over 4 years. For most of this time

Margin notes:
- The Mirabelle, London
- Talk of the Town, London
- A year in North America
- Alert for new ideas
- HCITB Scholarship winner
- 4 year apprenticeship + 706/1 and 706/2
- Part-time study

Outdoor catering

he was working for the Deansway Catering Company in Worcester. This gave Peter considerable experience of the problems of catering for outside functions (the company's business included a number of industrial canteens, army contracts, Masonic halls, functions at the Guildhall and in surrounding villages). He was responsible on many occasions for ordering and buying (and did an HCITB Storekeepers course) as well as cooking.

Peter was a student at Worcester Technical College. He spent a few months working as a commis chef (often acting as chef de partie) at the Lilleybrook Hotel in Charlton Kings, Cheltenham, before going to Switzerland on his HCITB scholarship. There he had worked for a year as a commis chef in the Hotel Belvue Palace in Berne. The arrangements for this were made by the British Hotels Restaurants and Caterers Asssociation.

The Forces

Royal Air Force

HCI Associate Membership

WING COMMANDER BARRY D. JONES MHCIMA is Assistant Director of Catering for the Royal Air Force. He joined the RAF in November 1959 after successfully completing a three year hotel and catering management course at Blackpool Technical College, where in July 1959 he passed the Associate Membership Examination of the Hotel and Catering Institute finishing second in the land and winning the Sir Francis Towle award.

After six months' officer training, Barry was appointed deputy catering officer first at RAF Coningsby in Lincolnshire (for two years) and then at RAF Finningley in Yorkshire for fifteen months. Both are large RAF stations and were then part of the RAF Bomber Command.

In 1963, when Barry was posted to a Station Catering Officer appointment and made responsible for the management of the catering service at RAF Hereford (the home of the RAF's School of Catering), he was elected a Member of the Hotel and Catering Institute.

Posted to Borneo and Singapore

A year later he was posted abroad to the Far East, where he spent the next four years. For a year at RAF Labuan in Borneo, where Barry was Station Catering Officer, he was responsible for the catering service with a staff of 100 (three outlets, in-flight catering for all aircraft using RAF Labuan, which was the RAF's principal base in Borneo during the confrontation with Indonesia). Subsequently in Singapore, he was manager of the Changi Creek Hotel, with a staff of 120. A 230 bedroom establishment, this was the RAF's hotel in Singapore, catering for entitled crews and passengers travelling between the UK and Singapore and throughout the Far East. The hotel supplied all in-flight catering requirements for the RAF.

In April 1968 Barry returned to Lincolnshire on promotion to Squadron Leader in charge of the management of the catering service at the RAF College in Cranwell, with a staff of over 430, seven food outlets (of which six were messes, all residential), and an annual food purchasing budget of £158 000. After two years at Cranwell, he was posted to the RAF Directorate of Catering at the Ministry of Defence, London as the staff officer responsible for the design of catering premises and the development of catering equipment for the RAF.

RAF Cranwell 430 staff

In May 1972, Barry returned overseas to Germany as a staff officer and in October 1973 was appointed Command Catering Officer for RAF Germany on promotion to Wing Commander. He was responsible for the direction and control of the RAF's catering organisation on the Continent, which had an annual food purchasing budget of £4 million, some 40 outlets and a staff of 900.

Command Catering Officer Germany

Following this appointment Barry was selected to attend a nine month senior RAF Staff College course at RAF Bracknell in Berkshire, before taking up his present appointment as Assistant Director of Catering for the Royal Air Force in April 1976. He is immediate deputy to the Director of Catering RAF who controls an organisation providing 32 500 meals per day in some 400 diverse outlets, with a staff of 8500 and an annual food purchasing budget of £20 million. Barry's particular responsibilities are for the planning, administration and organisation of personnel, accounting and audit aspects of the catering service for the RAF worldwide.

Assistant Director of Catering RAF

COMMANDER MICHAEL A. PEAREY MCFA is Command Supply Officer to CINCNAVHOME (Commander-in-Chief, Naval Home Command) and based in Portsmouth. Michael joined the Royal Navy in 1951 aged 18 as a Supply Officer. The first year's initial general training concentrated on leadership, seamanship, propulsion, and weapons systems; it was followed by 2½ years' supply training, covering all aspects of pay and cash, accounting, stores support, secretarial and administrative procedures and practices, law and catering.

Royal Navy

Commander Pearey subsequently enjoyed varied employment ashore and afloat, in the UK and overseas (including numerous trips to the Caribbean). He was involved in setting up the Polaris Submarine Base on the Gareloch in 1967/69 and was based in Malta when Mr Mintoff became Prime Minister and plans for the British withdrawal were being prepared.

Frequent travel

In 1971–74, as Training Commander in the Royal Naval Supply School, Chatham, Michael was in charge of all Supply

Royal Navy career
courses

and Secretariat training for officers and ratings and "Wrens" in
the Royal Navy. The *Royal Navy career courses* range from 7 to 32
weeks in length and lead to awards of the City and Guilds of
London Institute and the National Examinations Board for
Supervisory Studies. The Royal Navy, like the other Services, is
very selective during recruiting and the training is second to
none. Importance is attached to linking in with civilian
qualifications wherever possible, provided that this can be done
without detracting from the prime naval role. The Royal Navy
record in obtaining CGLI and NEBBS qualifications is
excellent.

During his time as Training Commander, Michael covered
two Hotelympias (46 awards to the Navy in 1972) and
implemented the transition to objective training based on
detailed job evaluations. He was responsible for policy, course
design, content, instruction and assessment, and the setting and
control of standards as well as character training. This included
hill walking in Snowdonia and the Lake District, pot holing,
canoeing week-ends and so on. The Supply School at Chatham,
HMS *Pembroke*, has over 100 staff and 500 students.

From 1974 to 1975, Michael was Supply Officer of assault
ship HMS *Fearless*, a mobile floating dock with a garage and
flight deck, accommodation for 750 in comfort, 1000 using
baths and passageways for sleeping. HMS *Fearless* is designed to
transport troops and vehicles (12 tanks, up to 100 lorries) for
assault landings. Michael recalls three particularly interesting
experiences from this time:

Replenishing at sea

"RN ships prefer to replenish stores and victuals at sea,
when all hands are available to take the gear in-board and
strike it down. We sailed from Plymouth for a major
NATO exercise with very little food on board, expecting to
RAS (Replenish at Sea) immediately on leaving harbour.
This is an exciting evolution, with loads of one ton being
dropped every minute by helicopter, to be removed from
the dropping area before the next load; and often
concurrently similar loads being hauled across from the
stores ship alongside, a feat requiring great skill and
concentration if the ships are to remain parallel and the
jackstay at the right tension to avoid dunking the supplies
in the sea, or, alternatively, snapping the jackstay. On this
occasion our support ship broke down! Storing for 1000
people for 3 weeks in 12 hours proved a good test of the
organisation. Luckily we were in a Naval Port and
alternative supplies were readily available — I have been
in a ship where Falkland Island sheep had to be rounded
up for our consumption! — but deprived of the use of
helicopters and jackstay transfer, we only managed by

Stores for 1000
people for 3 weeks
loaded in 12 hours

using every available boat: tank-loading craft, troop-landing craft, dockyard MFVs, ships, boats — anything we could lay our hands on that would float — and either hoisting loads in-board by crane, manhandling them up ladders or indeed hoisting the entire boat in-board, load and all, and unloading at deck level. One hundred and twenty tons of gear was embarked and was still being struck down and stowed as we steamed out into the Atlantic.

"At a time when the Greeks and Turkish governments were not talking, we were in the Eastern Mediterranean and needed the co-operation of both for exercise purposes. The solution was a formal luncheon for all parties concerned on a deserted beach on an un-named island at 6 hours' notice. We failed to provide the dancing girls but ice cold drinks greeted the guests at noon, and a four course lunch with all trimmings was served silver-service at 12.45. We got the co-operation we hoped for!

King and Queen of
Tonga for lunch

"Royal visit by the King and Queen of Tonga, a Prince and Princess. The King was reputed to be 33 stone. Special requirements included a church pew for him to sit on — nothing else was strong enough — and the you-know-what was reinforced with solid teak in case of need! The route required very careful planning to avoid vertical ladders and narrow passages. Just before the Royal Party embarked, we found that Tongan Royalty could not eat with Tongan commoners — lunch arrangements had to be altered at a rush. Incidentally the King asked for a typical Naval meal so had, amongst other things, Pot Mess — a delicious thick brown stew."

Traditionally, catering in the Royal Navy has been carried out by ratings, overseen by officers promoted from their own ranks. Commander Pearey was in the van of a new breed who entered as officers and specialised in catering. His previous job

Naval Catering
Adviser

was Naval Catering Adviser, covering all aspects of catering policy in the Royal Navy, and liaising with the other Services and many civilian bodies. Michael recalls going to his first management meeting of the Cookery and Food Association in fear and trembling, only to find the other members were human too! And that what he lacked in craft expertise was made up for in managerial experience.

Interest in rugby

Michael has been one of the Navy's representatives on the Rugby Football Union Committee since 1968 and is currently Chairman of the RFU Coaching Sub-Committee. The RFU administers rugby throughout England and has an influence worldwide; the problems, frustrations and comradeship have much in common with the Cookery and Food Association, Michael says.

Army Catering
Corps

LIEUTENANT COLONEL ANTHONY (TONY) R. ROE FHCIMA
ACC received his technical training at Westminster Technical
College, completing both the Professional Chefs' and
Restaurants Operations courses.

Tony was subsequently called up for National Service in the
Army Catering Corps. He was appointed to a commission in
April 1951 at the age of 19 and granted a permanent commission
the following year.

Tony was the Adjutant of, and responsible for, all personnel
matters in the Army Apprentices College Army Catering Corps
which trained 450 apprentices for Army service. He has been a
Specialist Catering Officer feeding from 800 to 2000 soldiers,
has acted as a Catering Adviser to Gurkha Brigade; served in

Experience in Far
East and Germany

Malaya, Singapore and Borneo, and later (1972-74) in
Germany where he was responsible for feeding 30 000 soldiers.

He has commanded and been the chief instructor of the Army

Army School of
Catering

School of Catering (1974-77) — arguably the premier Service
Catering School in the world, with an annual throughput of
2500 students.

Assistant Director
ACC

Tony is now the Assistant Director Army Catering Corps with
specific responsibilities for all technical aspects of feeding the
British Army. These include building design and equipment,
provisioning and accounting, research and development and
liaison with industry.

His interests are, not unnaturally, food, wine and travel. He is
a member of the Royal Society of Health, Cookery and Food
Association, the Institute of Meat, and the Army representative
on various Hotelympia committees.

Hospital Catering

JANE BULLOUGH BSc LHCIMA left school with nine 'O' levels
and four 'A' levels and went to the London School of Economics
where she studied for a degree in economics. After graduating in

BSc + HCIMA
Abridged course

July 1977 with a BSc Politics and History Jane decided she
wished to pursue a developing interest in catering and enrolled
at Leeds Polytechnic to take the one year HCIMA Certificate
course in Institutional Management, which she was awarded
with Special Merit in July 1978.

After leaving college Jane joined the National Health Service
as a management trainee. She was based at the London
Hospital, Whitechapel learning all aspects of NHS catering
management — practical, working as a cook, supervisor,
assistant manager, and theoretical, at the NHS residential
college. In May/June 1979 she set up a trial of a cook-chill
system of food service to patients on two wards at the London
Hospital in Whitechapel.

HCITB
scholarship

Study tour of
Canada

Jane used her HCITB travelling scholarship to spend two months studying innovations in hospital catering in Canada. Her first post has been at the 400 bed Henderson General Hospital in Hamilton, Ontario, where the traditional kitchen has recently been converted to a cook freeze production unit. Jane writes that she has found Ready Foods and Convenience systems widely utilised and has been most impressed by the quality of service and efficient operations, with a high degree of standardisation. She has also visited the McMaster University complex which used convenience foodstuffs. In Vancouver she has visited several other hospitals, and two in Edmonton. She also visited the Cedar Sinai Hospital in Los Angeles which operates an extremely efficient cook freeze/cook chill food service.

Since returning to England in August 1979, Jane has re-joined the staff of the London Hospital, Whitechapel.

ANDREW GAMON MHCIMA was awarded a National Diploma in Hotel Keeping and Catering at Hollings College, Manchester in 1966.

District Catering
Manager

As District Catering Manager in Central Derbyshire Health District, Andrew is responsible for the catering services in 18 hospitals — providing 5000 meals daily for patients and staff. He has a management team of three Catering Managers and 5 Assistant Catering Managers plus 250 other staff reporting to him. Wages account for a major portion of the annual budget of £1¾ million, for which Andrew is responsible to his District Management Team.

After college first
two years as
Trainee Catering
Manager

When Andrew Gamon left college he started his career as a Trainee Catering Manager with the Ministry of Health Manchester Regional Health Board. Then, after two years as Assistant Group Catering Manager in Coventry, he was appointed Catering Manager at the Nether Edge Hospital, Sheffield (1200 meals per day). After three years in this position and three years as Group Catering Manager in the Northern Sheffield Hospital Management Committee he was appointed to his present position.

Hospital Domestic Services

MRS MOIRA EDWARDS enrolled on an OND course in Institutional Housekeeping and Catering at the College of Arts and Technology, Newcastle in September 1972. When she sat her GCE in nine subjects that summer, Moira's ambition had been to become a domestic science teacher, but this required 'A' levels and there was no opportunity at her school to study domestic science subjects at 'A' level.

OND course

With six 'O' level passes including Mathematics, English, Biology and Chemistry, Moira was well qualified for the OND course. After the first year of the course, the students at Newcastle had a choice, for the college then offered two OND courses: Hotel and Catering Operations and Institutional Housekeeping and Catering. Moira decided upon the latter and in summer 1974 passed all her examinations and was awarded the diploma.

In her own words, Moira describes her career since:

DHSS Training Scheme

"I heard of the Department of Health and Social Security's Training Scheme for Assistant Domestic Services Managers and applied to the Northern Regional Health Authority for a place on the 1974/75 scheme. Having the necessary qualifications, I was accepted. I was attached to Gateshead Area Health Authority for my practical attachments. The four theoretical modules — which were for one or two week periods at a time — were held at Sheffield University Halls of Residence, and at the St Anne's Hotel, Buxton, Derbyshire.

Theoretical modules

Practical attachments

"I was soon to discover that all of the people on the course were in the same situation as me, having completed an OND course with very little knowledge and experience of work in hospitals. During the practical attachments I worked as a domestic assistant on wards and departments, then as a member of the floor team covering all areas of the hospital. I then worked as a Domestic Supervisor and finally as an Assistant Domestic Services Manager. The scheme ran from September 1974 to June 1975.

Appointed Assistant Domestic Services Manager

"When I completed the scheme I was appointed as Assistant Domestic Services Manager at the 400 bed Queen Elizabeth Hospital, Gateshead, where I had done the main bulk of my practical training. In September 1975 I was appointed as Domestic Services Manager (Grade I) for Dunston Hill Hospital, Gateshead with responsibility for two smaller hospitals. I remained there for three years.

Promoted

"The post of Domestic Services Manager (Grade II) at Queen Elizabeth Hospital, Gateshead became vacant and I applied in December 1978. I am presently doing this job. I am responsible for organising the Domestic Services at the Queen Elizabeth Hospital, Dryden Road Hospital and at Aidan House which is the Area Headquarters.

"I have two Assistant Domestic Services Managers, one Senior Housekeeper and six Domestic Supervisors under my control as well as 130 domestic staff.

Responsibilities

"One of the Assistant Domestic Services Managers also has responsibility for the Health Centres and Clinics run by the Gateshead Area Health Authority and the Community Domestic Supervisor is based at Queen Elizabeth Hospital. I therefore have certain responsibilities within the Community.

"The Queen Elizabeth Hospital will eventually become a Grade III post as the size of the building is increased by new developments (another 200 beds are being added).

The future
During this time I will be kept very busy commissioning new buildings and organising the Domestic Services within these areas. It is hoped to establish a new Housekeeping system in the new extension.

"The next stage in my career would be to become a District Domestic Services Manager."

Duties of Domestic Services Manager
Moira's duties and responsibilities as Domestic Services Manager at the Queen Elizabeth Hospital include: the recruitment of adequate staff (within the allotted budget), the maintenance of up to date work schedules, the maintenance of an acceptable standard of cleanliness throughout the area of responsibility, the control and issue of cleaning materials, equipment and appliances, the provision of adequate supervision during hours of duty, the training of supervisors and staff, the upkeep of various records, and the implementation and control, including quality control, of Domestic Bonus schemes.

Grade III is the top grade of a Domestic Services Manager — the grading of a particular post depends on the number of square metres under supervision.

District Domestic Services Manager
In her present position, Moira is responsible to her District Domestic Services Manager, Miss Joan Greenfield MBE MHCIMA. Joan Greenfield, who in fact comes from an Army background, has extensive responsibilities covering the whole area with its eight hospitals. She is responsible for laying down the lines on which individual managers will run their hospitals including methods, procedures, materials and equipment. She is responsible to the Area Administrator of Gateshead Area Health Authority.

DDSM responsibilities
Joan's specific responsibilities include control of the Domestic Budget, which covers staffing and materials, advising the Authority, research into up to date methods, responsibility for work study schemes, for contracts (including wall washing, window cleaning, pest control), for training the managers, and for giving advice when new buildings or major alterations are being planned and constructed on matters like suitable floorings, finishings, security, staffing levels, range and extent of service.

Joan Greenfield is Chairman of the Association of Domestic Management (see page 209).

School Meals Service

JOHN W. FRASER MBE FHCIMA is Head of the Education Catering Branch for the Inner London Education Authority.

ILEA One million meals a week

The Education Catering Branch of the ILEA provides the catering services at the Authority's schools and maintained colleges: over 1 million meals a week from about 800 kitchens and 250 dining centres to which meals are transported. John has a staff of some 8600 and an annual budget of approximately £25 million.

John started his catering career as a trainee chef spending three years working in kitchens before the Second World War intervened. After war service John was one of the first Diploma students at the Scottish Hotel School (1947-49).

Scottish Hotel School Diploma

A short period as a junior assistant manager with British Railways Hotels was followed by three years with the Grosvenor Caterers, Glasgow covering banqueting and outside catering, including ships' trials. His next move was in 1953 to enter the Royal Air Force as a catering officer.

RAF experience

John Fraser's appointments with the RAF included station catering (with 3-4 dining points plus satellite units), running a transit hotel and flight catering centre in Malta (where meal numbers ranged from zero to 10 000 a day), training officer in charge of steward training (RAF Catering School), food supplies officer for the Middle East (with responsibility for local contracts in Aden and the Gulf areas), and Staff (administration) appointments at the Ministry of Defence with responsibilities for kitchen planning, catering equipment, training and personnel matters, ration entitlements and accounting procedures.

When John retired from the RAF in 1969 with rank of Squadron Leader he joined the Greater London Council as their catering manager responsible for ceremonial catering and staff feeding at the County Hall and associated offices. He took up his present appointment in 1977.

MRS H. CLARE GOODEN MHCIMA became a student at the Polytechnic of North London in 1969 as a member of the first year of the new HND course in Institutional Management. Clare describes some of the aspects of her studies:

HND course described

"In Catering there was extensive practical work in the large scale kitchen and its attached restaurant outlet. Visits to the markets — Smithfield, Spitalfields, Billingsgate and Covent Garden — were included as well as exhibitions such as Hotelympia. The practical work in House Services ranged from the floor coverings within the department at college to the domestic duties covered by the management of a nearby students' hostel.

Three industrial
experience
elements

"The relevance of Management and Business Studies was underlined during my three week periods of industrial experience. At the end of my first year I spent eight weeks at the London head office of a large industrial firm. The Catering Manager had planned a full training programme so that I worked in all areas of the catering department. During my second year I spent twelve weeks in a college on a university campus working for six weeks on the domestic management side and for six weeks on the catering side. It was during this period that the decimalisation of currency took place and it was interesting to be involved practically in such an exercise of reorganisation. By my final year I felt that I should like to work with children and so it was arranged that I should spend six weeks in a children's home which was made up of a collection of family units under one manager."

+ CGLI 151

Clare who gained the City and Guilds 151 certificate during the course and qualified for her Higher National Diploma in June 1972 continues:

"The course had been very full, covering a wide range of subjects and the college's facilities were excellent. The teaching staff made the course very interesting and encouraged each student to find and develop their abilities to the full.

Finding a job

"When I started applying for my first post I found that although there were many posts vacant within the industry, the large majority were looking for qualifications plus experience which considerably limits the chances for a college leaver. My first post was in an ILEA boarding school for handicapped children where, as Residential Domestic Bursar, I was responsible for the catering and housekeeping. I was not supervised in the job and had very few guidelines to work to but I gained valuable experience of staff management and of working as part of a team."

Clare left this post after one and a half years; by then she was married and wanted a job offering regular hours, free weekends, and a well defined career structure with good promotional prospects. She applied to two County Councils. The first replied enclosing an application form for a teaching post, and the other invited her for an interview in the School Meals Department. Clare had not considered joining the School Meals Service until this point although, looking back, she had thoroughly enjoyed her school meals. She decided that the School Meals Service was not an old fashioned sector of the catering industry producing dull food in large quantities but highly professional, aiming to produce nutritionally balanced meals that are tasty, attractive and acceptable to the customer, whilst maintaining an

Moving on, Clare
considers School
Meals Service

extremely high standard of hygiene throughout the whole catering operation and keeping within the allocated budget.

Thus Clare joined Hertfordshire County Council's School Meals Department. She found that great emphasis is put on the training of staff at all levels to achieve an efficient service, and a career structure with good promotional prospects is offered. In **Appointed Divisional Training Instructor** 1974 she was appointed a Divisional Training Instructor to run one of Hertfordshire's six training kitchens, where all grades of HCC kitchen staff are trained in large scale practical work and the applied theory. Before running any courses herself, Clare was sent on the HCITB's ten day Instructor's Course and a Mid-Management Course for Supervisors of Manual Workers organised by the County Council. She then spent six weeks observing in another training kitchen before running her first two courses under supervision.

Then County Training Instructor In 1975 she became a County Training Instructor with more opportunity for "on job" training in different areas of the County. The work included retraining staff, reorganising kitchens and methods of service, setting up new kitchens and training new staff. During school holidays her work with the other members of the training team included compiling the HCC School Meals Metric Cookery Book. This involved collecting recipes from throughout the County, converting and testing them; usually they had to be adjusted in content, method or nutritional balance and then retested. The team was also involved in the design of new kitchens, setting up training meetings, giving cookery demonstrations and compiling handouts for the training kitchens. As a project, she made a visual display to introduce basic nutrition to junior and infant children through the school meal, and the team made four short films for the HCITB on metrication. These showed the use of metric weights and measures and how to use a metric recipe.

Clare, who left the HCC School Meals Department in 1978 to start a family, looks back and writes "Instructing in front of film cameras and preparing food for still photography in my project were only two of the many opportunities that I was given whilst a Trainer. As well as being hard work both physically and mentally, it was a very varied job with scope for using initiative and flair and it gave me great job satisfaction. I look forward to eventually returning to catering to continue my career."

IMA Diploma MRS JANE WALKER MHCIMA has worked in the non-commercial sector of the industry since being awarded her IMA Diploma in Institutional Management in 1967 (with Distinction). She was a student at the Northern Polytechnic (now Polytechnic of North London).

Jane's first post was as Assistant Domestic Bursar at Gipsy Hill

College in Kingston, where she was responsible for the hall of residence, and for the supervision of meal service in the attached catering unit. After some 15 months, family reasons required her to return to Devon in early 1969, where she worked for the Devon County Council for the next nine years, until shortly before the birth of her daughter in 1978.

In Devon, Jane worked first at the Exmouth School as Cook/Supervisor catering for over 400 senior school boys. After eight months she was then promoted to Assistant/Deputy Caterer at Rolle College in Exmouth, a college of education with about 900 students, a seven day a week meals service (breakfast, lunch and dinner) with additional special functions and, in the holidays, short vacation courses.

When her husband was transferred to Torquay in 1976 Jane Walker was appointed Supervisor at Innerbrook Central Canteen in Torquay, responsible for catering for about 1100 school children of all ages in five separate schools.

She has served on the committee of the Devon and Cornwall branch of the HCIMA for some time since her return to Devon. Her work for the Association has included arranging meetings in the East Devon area during the key membership scheme. Jane was a member of the HCIMA Council for some years, as the Devon and Cornwall representative.

Halls of Residence

In response to the question "What is your job?", ANNA GARRICK ROSS FHCIMA, Bursar at University Hall, St Andrews, replies "A job that defies job description". "One requirement", she continues, "is that you must like variety if you are Bursar of a Hall of Residence housing and catering for three hundred. The needs of university students and of conference visitors differ greatly, one from the other, and the ability to adapt is essential."

After Anna's two year training at the Edinburgh College of Domestic Science in institutional management and large-scale catering, she spent a year as Lady Cook in one of the College's residences. Following the closure of that residence, she then moved to the main storeroom of the College as Assistant Storekeeper. Two years later she was promoted to a newly created post of Superintendent Housekeeper in charge of the domestic staff and cleaning of the College, which until then had been under the Storekeeper's umbrella. These posts were all residential.

Anna moved to St Andrews in 1961 as Assistant Domestic Bursar and after a short time was promoted to Domestic Bursar. In her first year in Hall, a new extension was opened, the first in

Margin notes:

400 school boys

5 schools
1100 children

Member of
HCIMA Council

Halls of Residence

Atholl Crescent
student, then
College
Housekeeper

St Andrews, increasing the numbers accommodated from 120 to 270 women students.

"How thankful I am for the former training in Institutional Management given at Atholl Crescent", Anna writes. "A training which ensured a thorough grounding in craft as well as management. Grateful too for my subsequent staff appointments in the College, which helped to build up the needful experience. So when — at the eleventh hour — the chef is ill (fortunately a rare occurrence), to step in and prepare a banquet, with grouse as the main dish, is not as traumatic an event as otherwise it would be. On this occasion Her Excellency Mrs Armstrong, the US Ambassador, was among the 260 guests present, the banquet being held to mark the American Bicentennial.

Coping with the unexpected

"While such moments stand out, in the day to day routine a sense of humour and an understanding of and interest in people are also necessary if one is to reconcile the sometimes conflicting requirements and viewpoints of clientele and staff — not to mention current legislation!

An interest in people essential

"Finally one must recognise, promote and appreciate the value of the team spirit, for it is on this above all that a large-scale establishment depends if it is to run happily.

"Seldom a dull moment and never an idle one. 'Unsocial hours' have little relevance for a job such as this. But it has its own rewards and I am still in it!"

Never a dull moment

Contract Catering/Employee Feeding

ANDREW AVES BSc MHCIMA was appointed Catering Officer for the British Airports Authority at London's Heathrow Airport in June 1978.

Andrew took up this post directly from the University of Surrey, after graduating with a BSc degree in Hotel and Catering Administration. He was admitted to the second year of the degree course, in September 1976 (for two years of full-time study), in view of his experience and qualifications.

Surrey BSc degree special entry

Andrew had studied for the Intermediate and Final Membership examinations of the Hotel and Catering Institute on a full-time basis at Hendon College of Technology and after successfully passing all his examinations he joined British Transport Hotels in 1969 as a trainee manager. He worked for BTH for seven years altogether, in a number of hotels including the St Enoch in Glasgow, the Great Eastern and Charing Cross Hotels in London and in a variety of positions including personnel and banqueting managers.

after HCI Inter + Final + BTH experience

From this style of life, to adjust to a university environment on a Local Authority grant was not easy. But Andrew was aware of new technology, different management systems and techniques of which he had little or no knowledge, and wished to broaden his career opportunities into other sectors of the hotel industry and administration.

Andrew feels he gained more from a university education as a mature student than if he had entered direct from school. Towards the end of his course, however, he did fear he was at a disadvantage when attending interviews for jobs with other potential graduates. Employers recruiting graduates perhaps did not expect to find a 29 year old experienced hotel caterer, and while some companies offered shortened graduate entry schemes, they still felt he would be unaware of the company systems and must therefore undertake a training programme.

His present position with the British Airports Authority offers a challenge to both Andrew's academic training and his catering knowledge. The Authority does not undertake any catering itself but provides the premises, equipment and maintenance and contracts the job out to experienced catering companies.

Andrew Aves's work involves monitoring standards of hygiene, product quality and service, all of which must conform to predetermined specifications set by the Authority; investigation of marketing opportunities for the catering service and design of future catering facilities. Heathrow was designed to handle 6 million passengers and in 1978 handled 28 million. This number is increasing and the majority of Andrew's time is spent in the development of new or redevelopment of existing facilities.

MRS PENNY STEINER MHCIMA studied for three years at the North London Polytechnic, successfully passing her Higher Diploma in Institutional Management in 1975. In the two periods of industrial experience during her course, Penny worked in employee feeding operations (with Mullard Ltd and with the BBC), an interest she has since built upon.

Whilst studying for her HND Penny had a weekend job with London University as a cook supervisor in a hall of residence. For two years during term time she and a friend ran the catering, alternating weekends. With a staff of six they provided meals for about 250 resident students — breakfast, lunch and dinner. During the two summer vacations of her course, Penny remained in her flat at the University (which was part payment for her weekend work) and worked as Assistant Domestic Bursar. She and a staff of twenty provided the housekeeping services (no meals, just breakfast) for the hall of residence, which

The margin notes for the above paragraphs:
- Not all smooth going
- British Airports Authority
- HND student
- Enterprise

was turned into an hotel type operation during the summer for various groups of overseas students.

Although the University were keen to offer Penny a permanent job after she had completed her studies, and she had also been offered a job with the BBC, she decided to join British Petroleum on a one year training scheme. Only two HND students were accepted on to the scheme (the usual arrangement) on the basis of a one year contract at the end of which they would be offered a job if one was available. Penny spent this period at BP's offices in Moorgate in the City of London, where an average of 4000 luncheons are served a day from five food production areas. The staff dining facilities range from the staff restaurant to the hospitality and directors' dining rooms, and include the management dining room, salad bar area and coffee lounge. Penny spent about a month in each of these areas, a similar period in the kitchens, stores, cost control office, training office and in the restaurant management offices.

After eight months only of her training scheme Penny was offered a job as Restaurant Supervisor at the Moorgate Office. With the other Supervisors she rotated her duties between all the dining areas. In 1977, about 18 months later, Penny was transferred to BP Oil in Victoria as Restaurant Supervisor, directly responsible to the catering manager. About 1000 lunches a day are served in the Victoria office and Penny was beginning to find her work rather dull, each day following what seemed to be exactly the same routine, when BP offered her promotion to a new position in the catering division of the company, Regional Catering Supervisor.

The next year was spent working closely with the company Catering Manager, travelling to each of BP Oil's 36 employee feeding units, doing statistical work, monitoring the contract caterers, dealing with problems as they arose, becoming involved in negotiations with various trade unions on delicate matters like (small) price rises for meals. The 36 units, which vary in size, serving 8–100 lunches daily, are based at oil depots around the country from Inverness to Plymouth, Ipswich to Swansea. Penny's visits vary in length from day trips by plane, train or car, to overnight trips. The catering services at these units are undertaken for BP by contractors (three different firms are involved) in return for a management fee and full reimbursement of all costs.

Penny's work has also involved a number of specific projects, for example helping design the catering facilities at BP's computer centre in Hemel Hempstead, where the 15 year old kitchen was closed for a time, gutted and completely reequipped. This has meant learning a lot about equipment in addition to the qualities Penny Steiner has constantly to use in

BP one year training scheme

Appointed Restaurant Supervisor

Promoted to Regional Catering Adviser

36 units throughout UK

Specific projects

managing staff and motivating them, dealing with contract caterers and trade unions.

JOHN BIBBY is Catering Manager with the Civil Service Catering Organisation (CISCO) for the Premium Bond Office Staff Restaurant at Lytham St Annes in Lancashire.

CISCO

John joined CISCO in June 1973 as a Catering Manager grade IV(CMIV). Within two years he had been promoted one grade (CMIII) and transferred to Preston as a regional relief manager. From here he was promoted to CMII in charge of CISCO's operation at Lytham St Annes, in October 1977.

Promotion to CMII

A student at the then Hollings College (National Diploma in Hotel Keeping and Catering 1965–68), John spent his first period of industrial experience at a Gardner Merchant staff catering unit in Manchester. For the second period and also for some months after leaving college, he worked in hotels: in the Lake District and then as Assistant Manager at the Higher Trapp Hotel in Simonstone. John then joined Cadbury Bros in early 1969 and worked on the research and development of food products; his own responsibilities included the development of "Smash" instant potato mix.

Wide experience

"Smash" development

Before joining CISCO John worked again in the hotel sector, as Manager of the High Lawn Hotel in Darwen in Lancashire from late 1970 to 1973. This was a family business, and he was responsible for accommodation services, functions and banqueting.

MISS RUTH KIDSON is in charge of the staff restaurant at the Government Buildings in Chessington. She was transferred to CC Chessington in May 1969 as CMIII after passing her promotion board and within two years of joining CISCO. This is her third position with the Civil Service Catering Organisation: after completing her management trainee programme and project in late 1977 and passing the Grade IV promotion board she was appointed Catering Manager at Riverwalk House, Millbank. Eleven months later she moved to the Home Office in Queen Anne's Gate as CM support.

CISCO at Chessington

Ruth has had an interest in catering since leaving school. She spent some of the summer before commencing an Ordinary National Diploma course at Nelson and Colne College working in the catering department of a hospital, and helping out in the staff canteen of a supermarket. She worked in the industry at every opportunity while a student at Nelson and Colne, and later, while studying for the Final Membership examinations of the HCIMA on a two year sandwich course at Hollings College. These experiences included: working at various local hotels and restaurants at weekends, bank holidays and some evenings as a

OND + HCIMA Final

Not an opportunity missed

banqueting waitress, working as a general assistant at THF's Grand Hotel in Llandudno, a period of industrial experience at a Gardner Merchant unit in Manchester, another as catering assistant for Marks and Spencer Ltd (in the evenings Ruth worked as a bar-maid at an hotel), and for a week between Marks and Spencer and returning to college, she worked for Ring and Brymer (an outdoor catering specialist firm, subsidiary of THF) at the Farnborough Air Show, as waitress, bar-maid and general helper in one of the chalets for French VIPs.

Ruth finished her course at Hollings in June 1977 and after spending the summer in the Yorkshire Dales working in a friend's restaurant and also as a caterer at a children's holiday camp in Surrey, she joined the Civil Service Catering Organisation as a management trainee. As she had failed two of her HCIMA Final papers in June 1977, CISCO sponsored her to study again — by correspondence course with Metropolitan College, Reading — and re-sit the two subjects the following June. She passed on this occasion.

CISCO sponsor correspondence course for two re-sits

Ruth had decided in her first year at Hollings that it was the industrial sector of the industry that she wished to make a career in, but she determined in the meantime to gain the widest possible experience of other areas.

STEPHEN ALBERTINI MHCIMA joined the catering industry because he wanted to combine practical work with administrative work. Other members of his family are also caterers.

HND in Institutional Management

When Stephen left the Polytechnic of North London in 1975 with an HND in Institutional Management he joined a small firm of catering contractors based in Twickenham as a trainee manager. R & S Catering have some 60 units in London and the south-east varying in size with about 300 meals a day at the bigger units, and 100 meals the average. During his eighteen months with the firm, Stephen worked for a lot of the time as a relief chef manager, responsible for all managerial functions as well as cooking. He feels he learned a great deal.

Contract catering

Joins the Post Office

In 1977 he joined the Post Office — a very large organisation with greater opportunities. In view of his HND qualifications and experience, Stephen commenced as a Grade E Manager (entrants start on a higher or lower grade depending on qualifications and experience). His first job was at a medium sized unit, the Telephone Exchange in South Kensington. With a cook on his staff of five, Stephen was responsible for providing about 100 meals a day. In addition he regularly deputised for the Group Manager, who was in charge of four similar units in the South Kensington area.

Staff of five, 100 meals a day

Staff Restaurant
Manager

After a period of eighteen months at South Kensington, Stephen wanted to move on and he was therefore transferred for further development to St Paul's in May 1978 as Staff Restaurant Manager. At this unit about 150 lunches a day are served on a six day week basis. A trolley service is also provided and the conference room gives scope for buffet and other function work. This room is available for entertaining guests of the Post Office's Telecommunications Executive and for meetings and conferences when a wide range of catering requirements are called for.

Clubs

GARY CHISHOLM chose catering for a career because he wanted to be of service to the public and felt that was precisely what catering was about, at whatever standard or level. Not sure whether to go directly to college and study for four years (OND then HCIMA Final), Gary wrote numerous letters to various potential employers and after many interviews decided to join Boodles Club, St James's, London SW1, on a four year trainee manager's course. That was August 1975. During the coming four years Gary was to spend between six and twelve months in each department covering different aspects of catering.

College or straight
into industry?

4 year trainee
manager's course
at Boodles

The first six months were spent in the kitchen where in addition to learning the basics of cookery, Gary gained first hand experience of the problems encountered in the daily routine of a busy kitchen. His work consisted of many tasks, preparing sauces, vegetables and even ordering the following day's supplies. Trips to each of the markets were arranged with a 5.30 am start and the Club's buyer would show Gary all the things to look for and how to select the best quality goods.

The second half of the first year Gary spent working with the valets in the Club's chambers (rooms), learning many aspects of the organisation and control of this side of the operation.

During the following year, when Gary moved to the restaurants to work directly with the Restaurant Manager, he decided to enrol at Westminster College (September 1976) and study for the City and Guilds of London Institute certificates: 707/1 Food Service, 707/2 Advanced Serving Techniques and 707/3 Alcoholic Beverages. With excellent results Gary was awarded Part-time Student of 1976/77 at Westminster College.

CGLI studies

Once Gary had completed the course he returned to Boodles full-time in the restaurant and his third year began with cellar management where he worked with two younger trainees controlling the wines and spirits, binning all in-coming wines, ordering spirits and minerals and issuing stocks to the cocktail

Wine and Spirit
Education Trust
Course

and dispense bars. In September 1977 Gary enrolled on a Wine and Spirit Education Trust Certificate course at their training school near Mansion House; the course lasted for eight weeks, one afternoon a week, and gave Gary a chance to further his knowledge about wines and understand the production aspects of wines and spirits better.

Varied work

The last six months of that year were spent back in the restaurant doing banqueting. With large and small functions at the Club on most days, Gary found that a lot of work was involved in making sure there were no hitches, planning the menus carefully, laying up and providing the highest standards of service.

HCIMA Part A

In his fourth year at the Club, the final of the management training scheme, Gary has been working through the different departments again, helping to control costs (from food to stationery) and planning budgets for the following year. In September 1978 Gary Chisholm enrolled again at Westminster College, on the HCIMA's Part A course. When he has completed this course, studying over two years on a day release basis, Gary plans to continue his studies for full membership of the HCIMA by studying for Part B on a one year full-time course.

Public Houses

BSc degree

NIGEL A. GREENWOOD BSc MHCIMA graduated from the University of Surrey with a BSc degree in Hotel and Catering Administration in 1970. His "very useful and informative" industrial year was spent with the Catering Division of J. Lyons and Co. Ltd.

Charrington & Co.
Assistant District
Manager

Nigel joined Charrington and Co. as a management trainee after leaving Surrey. His first few months involved working in public houses, stocktaking, and getting to know most departments in the brewery from the bottling line to the sampling room! In February 1971 he was appointed an Assistant District Manager, administering and controlling pubs in London's East End, and proceeded to forget all about food preparation and service. Customers drank heavily but rarely consumed anything of more substance than a sausage!

Promotion
and discos

Nigel became a District Manager (still in the East End) in 1972, the time when pub-discotheque operations were at their height. With responsibility for 48 pubs (Tenanted and Managed) of which 36 had some sort of disco operation, his knowledge of modern music increased modestly. He also observed that drinking trends originate in the East End: the fashion for Southern Comfort, Vodka and Dry Martini being examples.

Derek Taylor, Grand Metropolitan.

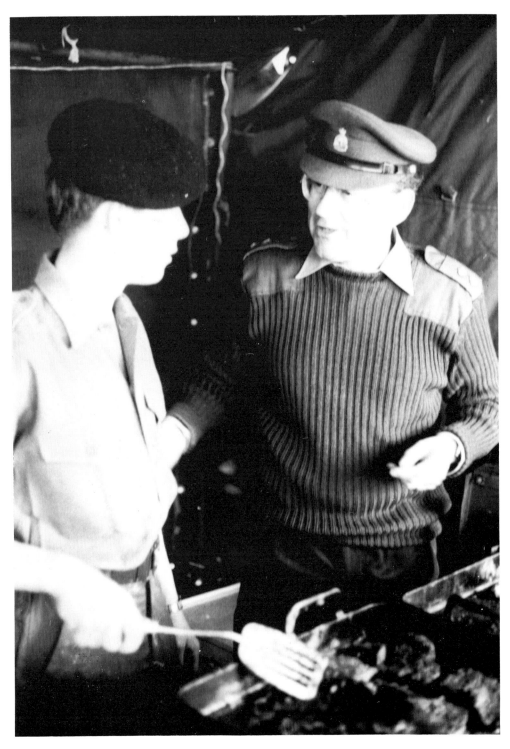

Lieutenant Colonel Tony Roe, Army Catering Corps.

Anna Ross, University Hall, St Andrews.

Michael Robertson, HCITB Travelling Scholarship winner 1978.

When he was appointed District Manager in Central London in 1974, Nigel suddenly realised that customers liked to eat as well as drink, and was at a loss to cope with this new demand until internal "rehabilitation" was carried out. In 1977 he was promoted to Regional Services Executive advising on control methods and taking on "one-off" promotional activities. Although he found this work frustrating, it did broaden his outlook.

Area Manager
140 pubs

Nigel Greenwood was promoted to his present position of Area Manager for Charrington & Co. in 1978, with responsibility through four District Managers for 140 pubs, Managed and Tenanted, throughout the City of London and its boundary. He has found the nature of trade in the City to be totally absorbing and unpredictable and indeed has found the positions of both District and Area Manager satisfying, demanding a wide knowlege of management — recruiting, training, selling, marketing, motivating, controlling and developing. Something of an exception to the rule by staying with one company since graduating, Nigel has "moved-on" within the company at the right time. (Perhaps this accounts for a developing interest he has taken in Pension Funds!)

Self development

In his career with Charrington & Co., Nigel has attended several in-company training courses as well as two externals: a four week Management Development Course at Ashridge Management College and a one week Law for Managers Course with Greville Janner MP organised by Incomtec Ltd.

The Specialists

A "National"
student

MISS HILARY CHARLES was a student at the National Training College of Domestic Subjects. After taking her Part I examinations (at the end of the two year full-time college course), Hilary spent her compulsory one year's industrial experience working as an assistant cook at Birmingham University. She recalls having only three weekends off in the whole year, working on her weekly "day-off" from 7 am to 10.30 am, and being paid a princely salary of £150 p.a. In 1954 after her Part II examination, she was awarded the IMA Certificate in Institutional Management and Housekeeping with First Class Honours.

£150 p.a.

Hospital catering

Although Hilary had been planning to carry on the family tradition of entering the medical profession and becoming a dietician, she decided at this time that the field of dietetics was too narrow for her and obtained a job as an assistant catering officer at the Princess Alice Hospital, Eastbourne. She worked there for $2\frac{1}{2}$ years under a boss who allowed her scope for developing her own ideas as well as considerable authority.

Joins Batemans

Her next experience, as assistant catering officer at New End Hospital, Hampstead, was less happy and in 1957 she joined Batemans as a trainee manager — "go anywhere and do anything because it is good experience" was what this meant. She was then made manager of a staff restaurant in Holborn, but after a year again got itchy feet and joined the company's relief force as a trouble shooter.

A temporary appointment at head office in control of the relief team led to Hilary Charles entering the personnel field.

Now Director of
Human Resources
Bateman
Grandmet

Today she is Director of Human Resources for Bateman Grandmet Holdings Limited. From a one-man band she has gradually built up a slim, but hardworking personnel department. In 1975 the department was decentralised within the UK, into divisional and regional departments, all of whom have a functional responsibility to Miss Charles. The Personnel and Training Department alone has a staff of 35 — a central training function was retained — excluding secretarial and clerical support.

Self development

Hilary, as well as being a Fellow of the Hotel, Catering and Institutional Management Association, is a Fellow of the Institute of Personnel Management and a Member of the Institution of Training Officers, and also now serves as a member on Industrial Tribunals. When she entered the personnel field, she attended numerous short courses as well as taking the IPM course at Ealing Technical College and later at Battersea College of Technology (at the time it became the University of Surrey).

Looking back on her long career with Batemans, Hilary writes: "There have been enormous changes in this time, no two years have been the same. I have had the most magnificent

World travel

opportunities to travel having literally been around the world, in some cases studying employment laws and conditions in countries where we operate, and in other cases recruiting 'Third Country Nationals' to work in Middle Eastern countries where local labour is not available."

When DEREK TAYLOR MA FHCIMA left Cambridge University with a degree in History, he had no plans for a career in the hotel industry. By sheer accident he joined a small group

Salesman

of London hotels owned by Maxwell Joseph as a salesman, soon to be appointed sales director.

Derek's office at 16 Half Moon Street in Mayfair quickly became the centre of a hive of activity, at a time when it was

A respected pioneer

almost unheard of for an hotel company to promote its sales. His assistant's task was to visit existing clients, write to potential clients and to telephone them in order to persuade them to spend money on accommodation, food and drink at the hotels within the group. His group sales manager concentrated on planning group bookings from Europe and North America.

Maxwell Joseph had entered the hotel business in 1946, eight years before he employed Derek Taylor, when he took over the Mandeville Hotel, London with only 6 bedrooms in use. By 1954, he had taken over the Washington Hotel in Curzon Street, modernised it at a cost of £50 000 and acquired Honeywood Hotels for £135 000. Grand Metropolitan Hotels (of which Derek Taylor has been a director for some years) was formed in 1962. It is now part of a giant organisation alongside Watneys, Trumans, Mecca, Berni, Express Dairies and IDV, to mention but a few of the household names that form part of the Grand Metropolitan group. In the year to September 1978 turnover was £1850 million with pre-tax profits of £115.9 million and the group gave employment to more than 100 000 men and women.

Derek Taylor is author of a number of books including *Hotel and Catering Sales Promotion*, *The Golden Age of British Hotels* (with David Bush), *Fortune, Fame and Folly* and *How to Sell Banquets*. He recalls spending his first year's salary on a six week trip to America (he was given unpaid leave for the purpose) to find out how the Americans tackled the business of selling an hotel's facilities — and pawning his typewriter to get back!

In September 1979 Derek Taylor was appointed visiting professor at the University of Surrey. He is a member of Food, Accommodation and Related Sciences Board of the Council for National Academic Awards (see page 204).

DERMOT MATHIAS BSc MHCIMA is a Director of Horwath and Horwath (UK) Ltd., responsible for supervising and conducting consultancy assignments in the hotel and tourism industries.

Dermot joined Hesketh, Hardy, Hirshfield (now Stoy Hayward & Co.)., the parent company of Horwath and Horwath, in 1973 as an articled clerk. That summer he had graduated from the University of Surrey with a BSc Honours degree in Hotel and Catering Administration. In addition to the year's industrial experience during the Surrey course, which Dermot spent with the Grand Metropolitan Hotels as a trainee manager working in both the St Ermins and Waldorf Hotels, he had worked for a year between school and university as a management trainee with the Forte organisation. He also spent three months in the United States, travelling extensively and work for a period as night auditor and manager of a Connecticut hotel.

While training and studying to be a Chartered Accountant Dermot spent part of his time on hotel consultancy projects for Horwath and Horwath, and was transferred to the company on a full-time basis once he had passed his final accountancy examinations in September 1976.

Dermot Mathias has specialised in the financial and marketing aspects of consultancy assignments. His work has included hotel feasibility studies for major international hotel companies in Denmark, the UK, Greece, Spain, Kuwait, Dubai, the United Arab Emirates and Yemen. He was recently involved in a study for the English Tourist Board on governmental financial treatment of hotels in England and several European countries. Tourism surveys Dermot has been involved in abroad include a tourism and hotel survey for an envisaged tourist complex in Bali, Indonesia, advice on a major tourist development on a Greek island, and an investigation into the Maltese tourism industry.

Frequent travel on assignments

MICHAEL PICKARD FCA joined the hotel and catering industry in 1967 when he was appointed managing director of Trust Houses. Previously financial director of British Printing Corporation, he attributes his success to accountancy training. He says: "I joined a smallish accountancy practice in the City as an articled clerk which gave me an insight into the way a whole range of companies were run, and with very varying results. It enabled one to have responsibility at a comparatively young age for individual audits and, more importantly, enabled one to understand what made companies successful and, equally important, unsuccessful."

Importance of accountancy training

Ingredients of success

Michael established his own catering business in 1971 and now employs over 600 staff in an expanding chain of family roadside restaurants. Each of these "Happy Eater" units is geared to the needs of the travelling family with reasonable prices, quick service and a special menu and play area for the children. His other business interests include the Pickard Motor Hotel in Epsom, recreation and motor business.

Family roadside restaurant business

One of Michael Pickard's priorities is good staff relations and he takes a personal interest in training. Each Happy Eater unit has an on-the-job training team, including the manager and experienced staff.

MICHAEL STAPLETON FCMA is Operations Accountant, London Hotels, for Trusthouse Forte Ltd., based in Sherwood Street, London W1. He recalls facing "the awful realisation after ten blithe years at public school that he had to decide on how to earn his way in the world". Determined that the industry he chose would be one where the "product" was people, of a highly personal nature, with a minimum of routine, Michael decided the hotel industry fitted these requirements perfectly

Joins people industry

and knowing nothing of the trade took practical advice both on the industry itself and the best way to enter it.

On the basis that college could teach aspects of the industry there would rarely be the opportunity of learning when in a working environment Michael enrolled in September 1969 with the first students on the new Higher National Diploma course in Hotel and Catering Administration at Westminster College.

The three year course contained immense subject matter (Michael feels there was perhaps insufficient emphasis throughout his course on the food production and service element of the industry) and it included two three month periods of industrial release which he spent at the Europa Hotel, London and with the Catering Division of the then J. Lyons & Co. Ltd. Like many other students Michael "moonlighted", thereby gaining an excellent insight into the trade, and, at the same time, the opportunity of working at such places as Buckingham Palace, Windsor Castle, at the Wimbledon Tennis Championships and at various race-courses.

After successfully gaining his HND and feeling his choice of industry confirmed, the thought of interminable periods of duty management made Michael decide to move into the ancillary, yet essential side of every industry, accounts. Resolved to retain a direct link with the operational side of the industry he returned to J. Lyons & Co. Ltd. as a trainee management accountant. Here, after a very few months, he first encountered an effect of the high staff-turnover of the industry, and was placed rather sooner than he might have expected in charge of the HO accounting function of the Leisure Catering Division. This division included an expanding series of catering concessions in safari parks, zoos and stately homes and involved him not only in the existing units but the development and appraisal of future projects. Before leaving Lyons two years later he had carried out a similar function for such diverse areas as a supermarket, a country hotel and the industrial catering division. Throughout this period when it was paramount to establish effective liaison with every level of operational management, Michael felt his practical experience in the industry invaluable. He decided at this time to formalise his accounting knowledge and joined the Institute of Cost and Management Accountants, passing the final examinations in 1977.

In 1975, in order to broaden his experience Michael joined the British-American Tobacco Co. Ltd. and worked on the Territorial Accounts team for South America which included collating accounting information from the subsidiary companies and an extensive involvement in development and expansion programmes. After eighteen months during which he gathered an insight into the highly sophisticated accounting

---

HND course

Moonlighting

Into accounts with J. Lyons

Institute of Cost and Management Accountants

BAT experience

techniques of one of the world's giant manufacturing companies, he returned to the catering industry and, after a brief flirtation with a small catering company, joined Trusthouse Forte Hotels Ltd.

Chief Accountant
at THF hotel

He was appointed Chief Accountant at the 530 bedroomed Kensington Close Hotel in spring 1977 with his first opportunity of direct unit responsibility (within the standardised procedures and Head Office reporting systems — each of THF's London Hotels has a large degree of autonomy). Responsible to the Hotel General Manager yet at the same time reporting to the THF Divisional Financial Controller, the accountant in an hotel of this size is considered a member of the senior management team with an absorbing and multifarious role. Besides controlling the accounts office staff, covering income and food and beverage control, bought ledger, a complete in-house sales ledger, the wages department, all cashiering and audit functions, the major role is the provision of information enabling management decision-making, and advising all operational management. As a 24-hour day operation, with a cosmopolitan and ever changing work force it is a very rare occurrence that everything runs perfectly, Michael says. The result of this is that the accountant spends substantial parts of his day perhaps reviewing liquor controls with the catering manager in an attempt to resolve a pilferage or cash-shortage problem, or discussing costings on a redevelopment project with the works manager, or evaluating the cost of a potential bonus scheme with the personnel manager. Involvement such as this, together with on-going review of the efficiency of systems, the use of Electronic Data Processing, detailed involvement in the compilation of corporate plans and feasibility studies, provided Michael with a very satisfying job.

A very satisfying
job

Promoted to
Operations
Accountant for
16 THF London
hotels

After nearly two years at the Kensington Close Hotel, Michael was promoted to Operations Accountant, London Hotels, covering sixteen hotels within London ranging from 70 to 1100 bedrooms and from three to five star categories. He is now responsible to the Operations Director, retaining the reporting role to the Divisional Financial Controller. Where in the hotel he had provided unit management with accounting information, he now carries out this role for all 16 hotels' results to the Operations Directors, and provides a liaisonary service back to the hotel managers and accountants in addition to carrying out *ad hoc* exercises in a continuing effort to improve procedures and optimise profitability whether it be by generating revenue or improved cost control.

Whilst Michael says he still nurtures the common ambition of one day owning his own hotel company and living by his own decisions, in the shorter term he hopes to progress within

Trusthouse Forte Ltd., by orientating further towards operational responsibility but at all times retaining both accounting and unit level involvement.

ROBERT KERR is Group Training Manager for Holiday Inn International with direct responsibility to the company's Regional Director (who controls the seven "Inc" UK Holiday Inns, and one in France).

Robert started working in the hotel and catering industry when he was nine years old and had to spend each morning of his school holidays preparing three bath tubs of potatoes, one for roasting, one for boiling, and one for chips. Although his step-father's hotel (The Commodore in Bournemouth) did have a peeling machine, it was Robert's task to remove the eyes etc. before being allowed to join his friends on the beach. At the age of fourteen he had his own station of thirty covers in the restaurant.

When he left school "hating the hotel and catering industry", Robert joined the Army on an officer's course — but after two years he resigned and studied for a National Diploma in Hotel Keeping and Catering (1957-61) at what was then called the Municipal College of Technology and Commerce in Bournemouth. It was a 4 year sandwich course, with periods in industry in the second and third years.

After gaining his Diploma, Robert went to the 390 room Mayfair Hotel in London (Grand Metropolitan) as junior food and beverage manager. A year later he was promoted to Catering Manager (the hotel has five food service outlets and weekly food revenue at that time was in the order of £10 000).

Robert's next move was to the Kennedy Hotel, near Euston (320 rooms), as Rooms Division Manager, then to the 160 room Washington Hotel as Personnel Manager. At the age of 27 he was appointed General Manager of the independently owned 120 room Norfolk Plaza Hotel.

Before joining Holiday Inn International in 1978, Robert worked for the company's South African franchise holder for nearly three years. Based in Johannesburg he was responsible for training, helping to open many of the country's 22 Holiday Inns, personally training all the staff at two Inns, and occasionally even bush fire-fighting. Robert also worked for the Best Western operation in South Africa (as Education and Systems Manager) before returning to the UK.

As Group Training Manager, Robert sees his job as developing people — sometimes this means some hard-selling because training can never produce a return on investment in pure cash terms, although some of its benefits (e.g. less staff turnover, higher productivity) can be measured, and Robert finds his work enormously challenging and satisfying.

Margin notes:

Holiday Inn Group Training Manager

An early start

First an Army officer's course

Food and Beverage Manager

General Manager at 27

South Africa

Developing people

4

The Evolution of Catering Education

The first schools of cookery. The forerunners of the craft courses of today, a brief description of the early initiatives of the City and Guilds of London Institute and the Hotel and Catering Institute, and subsequent developments. The first membership courses of the IMA and HCI. The National Diploma in Hotel Keeping and Catering. HCI Intermediate and Final. University degree courses. Ordinary and Higher National Diplomas, thinking behind TEC, the new HCIMA Professional Qualification. CNAA degree courses.

CATERING education in the United Kingdom has a short but eventful history. The first major landmarks were the formation in 1873 of The National Training School of Cookery in South Kensington, and the formation in 1910 of the School of Cookery at the Westminster Technical Institute in Vincent Square. It is in the period since the Second World War, however, that the greatest strides have been made. Change has become a regular feature, with important developments in each decade.

"The National"

Until the first classes began at the National Training School of Cookery in 1874, instruction in cookery and other aspects of household management had been unsystematic and very limited. It was not unusual for girls in orphanages and charitable institutions to be thoroughly instructed in cookery, there were a number of examples of private enterprise, some industrial schools were equipped with kitchens and washhouses (until in 1860 the Privy Council concluded they were too expensive to equip and maintain and directed that attention should be concentrated on needlework). The general public was deaf and blind to the importance of the matter.

Then the subject of food was included in the programme for the International Exhibition of 1873 in South Kensington. An accomplished lecturer on technical subjects, much in demand at the Mechanics' Institutes, J. C. Buckmaster was approached to conduct a series of lecture-demonstrations on cookery. At this first Exhibition, Mr Buckmaster confined his part to the actual lectures and arranging for them to be illustrated by a French chef.

The 1873 Exhibition was visited by half a million people, and the cookery section caught the public imagination. There was a charge of 6d for a seat in the front row, with permission for tasting, otherwise attendance was free. Recipes were also sold and the final takings amounted to £1765. Queen Victoria attended one demonstration, but it is recorded that "while waiting unwillingly for a demonstration of how to cook an omelette she had to listen to a rather tiresome lecture".

The man behind the cookery lectures was Henry Cole, a leading member of the Royal Commissioners for the Great Exhibition of 1851. Assessing the public's response to the lectures, and believing their success could be exploited to the benefit of the nation, he persuaded the Committee responsible for the lectures to back his idea of establishing a national training school of cookery. The Marquis of Westminster (later the first Duke) lent his home in Park Lane, Grosvenor House, for a public meeting on 17 July 1873.

It was unanimously resolved "That the establishment of a Training School for Cookery . . . is most desirable at the present time; that the aim of the proposed School should be to teach the best methods of cooking articles of food for general consumption among all the classes". It was proposed to commence the work of the National Training School of Cookery as soon as possible in Exhibition Road, South Kensington (now the site of the Imperial College of Science), in the building used for the lectures, which the Commissioners had placed at the disposal of the School for a limited period.

On 23 March 1874 the National opened with its first class of 14. The fees were three guineas for this first course, which lasted a fortnight. The morning session, from 10 am to noon, was on cleaning methods, management of ovens and flues and basic cookery processes. From 2 to 4 pm a lecture demonstration was given on a variety of dishes. Once a month, all who wished could attend a written examination in the theory and practice of cookery (fee 2s 6d); in the first twelve months, 176 students passed.

Working conditions in the building were rigorous, with no proper ventilation, a leaky corrugated iron roof and neither larder nor storeroom.

Westminster

There is a record of the Cookery and Food Association opening an "International College of Cookery" in Vauxhall Bridge Road in 1909. Certainly by the following year Herman Senn, founder of the Cookery and Food Association, had persuaded the London County Council to open a School of Cookery at the Westminster Technical Institute. The Baroness Burdett-Coutts was another driving force.

The Times of 16 November, 1911 reported: "The original course was for three years and the boys had to be between 17 and 16 years old when admitted. In addition to Practical Cookery, French, the language of the kitchen was taught with other general subjects."

A year later the same paper carried the report: " 'BC' Bachelor of Cuisine may be the next degree at the Universities . . . . Arrangements have been made at the Westminster Technical Institute for awarding a diploma in cookery to the student apprentices who pass next Easter their final examinations in the theory and practice of cookery. There are 44 of these students, first, second and third year men. The present third year, 15 in number, entered the Institute in the Spring of 1910 when the LCC offered 5 scholarships to boys . . . who wanted to be chefs . . . 5 scholarships are awarded every year to students . . . each worth £10 for the first year, £15 for the second and for the third. For those who did not get scholarships the fees are £9 per year. Most probably all who get diplomas will at once get positions in the big hotels of London."

The report continued: "The student waiters, of whom there are 12, are boys who competed last year for 12 scholarships of £10 each, open to boys of between 14 and 16 for a year's course in waiting . . . . Members of the Incorporated Association of Hotel Keepers, which includes the most prominent hotel owners of the kingdom have agreed to employ all the student waiters who pass their exam in table service, pastry work, menu work and accounts, starting them at 6s a week with board etc., for the first year of service, 8s for the second, 10s for the third, and further according to merit."

In the following year, when Iwan Kreins Head Master of the School for the first 26 years of its existence retired, proposals were advanced to build a 20 bedroom hotel to be linked with the School, but the hotel was never completed. The shell of the building, which had been constructed in Vincent Square adjacent to the college's other building, was used to provide a hall, additional restaurant and kitchen space and further classrooms.

A Scottish Story

One of the earliest students at the National was Miss Christina Guthrie Wright. She had a very definite purpose in mind, the opening of a similar school in Edinburgh.

At a meeting on 21 April 1875, with the Lord Provost of Edinburgh in the chair, a motion was moved "That in view of the great success which has attended the establishment of schools of cookery in London and elsewhere . . . it is desirable that some means should be provided in Edinburgh for acquiring a systematic knowledge of the general principles of this art".

The large audience, mainly composed of ladies, heard: "If the human body was not provided with properly cooked food to sustain its various operations, a demand, an irresistible craving existed for stimulants, and men had no alternative but to enter a dram-shop to satisfy their wants. It was now proposed to train the wives of the working men to induce their husbands to their homes by proper cookery, thus giving the men food they could relish and digest."

Shortly after Miss Guthrie Wright returned to Edinburgh, no doubt a little pleased by her achievement in gaining 965 marks out of 1000 in The National's examination, the Edinburgh School of Cookery opened publicly (November 1875).

In the session 1876/77 a ticket for a course of 12 demonstration lessons in High Class cookery was 1 guinea. On a Friday afternoon between 2 pm and 4 pm, the course of lessons covered entrées, fish, soups, pastry, jellies and creams, puddings, omelettes and soufflés, cakes and vegetables, sweet dishes, national dishes and sick room cookery. The Instructress cooked and explained the dishes, learners were expected to take notes.

Demonstration lessons were also offered in Plain Cookery and Artisan Cookery and Practice Lessons offered at an additional fee to those who had attended or were attending Demonstrations.

By August 1891 the Edinburgh School of Cookery and Domestic Science had moved its headquarters to Atholl Crescent and opened a boarding house for the benefit of lady students coming from the country. In the report to the Annual General Meeting of Shareholders for the year ended 31 August 1901, the list of subjects taught included: artisan, plain and high class cookery (demonstration and practice); starching and ironing; dress-fitting, cutting and making; the various branches of plain and fancy sewing; millinery; lectures on sick nursing, on household hygiene and on the method of teaching. Lessons were given on house book-keeping, also courses of lectures on elementary hygiene, chemistry of food and physiology of digestion, and on housekeeping (in connection with the practical training of Housewives and Lady Housekeepers).

During the year, the Staff Teachers had given 3290 demonstrations and Practice Lessons, and had heard and criticised 154 Test Demonstrations by Teachers in training.

In 1930 the name of "Atholl Crescent", as it was fondly called, was changed to the Edinburgh College of Domestic Science. Forty years later, and two years before changing its name again, this time to Queen Margaret College, the college moved to a new building in Clermiston.

The Early Development of Craft Training

The first schools of cookery opened in the last quarter of the 19th century . . . the first hotel school opened in 1910 . . . a new body was formed for the promotion of technical education throughout the country in 1878 . . . these are three strands in the early development of craft training for the hotel and catering industry.

Two further initiatives began to unite the efforts: an approach to the City and Guilds of London Institute by the catering branches of the Army, Navy and Air Force for a national syllabus and examination in cookery during the Second World War, and the formation of the Catering Trades Education Committee a few years after.

First, the schools of cookery. The National, one of the earliest, had an important and lasting influence on the pattern of further education in catering. Its own contribution was curtailed when financial pressures forced the college, a voluntary one, to close. The story of Queen Margaret College is therefore a more typical one, and certainly happier. Many of the hotel and catering departments in the polytechnics and colleges of today trace their history back to schools of cookery, even if frequent name changes do sometimes obscure the fact. (Brighton Technical College, known by that name since 1897, is one honourable exception.)

Second, the Schools of Cookery and Waiting of the Westminster Technical Institute. The School of Cookery was the first to be specifically established to provide well trained British craft workers for the hoteliers of the locality.

The involvement of the City and Guilds of London Institute, the third strand, in technical education has been almost as long as the existence of the first schools of cookery. Two years before the formal constitution of the City and Guilds of London Institute for the Advancement of Technical Education (as it was then called), at a meeting held at the Mansion House on 3 July 1876 by the Corporation of London and certain of the Livery Companies, the following resolution was adopted:

"That it is desirable that the attention of the Livery Companies be directed to the promotion of education not only in the Metropolis but throughout the country and especially to technical education, with a view of educating young artizans and others in the scientific and artistic branches of their trades."

The move of the Institute to establish a national syllabus and examination in cookery was made with the assistance of a committee that included representatives of the Army, Navy and Air Force catering branches, trade organisations (including the Hotels and Restaurants Association), educationalists and the Board of Education. The request for such a scheme had come from HM Forces. The impetus for the introduction of City and Guilds examinations and certificates in cookery was the need to facilitate the resettlement of Service Personnel in civilian life after the war. Thus it was in the academic year of 1944-45 that the Institute first introduced its Programme I: Cookery Subjects, which consisted of Subject 150 Plain Cookery, Subject 151 Cookery for Hotels and Catering Establishments and Subject 152 Advanced Cookery for Hotels and Restaurants.

Cookery was not the only technique in which instruction was needed, hence the fifth strand. Wider issues were facing the industry, the key to which was why should not "catering" take its place with other great national industries, why should it not develop its own scheme of technical education, and take advantage of the technical colleges established throughout the country by Local Education Authorities?

The Westminster School of Cookery provided the industry with a splendid example of the success of technical training, and the need for such training was obvious in an industry recovering from the upheaval of the Second World War with a desperate shortage of "home grown" staff.

A meeting took place on 10 December 1943, addressed by R. A. Butler, President of the Board of Education, and it was agreed with the support of almost all national associations in the industry to set up a Catering Trades Education Committee (CTEC).

This Committee formulated the principles of basic training for the industry and set about the organisation of training courses in technical colleges throughout the country.

By the time the Catering Wages Commission Report *Training for the Catering Industry* was published in 1946, some differences of opinion had emerged between the CTEC and the National Society of Caterers to Industry which had therefore withdrawn. The Hotels and Restaurants Association was not a member either.

The Commission, finding that no point of principle in connection with basic training seemed to divide the three bodies, made a strong plea for unity which was sympathetically heard, and acted upon. To reflect these happier circumstances, the CTEC was renamed the National Council for Hotel and Catering Education (NCHCE) in June 1947.

In its report for the year ended 31 March 1947, the National Council stated that there were more than 70 colleges and schools at which training for some aspect of the industry was being carried out. If account is taken of both full-time and part-time courses, there were at least 1500 students taking definite courses for the industry.

The majority of the students were taking either the City and Guilds 150 or 151. The full-time college courses in existence then, of two or three years duration, covered the syllabus, and included the examinations for the 150, 151 and, on longer courses, the 152; in addition certain administrative and managerial subjects were covered, for example hotel organisation, book-keeping and reception.

The National Council concentrated on the introduction of examinations in those subjects not covered by the City and Guilds of London Institute. The first developments proposed were courses for waiting to be divided into Parts A and B, the Council's Craftsman Certificate to be awarded to those who passed both examinations, and an Hotel Book-keeper Receptionist course.

Shortly after the formation of the Hotel and Catering Institute in November 1949, the NCHCE was dissolved (the idea of a professional body had been revived by one of the Associations represented on the National Council, and the project went ahead under the aegis of the full Council).

When the HCI took over the educational work in 1950, there were 1500 full-time and 3500 part-time students under training. Seventeen colleges were offering full-time courses and part-time courses, and 53 colleges were offering part-time courses only. In the same year, 328 candidates sat the City and Guilds 150 examinations, and 573 the 151. The total number of candidate entries to the Institute's examination, by comparison, was 81 080.

One of the first matters the HCI Council turned its attention to was continuing the educational work of the NCHCE. The first examinations in Waiting had been held by the National Council at Brighton Technical College in July 1949 (on a pilot basis). In 1951, the first examination in Hotel Book-keeping and Reception was held, while work continued on establishing a National Scheme for Apprenticeship for Cooks.

In 1952 the National Joint Apprenticeship Council for the Hotel and Catering Industry was established; the Hotel and Catering Institute was closely associated with the scheme in that it nominated employers' representatives to the NJAC, and for a time provided office accommodation and secretarial support.

The Apprenticeship Scheme was for five years, it included two months in Butchery Preparation, two months in Fish Preparation, two months in Poultry and Game Preparation, nine months in the Larder, six months in the Soup Corner, four months in the Roast and Grill, six months in Vegetables, Eggs and Farinaceous Cookery, eight months in the Fish Corner, nine months in the Sauce Corner, nine months in the Pastry Corner and three months as a Relief Cook.

Apprentices also attended college to prepare for the City and Guilds 150 and 151 certificates, and if they advanced exceptionally well, they could also prepare for the 152 certificate.

The HCI Journal announced in summer 1954 that 108 technical colleges throughout Great Britain were offering courses in training in hotel and catering subjects, and that 7500 potential new entrants and employees in the industry were taking such courses. These, the Journal continued, were record figures, unequalled in any European country and comparing very favourably with the position in the USA. At about this time City and Guilds revised the 150 scheme to form The Catering Trades Basic Training Course.

In 1957 a new national three year scheme for training cooks was inaugurated. It was the result of discussions between the Institute and the British Hotels and Restaurants Association, and was administered by the Institute through a National Committee assisted by regional committees. The BHRA, the Caterers' Association and other national trade organisations nominated representatives.

Two years later, an Apprenticeship Scheme for Waiters and Waitresses was inaugurated nationally (administered by the National Joint Apprenticeship Council of the Hotel and Catering Industry through regional committees). Briefly the scheme provided for a comprehensive three year training in establishments approved by the Council for this purpose, combined with part-time release studies at a technical college.

By 1961 there were only a handful of apprentices on these schemes: 34 in number, all waiters. However, over 1500 apprentice cooks had taken part in the 5 year scheme; the number of trainee cooks taking part in the 3 year scheme since its inception was 263, of whom, sadly, 52 had withdrawn. There were at the time, 2 girl apprentice cooks (5 year scheme), 19 girl trainee cooks (3 year scheme), but not as yet any apprentice waitresses.

The Early Development of Management Training:
First IMA Courses

It had become clear during the formative days of the Institutional Management Association, interrupted as they were by the Second World War, that if real progress was to be made in establishing institutional management as a profession, it was necessary to have some national qualification which would be recognised over the whole country as the appropriate professional entry.

The IMA decided in 1943 to call together a committee of enquiry consisting of representatives of employers' associations and other interested bodies as well as of educationalists which set out with the active support of the then Ministry of Education and the approval of the Ministry of Education for Northern Ireland and the Scottish Education Department to develop a syllabus for training and recommend the qualifications needed to fit a student for a career in institutional management.

As a result of the work of this committee, the IMA was recognised as the national examining body for institutional management in 1947.

The course, which started for the first time in 1947, was a two year full-time college course followed by a compulsory third year in appropriate employment. The Part I examinations (written and practical) were taken at the end of the period in college. The Part II examinations — taken at the end of the third year — consisted of a thesis or report written during the students' period in industry and a viva voce. Successful students were awarded the IMA Certificate in Institutional Management and Housekeeping.

In 1949 the IMA introduced the Matron-Housekeeper's Certificate: a two year full-time college course followed by a year gaining practical experience in approved employment. The course was designed for girls who wished to work with children in boarding schools or children's homes. No specific educational qualifications were laid down for entry until 1966, when the requirement was set at three GCE 'O' levels.

HCI Introduces Its First Membership Examination

The Annual Report of the Hotel and Catering Institute for the year ending 31 December 1952 announced that the Institute was preparing a syllabus for an examination for Associate Membership. Mr B. C. Edwards, Secretary of the Institute, explained at a meeting earlier in the year that the examination would have a managerial bias. He added that the Institute wanted Associate Membership and the letters AMHCI to indicate that the holder was a really well qualified person, just as Associate Membership of the Institute of Chartered Accountants and the letters ACA denoted the well qualified accountant or auditor.

The new system — requiring possession of two craft certificates, including the CGLI 151, success at the Institute's Associate Membership examination, and a minimum of two years' approved experience in the industry — was not put into full effect until 1955. The first examinations (which could then be taken direct as attendance at a course was not compulsory in the first years) were offered in March 1953. The fee for the examination, three papers of 3 hours' duration each, was 3 guineas.

The Late 1950s and Early 1960s

The principals of some of the colleges in which IMA training was given suggested in the late 1950s that the time spent in college by students was insufficient. They felt that the IMA Certificate course should be extended to three years' tuition, broken only by brief spells of practical work outside college.

Preliminary details of the new courses were published in the IMA Journal of December 1959:

1. IMA Abridged Course for older entrants
    "A one year course extending over three terms, and including some vacation work. Minimum age of entry 25 years with good professional qualifications or considerable practical experience and a reasonable standard of education."
2. IMA Diploma in Institutional Management
    "Candidates should be 18 years of age with a good general education and a General Certificate of Education to standards laid down. The course will be a three year full-time training at one of the colleges approved by the IMA."
3. The IMA Certificate in Institutional Housekeeping and Catering
    "This will be a certificate of national standing with less emphasis on management and more on craft. The course will be a two year full-time training in one of the colleges approved by the IMA. Conditions of entry: candidates will not be less than 17 years of age, with GCE passes in at least 3 subjects at 'O' level."

National Diploma in Hotel Keeping and Catering

Negotiations and planning for a National Diploma in Hotel Keeping and Catering had been protracted. The 1949 Report of the National Council for Hotel and Catering Education had expressed the hope "that with the establishment of the Hotel and Catering Institute and subject to the approval of the Ministry of

Education it would be possible to institute a National Diploma and National Certificate in Hotel and Catering Services. Preliminary work has already been done in connection with these and it is hoped that eventually National Diploma courses will be substituted for a certain number of existing full-time courses in hotel and catering subjects, which will thereby gain greater professional status."

When the National Diploma was finally approved for a start in September 1959 the entry requirements were stated as 3 GCE passes at 'O' level, including English language. These were later raised to five. The aim of the course was to give a sound initial training to students who, after gaining experience in the hotel and catering industry, would aspire to managerial and supervisory positions.

The three year full-time, or longer sandwich course, included the study of the theory and practice of trade cookery, kitchen and restaurant operation and service, housekeeping, reception and office organisation, hotel and catering planning, maintenance and engineering and the scientific aspects of the industry as well as an introduction to management and the subjects of accounting, economics and law as they affect the hotel and catering industry. A substantial part of the course was practical and the examinations included practical tests in trade cookery and restaurant operation and the service of food and drink.

How Many?

In 1961 five colleges offered the National Diploma courses; the first 100 students were awarded the Diploma in summer 1962.

The HCI Journal of Summer 1961 reported that there were some 4500 students on full-time college courses, and another 6500 on part-time courses in hotel and catering. Elsewhere in technical education, Ordinary and Higher National Diploma courses had already begun. In 1958–59 about 1600 students were enrolled on OND courses and about 3100 on HND courses of an industrial character. Almost 140 000 students were enrolled on Ordinary National Certificate, and over 40 000 on Higher National Certificate courses of an industrial character.

When the first IMA Diploma in Institutional Management courses started in 1961, thirteen colleges had been approved to offer the course. Fourteen had been approved to offer the Certificate in Institutional Housekeeping and Catering, for which courses started in the same year; four the Certificate (One Year Abridged Course) in Institutional Management (the first course started in 1960 at the Northern Polytechnic, London with eight students between the age of 25–54). Two colleges had been approved to offer the IMA Matron-Housekeepers Certificate Course.

At the IMA Council Meeting in November 1962 it was reported that 1264 students were in training: 379 on the Diploma course, 359 on the new Certificate course (107 on the old plus an additional 349 in the final year's industrial experience); 60 were taking the Matron-Housekeepers course, and 10 the Abridged course.

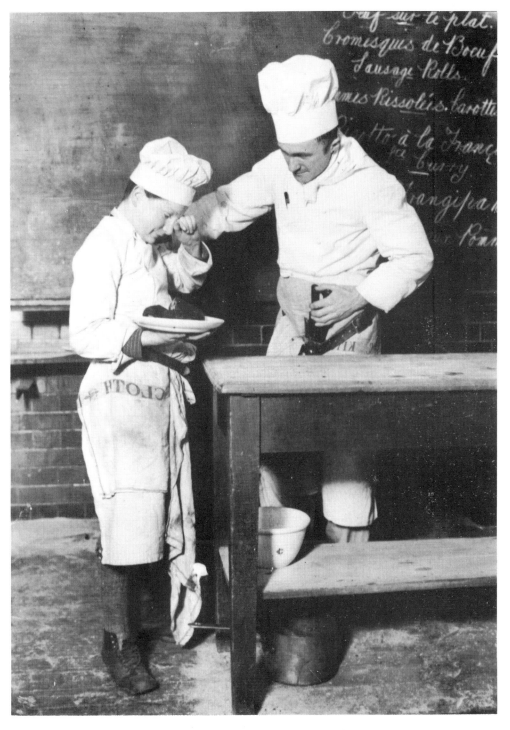

A young trainee chef at London County Council's School of Cookery at Westminster
Technical Institute *c.* 1920.

Students and instructor at Westminster Technical Institute c. 1930.

Practical session in a training kitchen at Westminster Technical Institute c. 1930.

Students in the Edinburgh School of Cookery c. 1900.

Other Developments in the 1960s

There were three other important developments in this period: the first two involved the Hotel and Catering Institute, the third was the commencement of the first degree course in hotel and catering studies at the Universities of Surrey (1964) and Strathclyde (1965).

In 1962 the HCI replaced the Associate Membership examination with an Intermediate Examination which candidates had to pass before being admitted to a course for the Final Examination. The Intermediate was normally a two year full-time college course, the Final one year full-time or two years part-time. It was sometimes possible to take the Intermediate in one year, and a number of colleges included the Intermediate Membership examination as part of a full-time course at the end of the second year. All candidates had to obtain the City and Guilds 151 certificate before sitting the Intermediate examination and it was later also made a preliminary requirement to have GCE 'O' level English.

Certain two year full-time general catering courses were approved for exemption from the Intermediate examination and it was the move to provide a national certification for these courses which involved the HCI. In 1964 the HCI General Catering Diploma was introduced, a two year course suitable for young people who were aspiring to supervisory levels in the industry after appropriate industrial experience. Students admitted to the course were normally 16 years of age with three GCE 'O' level passes. The subjects studied included trade cookery and kitchen operation, restaurant service, book-keeping and food costing, hygiene, nutrition, French, English and general studies. Housekeeping was an optional additional subject.

Degree Courses

The Scottish Hotel School at Ross Hall in Glasgow which opened in September 1944 was the second hotel school to be established in the UK, and like Westminster the Hotels and Restaurants Association had played an important role in this development. The School was attached to the Glasgow and West of Scotland Commercial College and M. Roger Dutron, a famous French Hotelier, was the first director.

The fees for the first course offered at Ross Hall were £20 per session. It was a two year full-time course, including theoretical and practical instruction, available to young people of both sexes, 16–17 years of age.

The school operated then as a residential hotel school (although day students were also accepted). The students were divided into two groups. Week about, to a strict rota of duties, while one half — the "guests" — studied theory in class, the other half — "staff" — undertook the entire practical work, running the school on hotel lines as they helped operate the front office, kitchen, restaurant and housekeeping departments. Each student had to keep his or her bedroom tidy and clean (they were inspected) and each week received a detailed "bill" from fellow students on office rota.

The first year theory included book-keeping and commercial practice, hotel accounting and control, typewriting and correspondence, French, food science, tourism, wines, hotel organisation, law and engineering, hygiene, technology and kitchen theory. The second year theory elaborated on all essential subjects and concluded with hotel management.

Practical training covered all hotel duties, from a hall porter's responsibilities, enquiries, reception work, reservations, record-keeping and the care of flowers to the intricacies of housekeeping — including repairs and maintenance, furnishing, linen upkeep and sewing room requirements — to the many kitchen duties of cooking, baking, costing and washing up. In the restaurant, students were given training in waiting — à la carte, table d'hôte and banqueting. Cellar duties, including dispense and American bar techniques, general organising, buying and binning, were undertaken. For twelve weeks each year students took jobs in hotels in various capacities, the first year in Scottish hotels, the second usually in the south of England or on the Continent.

The Diploma course, which had been extended to three years full-time from 1959, was converted into a BA degree course in Hotel and Catering Management from 1965.

In 1956 when Battersea College of Technology was designated a College of Advanced Technology, the work of the department of hotel and catering management, established a few years earlier, was given new standing. The previous three year full-time course was changed into a four year "thick" sandwich course leading to the Associateship Diploma in Hotel and Catering Management, and in 1964, once the college had been assured of university status as the proposed University of Surrey, it was converted into a BSc degree course in Hotel and Catering Administration.

The University of Surrey has a strong link with the National through its BSc degree course in Home Economics and some of the souvenirs of the National including the Grant of Arms are housed at the Home Economics centre. As the plaque states: "This Centre, for the Degree in Home Economics based on an original scheme of the National Training College of Domestic Subjects Trust, was given to the University by the Trust to perpetuate the aims and ideals of the above College. The Centre was opened by the Vice-Chancellor, Dr D. M. A. Leggett on 9 June 1973."

Behind the Degree Courses

The upsurge in demand for degree courses following the Second World War had seen not only the development of external degrees of the University of London, but the formation in 1955 of the National Council for Technological Awards (NCTA).

This independent and self governing body was formed to create and administer technological awards having a national currency available to students in technical colleges who successfully completed courses approved by the Council. The NCTA broke with tradition and operated in an entirely new way. It did not act as an examining body, supervising syllabuses and setting examinations, as was the practice of the University of London, but let the colleges themselves have the responsibility for constructing courses and for conducting their own examinations. The NCTA rigorously scrutinised the colleges' proposals and applied exacting standards before granting approval. The Council's Diploma in Technology award was set at honours degree standard and accepted as equivalent by the universities and employers.

In 1961 with student demand for university places still outpacing supply, the government set up a committee under the chairmanship of Lord Robbins to enquire into higher education. Included in the committee's report, published in 1963, was the recommendation that the NCTA should be replaced by a new body with the power to award degrees. The opportunities for advanced work outside the universities was to be extended from science and technology to the arts, humanities, social studies and related areas. Thus the Council for National Academic Awards (CNAA) was established by Royal Charter in 1964.

The Robbins Report amongst many other matters had enunciated the fundamental principle that higher education in the UK should be expanded to meet the demand from students qualified to enter and who wished to do so.

The effect on catering education was almost immediate, with the formation of the Universities of Surrey and Strathclyde, and the two new degrees in hotel and catering, and 1971 saw the approval by the Committee for Science and Technology of the CNAA of the BSc degree in Catering Studies at The Polytechnic, Huddersfield.

The Late 1960s and Early 1970s

As the 1960s drew to a close, catering education for supervisory and management levels underwent another period of major change. The HCI reviewed the structure and content of its membership examinations. The IMA's work as an examining body was substantially reduced. Both professional bodies were involved in the development and introduction of Ordinary and Higher National Diplomas. The HCI dropped its work as an examining body at craft level to concentrate on its role as a professional body for managers in the industry. The two Associations merged to form the Hotel, Catering and Institutional Management Association (1971). The Report of the Committee on Technician Courses and Examinations (Haselgrave Report) was published recommending the establishment of a Business Education Council and a Technician Education Council (1969). The first Council for National Academic Awards degree course was approved in catering (1971).

Revised HCI Membership Examinations

The results of the review of the structure and content of the HCI membership examinations were brought into effect in 1969. The Intermediate (entry requirements now set out at four GCE 'O' levels) became only a part-time or block release course, normally over two years, or three years if offered on an evening only basis. The Final could be offered on a full-time, sandwich or part-time basis over one or two years.

The syllabus of the Intermediate was divided into five areas: Preparation and Service of Food and Beverages; Food Hygiene and Nutrition; Provision and Service of Accommodation; Book-keeping; Food and Beverage Control. The aim of the course was to provide a sound knowledge of the technical aspects of hotel and catering operations.

The aim of the Final was to give those in industry an opportunity of obtaining a fundamental knowledge of the administrative aspects of hotel and catering operations. The syllabus was divided into the following six areas: Provision of Food and Beverages; Planning and Provision of Accommodation; Law for the Hotel and Catering Industry; Economic Aspects of the Industry; Introduction to Management; and Accounting.

When the HCI and IMA merged in 1971, the Intermediate and Final were adopted as the membership examinations of the new professional body and continued until 1978, when the HCIMA introduced a new course structure.

ONDs and HNDs in Institutional Management

Two joint Committees were formed in 1978 to administer the new Higher and Ordinary National Diplomas in Institutional Management. As the new courses commenced so new intakes on to the IMA Diploma and Certificate courses ceased. (The IMA Matron-Housekeepers course also stopped at this time.)

The aim of the HND in Institutional Management (which commenced in Scotland in 1968 and south of the border in 1969) was to provide an education in the principles and practice of management in relation to the domestic administration of residential catering establishments, including university halls of residence, colleges of education, residential and day schools, hospitals, hotels, residential clubs, the school meals service and industry. It was a three year full-time course, which normally included some industrial experience. Entry requirements were set at five GCE passes, including one at 'A' level.

Courses leading to the OND in Institutional Housekeeping and Catering commenced throughout the UK in 1969. In Scotland, where "Catering" usually comes first in course titles, the OND was called Institutional Catering and Housekeeping. The aim of the course was to prepare students for supervisory positions in residential or other large institutions, the school meals service or other catering establishments. The entry requirements were four GCE passes at 'O' level. In Scotland the two year course included a period of approximately twelve weeks, industrial experience outside college.

ONDs and HNDs in Hotelkeeping and Catering

The HCI had been involved since 1959 in the administration and control of the National Diploma courses, and acted as secretariat. The standard of this award was between that of an Ordinary National Diploma on the one hand and a Higher National Diploma on the other. As the 1961 statistics quoted earlier plainly indicate, elsewhere in technical education the OND/HND and indeed the Ordinary and Higher National Certificate structure was well established. It was important for the hotel and catering industry that the provision of courses should meet the needs and abilities of young people, as well as providing a suitable education. The entry requirements for the Diplomas of Battersea and Ross Hall were at degree level, but places were limited. The entry requirements for the National Diploma were five GCE 'O' levels, and the need for a more academically stimulating course had emerged clearly. That there was also a need for a course with less demanding entry requirements had been expressed in the development of the HCI General Catering Diploma.

In Scotland there had been no National Diploma course and therefore no Joint Committee. In 1964 it was reported in the HCI Journal, the Institute approached the Scottish Education Department with the aim of establishing a Joint Committee in Scotland to plan an Ordinary and Higher National Diploma in Catering and Hotel Keeping. The Joint Committee would be administered by the Scottish Committee for the Awards of National Certificates and Diplomas (SANCAD). A survey published in the July 1966 HCI Journal indicated that fourteen students were at the time of the survey studying for an Ordinary National Diploma in Catering and Hotel Keeping in Scotland.

The Higher National Diploma in Catering and Hotel Keeping started in Scotland in September 1968.

South of the Scottish border, the new OND and HND courses commenced in September 1969. The Ordinary National Diploma in Hotel Keeping and Catering was a two year full-time course (or the equivalent of a sandwich course) the aim of which was to train potential supervisors. The aim of the Higher National Diploma in Hotel and Catering Administration, a three year sandwich course, was to train potential managers. The entry requirements were the same as the OND and HND in Institutional Management.

How Many?

In September 1969, slightly under 400 students enrolled on the HND courses and 1500 on OND courses in Hotel Keeping and Catering in the UK. By comparison 440 students entered the second year of the National Diploma, 357 the third and 73 the fourth (where the course was longer than the usual three years because of the inclusion of a sandwich element).

Modifications

During the next decade the OND and HND courses were modified in a number of ways. In 1971 the number of Joint Committees were reduced from four to two; a few years later the administration of the Joint Committee for England, Wales and Northern Ireland was transferred from the HCIMA to the City and Guilds of London Institute's Unit. The similarities between the two schemes became emphasised rather than the differences and (except in Scotland) an OND in Hotel Catering and Institutional Operations and an HND in Hotel, Catering and Institutional Management were introduced; enrolments on the institutional diploma courses dropped off sharply.

In Scotland the two OND schemes were unified into one only from 1974: Hotel, Catering and Institutional Operations. A unified scheme was not developed at HND level and enrolments on the HND in Institutional Management remained strong there.

The Late 1970s

The Haslegrave Report, which was published in 1969, has had far reaching implications for all technical education. The late 1970s and early 1980s will see the effect of these on catering education, producing a number of major changes.

In 1973 the Secretary of State for Education and Science announced the establishment of the Technician Education Council (TEC) to be responsible for the development of policies for schemes of technical education for persons at all levels of technician occupations. In Scotland, after the report of the Hudson Committee had found "the whole system of courses for technicians had become too complex and diffuse", the Scottish Technical Education Council (SCOTEC) was established in June 1973.

Thinking Behind TEC

The Haslegrave Report found the pattern in the technical sector of further education "developing more and more along the separate Technician and National Certificate Diploma routes, each with its own system of courses and arrangements for administration. There is a tendency to meet every new expression of need by adding yet another course to the existing range of provision on one side or the other and, where necessary, creating yet another committee to be responsible for its administration. This proliferation makes the system even more complex and difficult for students and employers to understand, tends to encourage students to specialise earlier than necessary, and almost certainly prevents educational resources from being used to the best advantage. The lack of overall co-ordinating machinery means that courses are provided in one part of the system without full regard to possible implications for cognate courses in the other part."

A new, flexible and well-conceived pattern of technician courses and examinations should be devised, the Report states, "based on courses designed to help produce educated and trained technicians capable not only of meeting an immediate need for skill and knowledge, but of adapting themselves readily to meet changes in these needs as they arise . . . . The industrial and commercial bodies concerned with the training and associated further education should have full opportunity of collaborating with educational interests in the work of devising new courses and keeping existing ones up to date.

"The range of provision, although not necessarily the same for each sector of industry and commerce, should be sufficient to meet all reasonable demands and be capable of adaption to satisfy national, regional or local requirements. It should have regard as relevant to the requirements of professional bodies so as to achieve maximum application of the exemption system. It should not however, be allowed to become too complicated, and should lend itself to simplified administrative structures and assessment processes, and to the award of qualifications whose currency is readily understood and accepted by employers and students alike in all parts of the country . . . . The pattern should be effectively geared to the arrangements from time to time current for the period of transition of students from school to further education . . . . There should be provision for vertical and horizontal transfer within the pattern of courses itself and for transfer from and to other patterns (e.g. craft, professional) . . . . It should include arrangements for the different forms of study . . . . Any student who fulfils the entry requirements . . . and works reasonably hard and well during the course should be entitled to expect that he will pass the examination. The award of a technician qualification should never depend solely on the student's performance in a formal examination, the number of which should be kept to the absolute minimum. The measurement of performance on the educational course is only one part of the total assessment of the trainee's progress towards full preparation for the job."*

In Chapter 6 the new TEC and SCOTEC awards are explained fully.

New HCIMA Courses

The new HCIMA Professional Qualification is also explained in Chapter 6, for in 1978 the first students enrolled on two new courses, Part A and Part B which replaced the old Intermediate and Final Membership Examinations. That same year the last students enrolled on the HCIMA Certificate in Institutional Management (Abridged course), which was replaced from September 1979 by a new one year course suitable for non-catering graduates.

These courses brought to fruition a complete review of the membership examinations set up after the merger of the IMA and HCI. The syllabuses and course structure are the outcome of wide consultation with industry and education, including that embodied in the report *Tomorrow's Managers* published by the HCIMA in 1974, and in Paul Johnson's *Corpus of Knowledge* report published in 1977.

The Association introduced a more rigorous system of approval for vetting colleges seeking to offer the new courses, linked with demanding staffing criteria requiring appropriate academic qualifications as well as recent industrial experience.

Industrial experience was made a more important element of the courses. It is only possible to study for Part A while working full-time in the hotel and catering industry; to study for Part B on a one year full-time basis it is necessary to have had twelve months' full-time experience in the industry; there is no additional requirement for the longer two year sandwich course which includes six months' experience in the industry; for the part-time Part B course, or the correspondence course, it is necessary to be working full-time in the industry.

New Degree Courses

The Food, Accommodation and Related Sciences Board, one of the twenty-six subject boards of the Council for National Academic Awards Committee for Science and Technology, was first established in 1975. It was responsible by summer 1979 for eighteen courses with a first year enrolment (1978/79) of 428 and a total enrolment of 1026.

These included a four year sandwich BSc in Catering Systems at Sheffield City Polytechnic from 1974; a BSc in Institutional Management at the Polytechnic of North London from 1976; a second course at The Polytechnic, Huddersfield leading to a BA in Hotel and Catering Administration from 1976, the re-design of this Polytechnic's BSc degree and acceptance as a BSc Honours degree in Catering Science and Applied Nutrition; a BSc in Hotel and Catering Studies at Manchester

*Extracts from the *Report of the Committee on Technician Courses and Examinations* are reproduced with the permission of the Controller, Her Majesty's Stationery Office.

Polytechnic from 1978; a BA in Catering and Accommodation Studies at Napier College of Commerce and Technology, Edinburgh, from 1978; a BSc in Food Marketing Sciences at Sheffield City Polytechnic from 1978.

The first year enrolments on these courses had increased from 47 in 1975 to 189 in 1978, when total enrolments reached 395. Enrolments on the two single fields of Catering and Food and Nutrition at Oxford Polytechnic, approved in 1975, which can be combined to lead to a full-time BSc degree (modular degree), should be added to these figures. In 1978 the total enrolments for both fields was 136.

In 1979 two more CNAA degree courses were approved: a four year sandwich BA in Catering Administration at the Ulster Polytechnic and a four year sandwich BA in Food and Accommodation Studies at Leeds Polytechnic. At Oxford Polytechnic a new double field in Catering was approved at Honours level, as well as a Diploma in Higher Education in the Catering Double Field.

The BSc in Catering Systems at Sheffield City Polytechnic was reapproved at Honours level.

In 1977 a BSc Honours degree course in Institutional Management began at University College, Cardiff.

5

Craft Skills Training

Introduction. The City and Guilds of London Institute pattern for the 1980s. Description of all the Institute's catering courses, in food preparation, food service, alcoholic beverages, accommodation, hotel reception, as well as the Foundation Course and Organisation Studies course. Service Trade Qualifications for CGLI. Supervisory courses of NEBBS and SCOTEC. Description of the other opportunities, including various college certificates, examinations of the Regional Examining Bodies, the Wine and Spirit Education Trust, the Guild of Sommeliers, the Royal Institute of Public Health and Hygiene, the Royal Society of Health, the National Council for Home Economics Education, the Scottish Business Education Council, and Nautical Catering courses. Useful addresses.

Introduction

The opportunities to acquire good craft skills for a worthwhile career in the hotel and catering industry are many and varied.

There are full-time college courses readily available throughout the country at technical colleges. While GCE 'O' levels or CSEs are an advantage for entry to these courses, they are not essential.

There are part-time courses available on a day release basis (when the student is released from work with pay by the employer to attend college for one full day a week); part-time courses are also available on a block release basis (when students attend college full-time for a number of blocks of weeks). Some courses are available on an evening basis and these are suitable for those who have no choice but to attend college in their own time, or who cannot have their day off to coincide with the local college's day release course.

The range of courses available is extensive. Some are designed for the school leaver attending a full-time course, whilst others are adaptable and can be taken as part of a full-time course, on a block release basis, or by day release. The latter are most suitable for the young person already working in the industry.

Some courses provide a valuable opportunity for the mature person who has worked in the industry for a number of years, but without a school leaving qualification, to advance himself or herself by acquiring specialised craft skills, supervisory skills, or as a means for proceeding with management studies leading to professional recognition.

A number of courses are designed for people working in highly specialised jobs, and certain courses are more suitable for one sector of the industry than another, for example the licensed trade.

These courses all lead to certificates of one form or another. There are a number of awarding bodies involved.

The certificates available are for clearly defined areas of skills: for example food preparation, food service, wine and spirits, housekeeping, reception, food hygiene, nutrition and supervisory skills.

For part-time students the choice of course will bear a close relationship to the person's area of work. A trainee chef — courses in cookery; a waiter — courses in food service, wine and spirits; a floor housekeeper in an hotel — a course in supervisory studies; a second steward in the Merchant Navy — a course in supervisory studies.

The full-time college student will follow a broadly based course, usually including a special introductory course in the hotel and catering industry aimed at showing the student the wide variety of careers available, the different skills that will be called for in the range of jobs, and providing basic instruction in costing, applied business aspects and applied science. The course will usually also include instruction in cookery, waiting, housekeeping and reception.

Some students will already have studied a foundation course at school, which provided an introduction to many aspects of their working environment.

City and Guilds of London Institute
The statistics show the great advances that have been made since the days of the Catering Trades Education Committee.

In 1977–78 some 450 000 candidates entered the examinations of the City and Guilds of London Institute, compared to 75 000 in 1950 and 15 000 in 1900. Hotels and catering fell in fourth place in the 1977–78 league with over 38 000 examination entries (after Engineering with 208 000 and Construction and Vehicles). In 1961 and 1979 the corresponding figures for the hotel and catering subjects were:

Subject and number	Examination entries 1961	1979
Catering Trades Basic Training Course: 150	1867	
General Catering Course: 705		5414
Preliminary Trade Cookery: 147	832	
Basic Cookery for the Catering Industry: 706/1		9533
Basic Cookery for the Catering Industry: 151	2215	
Cookery for the Catering Industry: 706/2		8125
Advanced Cookery for Hotels and Restaurants: 152	42	
Advanced Cookery for the Catering Industry: 706/3		341
HCI Intermediate Waiting Certificate	1153	
Food Service Certificate: 707/1		4985
HCI Final Waiting Certificate	362	
Advanced Serving Techniques: 707/2		2933
Alcoholic Beverages Certificate: 707/3		2168
Housekeeping Certificate: 708		1345
HCI Hotel Book-keeping and Reception Certificate	200	
Hotel Reception Certificate: 709		2342
TOTAL	6671	37 186

The CGLI Pattern

Because of the great variety of opportunities available it is impossible to present them in a simple table. The City and Guilds of London Institute has, however, now placed its schemes into categories which correspond to four main career stages:

Career stage	Category of City and Guilds Award
1 Pre-employment or entry to employment	General Vocational Preparation
2 Training and education	Specific Vocational Preparation
3 Preparation for greater or wider responsibility	Career Extension
4 Professional Stage	Senior Awards

The Institute's Foundation Courses and the General Employment Award fall into the first category: General Vocational Preparation. The second category, Specific Vocational Preparation, embraces three levels of attainment, called Levels One, Two and Three. The third category covers the supervisory studies related to catering.

Thus the pattern of City and Guilds catering courses in 1980 may be shown as follows:

> *Career Extension*
> 771 Organisation Studies
> *Specific Vocational Preparation*
> Level Three: 706/3 Advanced Cookery for the Catering Industry
> Level Two: 706/2 Cookery for the Catering Industry
>   707/2 Advanced Food and Beverage Service*
>   707/3 Alcoholic Beverages**
>   708   Accommodation Services
>   709   Hotel Reception
> Level One: 705   General Catering Course
>   706/1 Basic Cookery for the Catering Industry
>   707/1 Basic Food and Beverage Service*
>   Specific Skills Schemes
> *General Vocational Preparation*
> 688 Foundation Course for the Food Industries

General Vocational Preparation

The City and Guilds of London Institute (CGLI) provides one course in this category of interest to readers: the 688 Foundation Certificate (Food Industry).

The Institute's Foundation Courses are designed for young people of average ability; they may be in their fifth year of secondary education, be staying on at school for sixth form studies, or may have elected to leave school for full-time further education. No precise age for starting the course is laid down, and the length of the course is the responsibility of the individual centre, but it is likely to be

*Provisional titles.
**New scheme, No 717 from September 1981.

between one and two years: the Food Industries scheme is based on approximately 900 hours of study.

The course is designed to develop the interests, abilities and talents of young people, to provide a basis for integrating and continuing their general education. The Food Industries scheme will give an insight into the nature and purposes of the food industries, the processes, procedures and materials involved, the various personnel involved and their functions. As well as giving the student an opportunity to develop simple practical skills, the course aims to improve the students' mathematical skills, to develop communication skills and to provide experience in designing and undertaking useful projects.

The student is assessed by means of multiple choice question papers, backed by coursework, in four of the six main components of the course. Candidates must take all components on their first entry; any individual ones they fail may be re-taken and a certificate is awarded when the candidate has obtained at least a Pass grade (there are two other grades: Distinction and Credit) in all the components.

General Employment Award Schemes

A mention should be made at this stage of the Institute's General Employment Award Schemes. These are intended for young people in employment for whom no current further education or systematic training schemes are available and no precise age or academic qualifications are specified.

The aim of the scheme is to develop young peoples' confidence and effectiveness at work for their own advantage and that of their employers. Pilot schemes leading to the Award are based upon a systematic approach to problem solving in work-related projects — assembling information, planning, then taking effective action and checking results. Project xontent is decided locally to meet specific needs of the employee and employer.

The Award is made to every young employee who completes five projects to the satisfaction of his college and firm, based on a programme agreed by the Institute.

Intermediate Craft (Level One)

The *705 General Catering Course* has been operated by City and Guilds for over a decade; prior to the re-numbering of the Institute's schemes in 1972, the General Catering Course was numbered 441. The last examinations for its closest predecessor, the Catering Trades Basic Training Course (No 150), were in 1970.

The aims of the course remain similar to those published when Course 150 was revised in 1957: to provide a broad basis of study for those who have just entered or are intending to make a career in the catering industry and a good foundation upon which later specialisation can be firmly based.

No specific educational qualifications are required for entry to the 705 General Catering Course: selection of students is within the discretion of the college. The scheme is based on one year full-time college study (duration 1000 hours), and the subjects include: food production and service, accommodation services, the catering industry (an introductory study of its nature and function), applied science, calculations, costing and control, applied business aspects and general studies.

The course is currently going through another revision, which will include updating the syllabus and modifying the examination structure. As with the 688 Foundation Certificate, candidates must take all components of the examination on their first entry, but also have the opportunity to re-take any they fail. Candidate's performance is graded (Distinction, Credit, Pass or Fail), and a certificate awarded to those who pass all components.

Specific Skills (Level One)

The development of courses for people whose work only requires a limited range of skills is one of the current tasks of the City and Guilds of London Institute. Schemes are being developed which will be suitable for room attendants, short order cooks/grill chefs, waiters, bar staff and uniformed staff — for example.

The Hotel and Catering Industry Training Board since its formation in 1966 has provided incentives for the training of craft workers in the industry through grant aid. The Board's Five Year Plan 1979–85 mentions the work being undertaken with the industry, City and Guilds and education, to provide opportunities for operatives (particularly those with limited range skills) to progress to craft levels and beyond.

Main Craft (Level Two)

Level Two is the minimum standard recommended for those aspiring to the usual form of industrial recognition, normally coinciding with the completion of an apprenticeship.

Details follow on the various schemes of the Institute at this level. The 709 Hotel Reception scheme was revised in 1978, the 708 Housekeeping scheme has been revised in 1979 and its name changed to Accommodation Services. The 706/1 Basic Cookery and 706/2 Cookery schemes are under review. The 706/1 is expected to remain a 500 hour course, and the length of the 706/2 will be reduced so that the period of study for these two certificates, on a part-time basis, will be reduced from four years to three.

The 707/1 Food Service and 707/2 Advanced Serving Techniques are also being revised and new schemes are expected to start in September 1980. The 707/3 Alcoholic Beverages scheme is being reviewed and once consultations with the other examining bodies in this field have been completed, the Institute proposes to introduce a new scheme, numbered 717, from September 1981.

The new pattern of courses in Catering Subjects that is being introduced following the Institute's Policy Statement of September 1978 allows for courses to be provided either full-time or part-time, by block release, either free-standing or as part of a broader structure of college courses in catering, or within industrial establishments.

The 706 schemes, Cookery for the Catering Industry, aim to provide a sound understanding of knowledge and expertise in professional cookery. They are presently planned to make possible such forms of study as day, day plus evening, or block release, or a combination. Many of the two year craft courses available at colleges include 706 schemes.

Basic Cookery for the Catering Industry (706/1) is a basic craft course in professional cookery, giving a broad introduction to the theoretical and practical aspects of cookery. No specific educational qualifications are required, selection of students is at the discretion of the college. The syllabus is designed to include about 500 hours of technical studies including general studies: general introduction to the catering industry, simple study of essential commodities, use and handling of the tools of a chef, kitchen equipment, personal hygiene, food hygiene, kitchen hygiene, safety, fire, first aid, nutrition, basic principles affecting menus, catering calculations, heat and fuels.

The revised syllabus places greater emphasis on the methods of cooking: stocks, soups, sauces and gravy making, boiling, poaching, stewing, roasting, baking, braising, pot roasting, steaming, frying (deep and shallow), grilling, cold preparations, hot and cold snacks and savouries, breakfast dishes, sweet preparations, and non-alcoholic beverages.

Practical work is an essential part of the course and success in this aspect contributes to the student's success in the certificate (alongside a multiple-choice test paper). The grades of performance are Distinction, Credit, Pass, Fail. Candidates who are successful in some but not all of the components of the examinations may carry forward their successes and need re-take only those components in which they failed. This arrangement applies to all the Institute's schemes.

Coursework assessment and a multiple-choice test paper will also form part of the examination components of the revised *Cookery for the Catering Industry scheme (706/2)*. Although no specific educational qualifications are required for entry to this course — the selection of students being at the discretion of the college authorities — the Institute does recommend that the students should previously have passed the 706/1 examination, or the General Catering Course examination (705), or a corresponding examination of the Regional Examining Boards.

Cookery for the Catering Industry is related to and an extension of Basic Cookery, the treatment of the syllabus deeper.

Students who qualify for the Basic Cookery or Cookery Certificate on a part-time basis and who are registered with the Hotel and Catering Industry Training Board (in 1977-78 there were over 2000 such craft trainees) receive a joint certificate issued by the Board and the Institute.

The HCITB is currently proposing to discontinue registration of individual craft trainees and training establishments, and instead to register the organisations (e.g. those leviable employers) which provide facilities and programmes of training combining courses of further education and industrial experience. A CGLI/HCITB certificate will be awarded when a trainee has gained both the City and Guilds award, e.g. the 706/3, and, during a period of industrial experience, reached a prescribed standard of skill on the job.

The schemes for the *707 Food Service Certificates* of the Institute (as published for 1978-79) are designed on the assumption that students will attend a technical college on a block release basis. They are intended for men and women undergoing training or already employed in the service of food and beverages.

The three schemes retain the same names as those introduced in 1970 (to replace the 435 Waiting Certificate and the 436 Advanced Waiting Certificate):

707/1 : Food Service Certificate (was 452)

707/2 : Advanced Serving Techniques Certificate (was 454)

707/3 : Alcoholic Beverages Certificates (was 453)

No specific education qualifications are required for these courses (the selection of students is within the discretion of colleges) but a good general education is required and it is important that students should be able to read, write legibly, add simple figures and have reasonable understanding of the English language. The Advanced Serving Techniques Certificate and the Alcoholic Beverages Certificate schemes are intended for students who have completed the 705 General Catering Course, or the 707/1 Food Service Certificate or have had industrial experience.

Many of the two year craft courses available at colleges include studying for these Food Service Certificates. The schemes are somewhat shorter than the Cookery Certificates: 240 hours for the Food Service Certificate, 120 hours for the other two. All include General Studies. The examination for each certificate has two components: a multiple choice test paper, and coursework assessment. A joint certificate is issued by the Institute and the HCITB when successful candidates are registered under the Board's scheme (there were just over 200 registered craft trainees on Food Service schemes in 1977–78).

The syllabus for the *707/1 Food Service Certificate* includes a broad survey of the industry, the different types of units, food service operations, safety and fire precautions, personal hygiene, food hygiene, social skills, some law, cleaning duties, food service equipment, billing and checking, preparation and service of non-alcoholic beverages, the menu, including interpretation of menu terms, serving correctly (and with the appropriate accompaniments), various menu items and courses, elementary portion control and the ability to carry out a series of tasks (identified by the HCITB in their Training Recommendations) including serving, billing, *mise en place* preparation and social skills.

The details of the revised scheme for the 707/1 which takes effect from September 1980 were not available at the time of going to press. The title of the new scheme is likely to be *Basic Food and Beverage Service.*

A revised scheme for the 707/2, called *Advanced Food and Beverage Service,* will also start in September 1980.

The *707/2 Advanced Serving Technique Certificate* (current scheme for 1979/80) aims to provide the knowledge and skills required in a range of advanced serving techniques, including final preparation of foods at a side table, lamp work and an introduction to supervisory skills (forecasting, planning, organising, leading, co-ordinating and controlling). Selling and social skills are covered (from dealing with reservations to presenting the bill). Serving tasks, merchandising and display tasks, lamp work and carving tasks, social skills and planning tasks are taught in addition to those in the 707/1 syllabus (correlating with those identified by the HCITB).

The *707/3 Alcoholic Beverages Certificate* also includes a list of tasks, for example, serving and pouring wines, beers and other drinks including cocktails, mixed drinks and liqueurs, preparing and serving liqueur and spirit based coffees as well as social skills and planning tasks. The syllabus includes a study of the origin, history and characteristics of wines as well as spirits and liqueurs, beers, mineral waters and fruit drinks, tobacco (cigars, cigarettes); aspects of buying and storing these items, controlling their movement and complying with the licensing laws.

The revision of the 707/3 scheme will not be completed until late 1980, and it is then expected to be replaced (from September 1981) by a new scheme numbered 717.

Although the Institute's now revised scheme, the 708 Housekeeping Certificate, was designed as an industry-based course, it was included in many of the two year full-time college craft courses. There were only 26 HCITB registered craft trainees on this scheme in 1977–78. If operated on a day release basis, the course extended over one academic year (240 hours).

The new scheme *708 Accommodation Services* has been devised either as a one year full-time course of not less than 750 hours of study, or as a part-time day or block release course of 300 hours of college study complemented by a minimum of 700 hours' planned training and experience in the industry. Full-time courses will usually include a minimum of four weeks, in one or more blocks, practical experience in the industry.

The 708 scheme is a comprehensive course for people who wish to make a career as housekeepers in conference centres, clubs, hospitals, hotels and both residential and non-residential educational establishments. No specific educational qualifications are required for entry to the course (which is at the discretion of the college); students on a part-time or block release course should be working in accommodation services.

The syllabus includes: introduction to housekeeping departments in the different types of establishments within the industry, social skills, health and safety, principles of cleaning and servicing, nature of dirt, characteristics of surfaces in relation to cleaning, industrial cleaning equipment, cleaning agents, operational cleaning procedures, organisation of cleaning procedures, specialised operation and procedures, checking and inspection procedures in housekeeping, work study, textile care, textile services and renovation, contract services (including cleaning services, maintenance services and labour services), security, interior design in relation to the work of the housekeeping department, cost control, communications, staffing and industrial relations (this section of the syllabus has been introduced in recognition of the growing importance of these developments and the increasing need of students to be aware of them). Communication skills and general studies are regarded as an integral part of the course (about 45 hours).

There are two components to the examination: a one hour multiple choice paper, a two hour written paper, and coursework assessment. Each candidate's coursework will be assessed by the lecturer responsible for the course and by a visiting assessor appointed by the Institute. There are four grades of performance for the components taken: Distinction, Credit, Pass and Fail. A joint certificate will be issued by the Institute and the HCITB to those candidates who are registered under the Board's scheme.

The first examination in the revised *709 Hotel Reception* scheme was in May/June 1978. The scheme has been devised for operation either as a one year full-time course of not less than 1000 hours' duration (when it is strongly recommended that students spend 4 weeks gaining practical experience in the industry after the twelfth week of the course), or on a block release basis with approximately 540 hours' in college to complement a minimum of 460 hours' planned industrial experience.

The Institute recommends that students for the full-time course possess minimum qualifications of CSE Grade 2 in English and Arithmetic, alternatively, a 705 General Catering Course Certificate (or equivalent qualification). There are six components in the examination in Hotel Reception: a multiple choice test paper, two other written papers (the second on book-keeping and cash control), a typewriter test, and coursework assessment on machine accounting, and personal attributes.

The scheme includes General Studies and the syllabus falls into four sections: hotel reception (principles and practice), book-keeping and cashiers' duties, safety and security and ancillary duties. Included in the first section are all aspects of an hotel receptionist's work, including legal aspects, salesmanship, communications, office practice (touch typing to a minimum standard of 25 w.p.m., using duplicating and copying machines, filing, use of telephone switchboard are some of the skills taught). Ancillary duties include non-reception matters, for example, restaurant bookings, lost property, wages procedure, restaurant accounts, housekeeping (housekeeping routine, emergency preparation of rooms, flower arrangement, for example), food service (including tea, coffee and other non-alcoholic as well as alcoholic beverages).

Of a typical 30 hour week on the course, 12 hours might be spent on hotel organisation and reception (including legal requirements), 5 on personal attributes and salesmanship, 5 on book-keeping and accounts, 6 on typing and office practice, and 2 on general studies.

Advanced Craft (Level Three)

The City and Guilds of London Institute has one course at present available at this level: *706/3 Advanced Cookery for the Catering Industry*. The scheme will be reviewed in the early 1980s and it is possible that similar schemes will be prepared for other aspects of catering.

The 706/3 scheme can be traced back to the 152 Advanced Cookery for Hotels and Restaurants scheme, which was itself revised a number of times.

The 706/3 is divided into two specialisms: Kitchen and Larder (about 480 hours) and Pastry (itself split into Part I and Part II, about 240 hours for each Part). Students should have previously passed the Institute's examination in 706/2 Cookery for the Catering Industry and have had five years' experience in industry if studying for the Kitchen specialism, or four years if studying for Part I of the Pastry specialism. Students for Part II of the Pastry specialism would normally be expected to have previously passed the Part I examination. There are three components to the examination for each specialism: written examination, practical test and coursework assessment. The specialisms are an extension and development of the knowledge gained during the 706/2 scheme. For the Kitchen and Larder specialisms it is also intended that there should be an understanding of the art of display, students are encouraged to develop creative ideas and for Part II of the pastry specialism there should be a real understanding of the principles and raw materials used in pastry work. Original display work plays an important part in this course.

The syllabus includes applied science (including types, purpose and legislation affecting food additives; storage of commodities, temperature control necessary for all types, speed of cooling with type of food, cook freeze regeneration, moisture control regulation etc.); hygiene (including main sources of bacterial and chemical food poisoning, methods of prevention, hygiene of premises and legal requirements); an appreciation of the Trade Descriptions Act, Food and Drugs Act 1955, Food Hygiene General Regulations 1970 and other legal aspects affecting food; design, decoration and display; food costing, related costs and quality control (including the cost and quality control of all commodities, classical recipes and finished dishes, effective use and costing of manpower, resources and profit generation); premises and equipment (including maximum efficient utilisation of equipment and work practices to achieve satisfactory flow of materials with adequate work distribution); safety.

Career Extension Awards

The City and Guilds of London Institute has one course available at this level: the catering option of the 771 Organisation Studies Certificate. Before 1978 the Organisation Studies Certificate was restricted to engineering, but the Institute did offer until 1974 (when the last examinations were held) the 720 Kitchen Supervision and Organisation Certificate.

The Kitchen Supervision and Organisation Certificate is probably more widely known by its pre-1972 number — 353 — and in this form dated back to 1967. When the scheme was up for review in 1972, the Institute's advisory committee took the view "that there should be an extension of supervisory studies to other areas of the catering industry than simply the kitchen. Therefore, in the future arrangements for examinations for supervisors in all sections of the catering industry shall be undertaken by the National Examinations Board for Supervisory Studies . . ." (City and Guilds Broadsheet No 72 of July 1972).

The NEBBS Certificate in Supervisory Studies and the similar course available in Scotland, the Certificate in the Supervision of Catering and Accommodation Services of the Scottish Technical Education Council, are described later in this chapter.

The City and Guilds *771 Organisation Studies* scheme is primarily intended for students who have followed a craft training and craft education route and who are being trained for a position of higher responsibility. The course is a demanding one; students who have completed a Level Two or Three craft course will normally attend college on a part-time or block release basis for a minimum of 240 hours but this might be reduced for more experienced students. The examination has three components: a 2 hour written paper of questions referring to a catering case study, a 2 hour general examination paper, and a project (a minimum of 30 hours should be spent on the project by each student).

Students are given an appreciation of the organisation as a whole by a study of key factors, some of which they are likely to have met already during their industrial experience, others of which they are likely to be involved in if given greater responsibility. These factors are: costing, estimating, work study, quality assurance, information processing, communication, industrial relations, group behaviour and human resources. The aims of these studies reflect the approach of the course. For example the aims of the study of human resources include: to provide the student with an outline of the ways in which organisations plan to develop the human resources on which their operations depend, and to show how the individual can use the opportunities provided.

The aims of the third factor, work study, include: (i) to enable the student to appreciate the part work study can play in the improvement of individual and group performance in the achievement of higher productivity, (ii) to understand the broad principles of the techniques involved in work study and the importance of a systematic approach rather than to become a practitioner of such techniques, (iii) to use the problems often encountered in the introduction of work study as a means of helping to understand the human aspects of an organisation, (iv) to use the rigorous analysis associated with work study as a means of studying the use made by organisation of men, materials, machines and money.

Keep up to Date!

The Institute emphasises that no one can receive a City and Guilds Certificate or Award unless he or she actually sits and passes the requisite examinations, and that as the courses are constantly under review and subject to modification, it is essential to be conversant with the current syllabus and regulations.

Service Trade Qualifications and City and Guilds Examinations

Although it is a requirement for entry to most of the Institute's examinations that candidates are undertaking, or have completed, the respective course at a technical college or other approved establishment, a special arrangement exists for certain Service technicians and mature individuals to make direct entry to the Institute's examinations.

In the Royal Navy a Leading Cook may make a direct entry to the 706/1 examination; a Petty Officer Cook and Petty Officer Caterer to the 706/2 examination. Suggested for further study are, respectively, the 706/2 and 706/3.

A Leading Steward may make direct entry to the 707/1, and the 707/2 is suggested for further study.

In the Army Catering Corps and the Royal Air Force the arrangements are as follows:

	Trade or category	Minimum trade standard	Direct entry to CGLI examinations	Suggested further study
Army Catering Corps	Cook	B2	706/1	706/2
	Cook	B1	706/2	706/3
	Cook	A1	706/3	
Royal Air Force	Cook	SAC	706/1	706/2
	Cook	Corporal	706/2	706/3

Communication Skills and Numeracy

The Institute held the first examinations in December 1978 for a new scheme: *772 Certificate in Communications Skills.* Approximately 60 hours, which may be taken from within General Studies time, are recommended for allocation to the course, at the end of which students should be able to listen to and understand oral messages and read and understand the various types of material with which they have to cope in everyday life. They should be able to express themselves clearly and effectively in speech and in writing, as well as be able to understand and produce simple sketches, diagrams and charts as clarification of verbal or graphical information. The scheme for the course and examination is intended to meet the needs of students at craft and operative level.

The scheme *364 Numeracy* was introduced in 1979 to meet the needs of young people who as a result of their lack of basic numeracy skills are finding it difficult to cope with the demands of their college course, their jobs or social lives, or who find difficulty in gaining entry to the course or employment of their choice. The length of the course, which may be run as a preliminary to other courses or in parallel with them, depends on the abilities of the individual student.

City and Guilds' Assessors

The introduction of the revised 709 Hotel Reception scheme in 1977 brought about an expansion of the use of assessors on the Institute's catering schemes. They are now used on the 706, 707, 708 and 709 schemes — not to examine, but to help advise the college on the operation of the course, and to help the Institute monitor and maintain standards. Each college who runs these courses has an outside assessor who pays a visit at least once a year and inspects the way the course is run by the college, how the students are benefiting from it and whether the course is meeting industry's requirements.

Supervisory Courses: NEBBS and SCOTEC

The *National Examinations Board for Supervisory Studies* (NEBBS) provides courses that are especially suitable for catering supervisors and supervisors in accommodation/domestic services/cleaning science. The Board (an independent, autonomous body established in 1964) has established a flexible structure by which it aims to assist the development of local initiative by encouraging colleges and industrial organisations to co-operate in devising suitable courses to meet specific needs. These courses are at Introductory, Certificate and Diploma level.

The *Introductory Course* (45 hours' duration) which started in 1977 seeks to provide a background of knowledge of the elements of supervision, to improve communication skills, to lay the foundation for professional and personal development and to introduce the student to adult methods of study.

The *Certificate in Supervisory Studies* (which started in 1965) is open to students of not less than 21 years of age on entry to the course; normally the student will be sponsored by his or her organisation.

A minimum of 240 hours for the course is required — on a full-time, part-time or block release basis. A residential period of at least two full days is required for all part-time courses, and is strongly recommended on all courses.

Project work is an integral part of the course, and although courses will be structured to meet varying requirements (national syllabuses are not offered in hotels and catering) they normally include principles and practice of supervision, communications, industrial relations, economic and financial aspects.

The Board provides a two way approach to the establishment of courses:

approving centres, which are then permitted to develop certificate courses without seeking the Board's approval, and approving specific courses.

The total number of successful candidates on the Certificate course in 1977/78 was nearly 6000 for all industries; over a tenth of these were for a catering NEBBS at approximately 100 colleges. The comparable figure for the NEBBS *Diploma in Supervisory Studies* was just over 500 (very few in catering).

Students for the Diploma course should have the Certificate in Supervisory Studies (or acceptable alternative) and a minimum of three years' industrial experience of which two must have been in a supervisory capacity. This course (180 hours) is also available on a very flexible basis, with a required residential period for part-time courses (and recommended for all). Diploma courses, which have to be approved by the Board, will cover the practice of supervisory management (about 70% of the time available), and a specialised technical subject and emphasis will be placed on the need for supervisors to recognise and deal with change.

In 1977 the *Scottish Technical Education Council* (SCOTEC) introduced a *Certificate Course in Supervision of Catering and Accommodation Services*. Over 40 students enrolled on the first course.

The course is designed for those employed (or likely to be employed) as first level supervisors within the catering and accommodation services industries and aims to develop an understanding of, and competence in, those techniques used in the co-ordination and control of the various types of operations.

SCOTEC do not specify any mode of attendance; the recommended number of hours when the course is offered on a day release basis is 240. In the session 1978/79 the course was available at Kingsway Technical College in Dundee on an afternoon/evening basis, one day a week, over an academic year; at Glasgow College of Food Technology it was offered on a day release basis, 9 am to 5 pm, over an academic year. Three other colleges offered the course on a day release basis in 1978/79 and more than five are expected to offer it in future years. The normal entry requirement to the course is satisfactory competence in relevant crafts with appropriate experience (entry is at the discretion of the Principal of the College).

SCOTEC provide a detailed syllabus for the course, which covers the following areas:

Financial Aspects (about 30 hours): a review of the principles involved in the supervision of cash and credit handling and of wages and tax compilation and a survey of the various techniques used in the industry.

Personnel Aspects (about 60 hours): the principles of health and safety, work study motivation of staff and legislation relevant to the work environment; the training facilities available and the roles of the Trade Unions within the industry.

Work Organisation (a) Business Aspects (about 30 hours): methods used in the industry to record business transactions; (b) Operational Aspects (about 90 hours): techniques and tools necessary for the effective organisation of human and physical resources in the industry.

General Studies (about 30 hours): to develop the students' communication skills and to develop an awareness and understanding of their own society with particular reference to their roles as individuals, citizens and workers.

The Work Organisation, Personnel and Financial aspects of the course are tested by means of two 3 hour written examinations; continuous assessment is used to test the General Studies. A pass in each is required for the award of a certificate.

Other Courses and Opportunities

There are many! Some of the Regional Examining Bodies offer examinations in catering subjects. These include the Licensed Trade Catering Course of the North Western Regional Advisory Council. The Brewers' Society, through its organisation Brewers' Society Training Centres Limited, offers five courses at its two residential training centres suitable for those in the licensed trade. The Guild of Sommeliers offers courses and examinations. The Wine and Spirit Education Trust offers a number of courses and examinations.

The Royal Institute of Public Health and Hygiene has offered courses leading to the Certificate in Food Hygiene since 1958; the more advanced Diploma Course for students specialising in the handling of food and holding more important positions in this field was introduced in 1962.

The Royal Society of Health offers a number of certificate and diploma schemes in hygiene and nutrition.

There are City and Guild schemes available in Food and Drink, including the 120 Bakery Certificate and the 130 Food Technicians' Certificate. The Institute also offers schemes in Home Economics and Creative Studies. For those undergoing training or employed as supervisors in the various sectors of the cleaning industry, the Institute has available the scheme 764 Certificate in Cleaning Science.

Inspection of college prospectuses reveals a variety of other courses. A typical two year college craft course has already been mentioned; some colleges offer a different combination, two examples follow:

Colquitt Technical and Nautical Catering College, Liverpool: after one year of full-time study Part I examinations include: City and Guilds 705 General Catering Course, Royal Institute of Public Health and Hygiene Certificate in Food Hygiene and the Handling of Food; after the second year, Part II examinations include: City and Guilds 706/2 Cookery for the Catering Industry, either the 707/1 Food Service Certificate or 707/2 Advanced Serving Techniques Certificate or 708 Housekeeping Certificate, Royal Society of Health Certificate in Nutrition in Relation to Catering and Cooking, and Union of Lancashire and Cheshire Institutes Basic Pastrycooks Certificate (Source 1979/80 Prospectus).

Waltham Forest College, London: examinations taken at the end of the first year: City and Guilds 705 General Catering Course, 707/1 Food Service Certificate, Royal Institute of Public Health and Hygiene Certificate in Food Hygiene, British Red Cross Certificate in First Aid; at the end of the second year: City and Guilds 706/2 Cookery for the Catering Industry, 707/2 Advanced Serving Techniques Certificate, 707/3 Alcoholic Beverages Certificate, Royal Institute of Public Health and Hygiene Diploma in Food Hygiene, and Royal Society of Health Certificate in Nutrition (Source 1979/80 Prospectus).

The National Council for Home Economics Education offers a Housekeeping and Catering Certificate and a range of other certificates and diplomas.

There are various highly regarded college diplomas.

Brief information follows on a selection of these.

College Diploma Courses

It would not be possible in a book of this nature to detail every college diploma course. The range is extensive from occasional one-off courses, perhaps organised in cooperation with the Manpower Services Commission's Training Services Agency, to special one term courses (one afternoon and/or evening, once or twice a week) covering topics like waiting and restaurant organisation, banqueting waiting, hotel book-keeping and accounting, and wine appreciation.

The two year college craft courses usually lead to a college diploma in addition to a collection of different certificates from national award-making bodies. There are, however, several exceptions including:

At *Westminster College* a two year full-time Restaurant Operations course available to young men and women with a good secondary education and proven ability in English and numeracy, keen to specialise in the field of food and beverage operations. This course has a long tradition dating back to 1949.

A three year full-time course leading to the Westminster Diploma in Professional Cookery, available to students with a good secondary educational standard (those with a CGLI 706/1 may be considered for admission on to the second year of the course).

At *Thanet Technical College* a one year full-time course, available to students with an OND or CGLI 706/2 who wish to study advanced cookery techniques and "haute cuisine" (including computer utilisation for menu costing).

At *Brighton Technical College,* a two year full-time college diploma in Hotel Book-keeping and Reception, a two year full-time craft diploma in Professional Cookery.

At *Highbury College of Technology* in Portsmouth a three year full-time course leading to the Diploma in Professional Cookery, and a two year sandwich course leading to the college Diploma in Restaurant Operations. During the second year of the latter course, students spend a 12 week period gaining experience in an approved establishment.

Regional Examining Bodies

The City and Guilds of London Institute does recognise success in the examinations of the Regional Examining Bodies as corresponding to success in its own examinations. Where examinations in cookery corresponding to the Institute's Basic Cookery examinations are held by a Regional Examining Body, a local education authority in membership with the REB will normally arrange that its students take the examinations of the Regional Body. Only where a specific request is made to City and Guilds by the Chief Education Officer will the Institute accept from such a local authority entries to the Basic Cookery examinations.

The North Western Regional Advisory Council for Further Education incorporating the *Union of Lancashire and Cheshire Institutes* offers such an examination: *706 Basic Cookery for the Catering Industry.* The syllabus is very similar to the City and Guilds 706/1 scheme, but it is divided into two years. The first year's syllabus includes those elements of the full two year syllabus which are examinable at the end of the first year. These examinations include a writen paper in Basic Cookery Theory and assessment of the candidate's practical work. Successful candidates receive a First Year Certificate.

The format for the examination at the end of the second year is similar, with continuous assessment of practical work. In the written paper questions may be set on any part of the full syllabus. Successful candidates receive a Second Year Craft Certificate.

The Regional Examining Body also offers three other courses: 711 Pastry Cooks' and Patissiers' Course, 714 Housekeeping and Catering Course, and 712 Licensed Catering Course. The first is intended for patissiers, pastry cooks and other people responsible for preparing sweets in catering establishments; the course is in two stages (each a minimum of 120 hours) with a written examination and coursework assessment for each.

The *714 Housekeeping and Catering Course,* which is two years full-time, is designed for students wishing to obtain posts in catering and domestic administration in residential establishments, hostels, residential clubs, colleges, hospitals, halls of residence for example. Nearly a third of each year's syllabus (300 hours) is devoted to the study of food — investigation of underlying scientific principles and methods, a comprehensive study of the essential constituents of foods and their functions and the composition of common articles of diet, supported by practical study including comparative costing. Each year, 180 hours are devoted to the housekeeping syllabus, 480 hours to general and related studies and 120 hours to be spent by students on supervised practical experience (in the first year, in the school meals service, industrial canteens or residential schools etc.; in the second year in welfare homes, hospitals, halls of residence etc.). Two written examinations are set at the end of the second year, coursework assessment is conducted throughout the two years.

The *712 Licensed Trade Catering Course* had been designed for licensees, intending licensees and staff of non-residential licensed etablishments. The course involves a minimum of 72 hours' attendance — ideally not more than two sessions a week of 3 hours each for twelve weeks. A two hour written examination is set at the end of the course, and coursework assessment also contributes to the award.

The syllabus has been devised to meet the requirements of the Licensed Trade and covers snack catering and main meals for businessmen's lunches and small functions. The following topics are emphasised throughout the course: quantities, costing and portion control, food hygiene, and safety factors.

The Yorkshire and Humberside Council for Further Education at present offers one examination relative to the hotel and catering industry: the 706 (Part I) Basic Cookery for the Catering Industry. This compares to the 706/1 scheme of the City and Guilds of London Institute.

There are six Regional Examining Bodies altogether. The West Midlands Advisory Council for Further Education (incorporating the Union of Educational Institutions), based in Birmingham, does not offer any examinations for the hotel and catering industry. Nor does the Northern Counties Technical Examinations Council, based in Newcastle upon Tyne (linked to the Northern Advisory Council for Further Education); nor the Welsh Joint Education Committee in Cardiff.

The East Midland Educational Union offers the following examinations in catering:

705 General Catering Course
706 Basic Cookery for the Catering Industry
713 Book-keeping and Costing
711 Pastry Cooks

The *705 General Catering Course* is a one year full-time college course of not less than 1000 hours' duration. No specific educational requirements are needed, entry is at the discretion of the college. The syllabus is similar to the 705 scheme of the City and Guilds of London Institute (as published for 1978 and 1979). There are three components to the examination, assessment of practical course work, a 2 hour written paper and a $2\frac{1}{2}$ hour written paper.

The *706 Basic Cookery for the Catering Industry* scheme has been devised on the assumption that a minimum of 420 hours will be available for technical studies, plus an additional 60–90 hours in general studies per year, and that these will be organised on a part-time or block release basis, while students receive planned experience in the industry. The first year examination has one component: assessment of practical work; the second year two: coursework assessment and a 2 hour written examination. The syllabus corresponds to that of the City and Guilds of London Institute 706/1 scheme (before the 1979 revision), as do arrangements for joint HCITB/Union certification. City and Guilds accept success in the Unions' examination as corresponding to success in the 706/1.

The Union's syllabuses and examinations in *Book-keeping and Costing (713)* are intended for use in colleges which offer courses such as the 705 and 706. The scheme is in two stages:

> Food Costing I (minimum of 100 hours) covers the basic principles of food costing, the fundamental systems of food and beverage control and the techniques involved. A 2 hour written examination (no electronic calculators permitted!) follows.
>
> Book-keeping and Food Costing II (minimum 100 hours) extends the study undertaken in Stage I: arithmetic, food costing — dealing with the control of cost elements, kitchen percentages, need for portion control in relation to price, treatment of staff meals, stock taking, goods ordering procedures; and covers the principles of book-keeping: double-entry, ledger accounts, tabular ledger, cash book, VAT, imprest petty cash, trial balances, wages, PAYE, banking. A $2\frac{1}{2}$ hour written examination (battery operated pocket calculators permitted) follows.

The *711 Pastry Cooks' Course* is intended for patissiers and pastry cooks in catering establishments. The course is again in two stages, of a minimum of 120 teaching hours each. Entry to either stage is entirely at the discretion of the college.

Stage I relates to basic pastry work. Assessment of practical work and a 2 hour written examination form the examination components.

Stage II is more advanced work, the syllabus is divided into theory and practice (as Stage I) with an identical examination structure.

Licensed Trade

Training courses for the licensed trade fall into three categories: part-time courses available at technical colleges in England and Wales leading to awards of the Licensed Trade Education and Training Committee (details from colleges, the Brewers' Society, or the regional offices of the Licensed Trade Development Association); residential courses operated by the Brewers' Society Training Centres Limited at two training centres in England: and occasional courses organised by the HCITB in conjunction with colleges and the industry.

As these courses are largely aimed at mature entrants to the trade, licensees, tenants and managers with experience in the trade, they are described in Chapter 8 — Catching Up.

Wine and Spirit Education Trust

The Wine and Spirit Education Trust (an Education Charity approved by the Department of Education and Science) offers a range of examinations for those persons over the age of 18, who are, or intend to be, engaged in or connected with the wine and spirit trade and ancillary trades.

Since the formation of the Trust in 1968 the number of students attending the Wine and Spirit Education Trust's courses has increased from 1000 in 1968 to 5000 in 1978 and is still multiplying.

Preparation for the examinations is by study assisted by courses (run by the Trust or by colleges on its behalf), and the Trust emphasises that considerable reading is necessary, especially for the higher level examinations, in addition to attendance at lectures. There are five courses:

Short Course for Companies' Group Training: an introductory course of five one hour lessons intended to teach the basic facts of wines and spirits (no examination).

Certificate Course: a four hour course which can be divided into seven sessions on completion of which the student will be able to answer general questions on the production of wines, spirits, beers and liqueurs, be able to name the principal wine-producing and spirit-producing areas of the world, interpret labels on bottles and make recommendations to customers. There is a one hour, multiple-choice examination. Some colleges offer this course, and it is also offered regularly at the Trust's Training Centre at Five Kings House in London on a one afternoon a week basis over eight weeks.

Wine Service Certificate Course: a pack of course material developed by the HCITB in collaboration with the Trust for the use of businesses or colleges wishing to train waiters in the basic essentials of wines and spirits together with their service.

Higher Certificate Course: a 30 hour course (at least three times this amount of time should be spent in private study) on completion of which the student will be able to answer specific questions on the culture of the vine in various parts of the world and the production and character of various wines, both light and fortified, also on spirits, aromatised wines and liqueurs. There is a two hour multiple-choice examination.

The Higher Certificate course is offered in two forms by the Trust: a one week block course, and a day release course over seven weeks.

Diploma Course: a two year course of study, the subjects being divided into two parts A and B, which may be taken in either order, but only one part may be taken in any calendar year because the knowledge required is so detailed. The course for each part consists of 30 hours of lectures supported by at least 150 hours' private study. In the examinations, which are both theoretical and practical, candidates are required to show an extensive and detailed knowledge, with a commercial background of particular wines and spirits and other subjects connected with the trade. Candidates for the Diploma course should ordinarily have passed the Higher Certificate examination or the HCIMA's membership examinations. The number of centres in which Diploma courses are presented is limited. Where it is impossible to attend a course, students can be allowed to register for the examinations and will be sent bookpacks and details of the wines shown at the lectures, and so with proportionately more private study (and coaching from local experts in the trade) may achieve the required standard.

Guild of Sommeliers

The craftsmen's Guild of Wine Butlers in the UK, the Guild of Sommeliers — established in 1953 — sponsors two courses through its branches: the Intermediate Course and the Sommeliers Certificate Course (Wine Waiters Certificate) and, thirdly, conducts an examination for the Master Sommeliers Diploma.

Sommeliers Intermediate Course: a three day course designed to provide the level of accomplishment and knowledge required for the candidate to eventually take the Master Sommelier Diploma examination.

The syllabus, based on 16 hours of teaching, covers viticulture, viniculture, classifications, the lesser known districts of France from which wines are now bought, the districts, soil, grapes and climate of the principal wine producing areas and countries, including Bordeaux, Burgundy, Alsace, the Loire, Champagne, Italy, Germany, Spain, and Portugal; the development and characteristics of wines from these areas and countries, and of sparkling wines; licensing regulations, carafe law, the Trade Descriptions Act, labelling regulations and the EEC. The course includes practical and theoretical tasting (to understand what is involved and why), and such matters as taking orders, opening and decanting, customer approach, *mise en place* and advising on why a wine should be chosen.

Sommeliers Certificate Course: a three day course which concludes with a one hour examination, success in which qualifies the student for the award of a Certificate (Honours, Credit, or Pass).

The syllabus covers wines of the world, geographical and historical background to the wine trade in England; methods of production of wines; the principal red and white wine producing countries, comparison of the main areas and wines; champagne, sparkling wines, areas and methods of production; sherry, port, methods of production, main types; various spirits, raw materials, principal methods of production; care and service of wines and spirits; liqueurs and cigars, storing and service; comparative tasting of wines; salesmanship as applied to the restaurant, job of the sommelier, customer communication and follow up.

Master Sommelier Diploma Examination: candidates have to be full members of the Guild, actively engaged in the profession, should preferably be sponsored by their employer, and have a minimum of five years' experience as a wine butler prior to the date of entry for the examination. The examination is divided into three parts; a candidate failing to pass all three may re-take the examination in the following two years at a reduced fee with due credit for passes.

An adequate knowledge of aperitifs, wines used in wine lists, liqueurs, spirits, and cigars must be attained by the candidate and the Guild recommend texts. There is no course, but it is expected that everyone taking the examination will have done the Intermediate course.

Part One of the examination covers the practical work of the Sommelier, setting up, use of equipment, presentation and service of wine, decanting, customer approach and ability to sell wine. This examination, conducted by a small panel, is entirely on the practical approach of the candidate.

Part Two is a theoretical viva voce conducted by a small panel. In addition to knowing the principal wines and areas of some ten countries and sub-continents, candidates must understand and know the principal grape varieties used for wine making, the laws relating to wine labelling and production, to have an in-depth knowledge of the principal districts and wines of the main areas of France, Germany, Spain, Portugal and Italy. An understanding of the reasons for Vintage Wines and the best years since 1965 is required for Bordeaux, Burgundy, Port and Champagne; and a good understanding of cigars, their manufacture, storage and presentation.

Part Three is a practical tasting before a panel to prove the candidate's ability to identify the style of wine being offered, to give a basic opinion on quality and to be able to identify faulty wine.

Passing this examination entitles the candidate to become a member of the Court of Master Sommeliers and to wear a personal Master Sommelier Badge.

Royal Institute of Public Health and Hygiene

The first courses leading to the *Certificate in Food Hygiene* of the Royal Institute of Public Health and Hygiene were set up with the assistance of local Medical Officers of Health. Interest in the courses has spread rapidly since 1958 and the Institute's 1979 list of approved centres names nearly one hundred for the Certificate course in Food Hygiene and the Handling of Food, and thirty for the Diploma in Food Hygiene. The list not only includes colleges and the Institute's headquarters, but Council offices. The Institute sets all examination papers and marks the scripts; oral examinations in the provinces are held locally.

Comprehensive lecture notes on the *Certificate course in Food Hygiene and the Handling of Food* have been published by the Institute since 1964 and the third edition of these is available at a modest charge. The minimum number of teaching hours for the course, which can be offered on a full- or part-time basis, is 16. All candidates for the examination must have attended the course.

The syllabus includes: making food safe; an introduction to bacteriology; food poisoning — types of incident, spread, body's defences, prevention, sources and control; laws relating to food hygiene, agencies concerned with the control of food; examples of outbreaks of food poisoning and food borne diseases; the protection of food — personal hygiene, cross contamination, design and cleaning of equipment and premises, infestations, destruction of germs in food, prevention of bacterial multiplication; and health education.

The examination is in two parts: a two hour written paper (long answer type questions) and a short oral interview of 5 to 10 minutes. Successful candidates are awarded a certificate and are entitled to Associateship of the Institute.

Lecture notes are in the course of preparation for the more advanced *Diploma course in Food Hygiene.* The minimum teaching hours for the course, which can also be offered on a full- or part-time basis, are 20–24. Students must hold the Certificate in Food Hygiene and the Handling of Food, or an equivalent qualification.

The syllabus covers: nutrition and diet; relevant legislation — including Food Hygiene Regulations, Unsound Food, Heat Treatment Regulations, Milk and Dairies Regulations; canning; accelerated freeze drying; quick frozen foods; preservation of foods — including preservatives, dehydration, gas storage; bacteriology; cleansing and sterilisation of equipment; retail food hygiene; hygiene of meat and meat products; bakery and dairy products; methods of education in food hygiene; complaints — nature, cause, remedy.

The examination is in three parts — two 2 hour written papers and an oral examination.

Successful candidates are eligible for Membership of the Institute and, after election, to use the designatory letters MRIPHH.

Royal Society of Health

The Royal Society of Health offers a range of examinations in the field of health, hygiene, nutrition and child care, a number of which are only available outside the UK. Three are of interest to the hotel and catering industry; the first two were introduced in 1945, the third in 1960:
   — the Certificate in Nutrition in Relation to Catering and Cooking
   — the Diploma in Nutrition in Relation to Catering Management
   — the Certificate in Hygiene of Food Retailing and Catering

In 1978, the numbers of examination entries were as follows: Certificate in Nutrition in Relation to Catering and Cooking, 347; Diploma in Nutrition in Relation to Catering Management, 36; Certificate in Hygiene of Food Retailing and Catering, 3270. During the same year fifteen more centres were approved to offer the third of these courses, which attracts by far the largest number of entries of all the Society's examinations (72% of the total in 1978).

It is a condition of entry to the examinations that candidates have completed an approved course of training. The Society does not specify the number of teaching hours for its certificates and diplomas, but courses may only be conducted by approved centres, for example colleges, some local public health authorities. Detailed syllabuses are prescribed by the Society, which sets and conducts the examinations.

Candidates will normally only be admitted to the test (which is in two parts, written and oral) for the *Certificate in the Hygiene of Food Retailing and Catering* if they are 16 years of age or over at the time.

The syllabus includes: the social aspects of food hygiene; the digestive processes of the human body; germs — appearance, size, reproduction; outline of types of food poisoning and sources; transmission of food poisoning organisms; how food is contaminated; protection of food against contamination; hygienic construction (design and layout of equipment); aspects and problems affecting food hygiene, including legal matters and personnel factors.

The test for this Certificate is arranged so as to make it possible to obtain a general certificate or a certificate covering a specified section (for example Bakery, Ice Cream, Fish and Poultry).

Candidates showing exceptional ability will be awarded a Credit Pass; all successful candidates are eligible for Affiliateship of the Royal Society of Health (Affil RSH). See Chapter 10.

There are no additional specific requirements for entry to the test for the *Certificate in Nutrition in Relation to Catering and Cooking,* but ability in written English is important.

The syllabus includes an introductory section, another on nutrients; on physiology; on the composition of foods — in relation to their nutritive value and cost in average portions, contribution to the nutrient content of the average diet, sources of nutrients in other types of diet, fortification, effects of different quantities and cooking and service methods on nutrient content, as well as the effects of processing, preservation and storage; menu planning and food hygiene.

The Certificate examination comprises one written paper (which includes some essay type questions) and an oral test. The test for the *Diploma in Nutrition in Relation to Catering Management* includes a second written paper and a higher proportion of essay type questions.

Before commencing an approved course of training for the Diploma examination, candidates must either (a) have taken or be in the final year of a full-time course in catering subjects of not less than two years' duration or (b) have the City and Guilds 706/2 or equivalent with a minimum of three years' supervisory experience in catering, or (c) have held an administrative or managerial post in catering for a minimum of two years. However selected students attending the Certificate course will be allowed to enter for the Diploma examinations on the recommendation of the course authorities.

The basic syllabus for the Diploma is the same as that for the Certificate, with an emphasis on acquiring a deeper understanding of the application of nutritional principles to catering management. For example candidates should be able to plan meals to fit prescribed requirements for common modifications of the normal diet; and be able to instruct subordinates in buying, storing, cooking and serving food so as to get and retain nutritive values, to check that these principles are observed and to be versed in practical methods of demonstrating to staff.

Exceptional ability in the Certificate or Diploma test will be acknowledged by the award of a Credit or Distinction.

A list of colleges approved to offer RSH courses is available direct from the Society; it is advisable to contact the nearest college for details on how the course is offered.

As the Society does not specify the number of teaching hours for its courses, it is only possible to generalise on course structure and length.

Certificate courses in Hygiene of Food Retailing and Catering are offered by a number of colleges on a part-time evening basis — one attendance per week (about two hours) for one term, or shorter attendances over a longer period.

Certificate courses in Nutrition in Relation to Catering and Cooking are offered by a number of colleges in conjunction with the Diploma in Nutrition in Relation to Catering Management, on a part-time evening basis, one attendance per week for one academic year; other colleges may require longer or more frequent attendances but reduce the length of study.

National Council for Home Economics Education

The National Council for Home Economics Education offers a full-time course leading to the Council's Housekeeping and Catering Certificate. The Council's other courses include:

Cooks Professional: a one year course intended for those who require a high standard of cookery for their career; qualified students, the Council state, may expect to be employed in the preparation of food and service of wine for receptions, directors' luncheons, private dinner parties etc. Entry to the course is open to those with an approved qualification in Household Cookery.

Certificate in Home Economics: a two year full-time course designed to provide a good basic knowledge of home economics leading to posts in industry and commerce as assistants with the fuel industries, manufacturers of foods, domestic appliances and equipment, detergents and textiles. The entry requirement is 4 GCE 'O' levels, one being English language/literature.

Diploma in Home Economics: a three year full-time course planned for students who wish to make a career as a professional Home Economist in industry or commerce, the consumer advisory services, or community services. The entry requirement is 5 GCE passes, including one at 'A' level, English language and a science subject.

The Housekeeping and Catering Certificate course (two years full-time) is open to students of 16 years of age or over and assessed as suitable by the college. The course, which is offered by about twenty colleges, is suitable for those wishing to take up appointments as assistant housekeepers and caterers in clubs, hostels, schools and colleges, halls of residence, hospitals, industrial canteens and other institutions.

The syllabus includes institutional establishments and their functions — development, functions, staff responsibilities; housekeeping and administration — including care of premises, furnishings and equipment, safety and hygiene, laundry work and linen room management; staff management and welfare; methods of purchase; stock control; accounts; office practice; kitchen organisation; large scale cooking equipment and catering methods; menu planning; costing; meal service; nutrition and cookery.

Students have a minimum of four weeks' practical experience in a suitable establishment. During the course, certificates are taken in First Aid and Home Nursing. The examination for the course itself includes three written papers and practical assessment.

Scottish Business Education Council – Hotel Reception Courses

Two courses in Hotel Reception administered by the Scottish Business Education Council (SCOTBEC) are available at a number of colleges in Scotland.

In the 1978/79 session some ten colleges offered the SCOTBEC Certificate for Hotel Receptionists (Stage I) and eleven the Certificate for Hotel Receptionists (Stage II). Some 191 students enrolled on the Stage I course and 183 on Stage II.

These courses, which have been offered by SCOTBEC since 1972/73, are being revised for the 1980/81 session. There are unlikely to be any significant changes to the entry requirements or structure of the courses as a result. However, the syllabuses will be amplified and clarified and it is possible that the number of teaching hours will be recommended for each subject.

The *Stage I* course is intended for young trainee receptionists and for persons intending to become hotel receptionists. There are no formal entry requirements other than that the candidate should have completed three years of secondary education, and satisfied the college on interview.

The course is offered either on a one year full-time basis (when the equivalent of five weeks' work experience is included, sometimes on a day release basis) or on a block release basis (with two blocks of college study and an intervening period of practical work in hotels) also over one year. The HCITB will endorse certificates in the latter case.

The Certificate is awarded to candidates who obtain passes in:

Communication (internal college subject, not examined by SCOTBEC as the others are);

Hotel Book-keeping and Accounts including double entry book-keeping; tabular ledger, cash handling; wages; an appreciation of the use of machines in hotel accounting; control procedures and VAT;

Hotel Organisation and Reception including the functions and operation of departments within an hotel and daily reception routine;

Typewriting and a *Modern Language.*

The *Stage II* course is designed for the well qualified school leaver with no experience in the hotel industry; it is only available as a one year full-time course.

The entry requirements are: 3 SCE 'O' grade passes including English; or SCOTBEC Junior Certificate; or CGLI 705 plus 2 SCE 'O' grade passes including English; or candidates aged 21 or over with a minimum of 2 years' appropriate post-school experience (at the discretion of the College Principal).

The course includes a minimum of five weeks' practical work in an hotel. The Certificate is awarded to candidates who obtain passes in:

Communication

Hotel Book-keeping and Accounts: including the principles of accounting with special reference to the hotel industry; the complete accounting systems for recording the transactions of an hotel; preparation of tabular ledger; mechanical billing; control;

Business Practice: to provide the student with a wide knowledge of business practice, the syllabus includes: business organisation, correspondence; telephone and telegraphic services; filing and indexing; business documents; sources of information; wages; income tax and social security; methods of payment; control of stationery and meetings;

Typewriting and *Office Machines.* A modern language may be taken as an optional subject.

The syllabuses for both Stage I and Stage II are under review (August 1979).

Nautical Catering courses

In 1892, Liverpool was the first local education authority to provide vocational education for ships' cooks. The name of the Training School for Ships' Cooks as it was called in 1906 has been altered three times since, the most recent change being in 1979 when the Nautical Catering College amalgamated with Colquitt Technical College to form the new Colquitt Technical and Nautical College. A very wide range of nautical catering courses — mainly leading to college certificates — is offered including:

Preparatory Stewards Course to prepare new entrants to the shipping industry in the duties and skills required as junior catering ratings, for which prospective students must have a reasonable education standard, be physically fit, be aged between 16 and $17\frac{1}{4}$ years, and be considered suitable for future employment at sea. The 12 week course includes pantry work, basic food and beverage preparation, food service, menus, cabin and public room service, first aid, general ship knowledge, life boat work, liberal studies, physical education, maintenance of furnishings and fittings.

Assistant Stewards Course: a two week course useful for junior catering ratings on, or prior to, their promotion to assistant steward, and for assistant stewards who have had little or no experience or training in food and beverage service.

Advanced Waiters Course: a two week course which includes the restaurant and its equipment, menu compilation, food and menu terms, reception, techniques of service, banqueting organisation, wines, storage and service, cookery at table, carving from wagons, food and personal hygiene and cost control.

A series of two week supervisory courses are available for those who have had a minimum of one year's experience at sea in a catering department, or appropriate experience in the hotel and catering industry ashore with at least three months' service in catering afloat. These include one for Second Stewards (Non Passenger) on successful completion of which the Merchant Navy Training Board Certificate for Second Stewards is awarded.

The food preparation courses include a four week Bread and Confectionery course designed to teach the finer points of bakery, confectionery and sweet production; Part I and Part II of the Ships' Cooks' Certificate of Competency, each six weeks long; a special six week long Refresher Course in Cookery; a six week Higher Grade Cookery Course; a two week Higher Grade Cookery Refresher Course and a six week Advanced Cookery Course.

Prospective students for entry to *Part I* of the *Ships' Cooks' Certificate of Competency course* must be aged not less than $17\frac{3}{4}$ years, and have a minimum of 12 months' sea service in the catering department. The course, which includes practical and theory of cookery, bakery and butchery, menu planning, hygiene and nutrition, care and maintenance of kitchens and equipment, leads to examinations for the Merchant Navy Training Board's Cookery Certificate.

To be accepted on to the *Part II* course, seafarers must have completed Part I successfully and have served a further 12 months at sea. The course, which takes to greater depth the areas of study of Part I and includes costing and kitchen management, leads to examinations for the Department of Trade's Certificate of Competency for Ships' Cooks.

For those who are aged 21 or over, and either completed five years' sea service in the purser/catering department of which one year has been at the rank of 2nd Steward or Chief Cook or higher, or had similar experience including related further education in the hotel and catering industry ashore, there is a six week course available leading to a NEBBS Catering Officers Certificate and the Department of Trade Ships' Captains Medical Training Certificate. The title of the course is Catering Officers (Head of Catering Department). A seven week course is available relevant to short sea trades.

In *Scotland* at Glasgow College of Food Technology block release courses leading to Ships' Cooks Certificate and Higher Cooks Certificate are offered, as well as the Merchant Navy Cooks Certificate. Aberdeen Technical College offers a short course for Merchant Navy Cooks. Other colleges offering nautical catering courses include Leith Nautical College, Edinburgh; the London School of Nautical Cookery; Marine and Technical College, South Shields; South Glamorgan Institute of Higher Education, Cardiff; Hull College of Higher Education; and, of course, the Royal Navy School of Cookery, HMS *Pembroke* (HM Naval Base, Chatham, Kent).

Useful Addresses

CITY AND GUILDS OF LONDON INSTITUTE, 76 Portland Place, London W1N 4AA (Tel 01-580 3050); the CGLI unit dealing with catering courses is based at 46 Britannia Street, London WC1X 9RG (Tel 01-278 2468)

EAST MIDLAND EDUCATIONAL UNION, Robins Wood House, Robins Wood Road, Aspley, Nottingham NG8 3NH (Tel 0602 293291)

GUILD OF SOMMELIERS, Five Kings House, Kennet Wharf Lane, Upper Thames Street, London EC4V 3BA (Tel 01-236 4610)

HOTEL AND CATERING INDUSTRY TRAINING BOARD, PO Box 18, Ramsey House, Central Square, Wembley, Middlesex HA9 7AP (Tel 01-902 8865)

MERCHANT NAVY TRAINING BOARD, 30/32 St Mary Axe, London EC3A 8ET (Tel 01-283 2922)

(For addresses of colleges, see Chapter 9.)

NATIONAL COUNCIL FOR HOME ECONOMICS EDUCATION, 214 Middle Lane, Hornsey, London N8 7LB (Tel 01-340 4823)

NATIONAL EXAMINATIONS BOARD FOR SUPERVISORY STUDIES, 76 Portland Place, London W1N 4AA (Tel 01-580 3050)

NORTH WESTERN REGIONAL ADVISORY COUNCIL FOR FURTHER EDUCATION (INCORPORATING THE UNION OF LANCASHIRE AND CHESHIRE INSTITUTES), The Town Hall, Walkden Road, Worsley, Manchester M28 4QE (Tel 061-702 8700)

ROYAL INSTITUTE OF PUBLIC HEALTH AND HYGIENE, 28 Portland Place, London W1N 4DE (Tel 01-580 2731)

SCOTTISH BUSINESS EDUCATION COUNCIL, 22 Great King Street, Edinburgh EH3 6QH (Tel 031-556 4691)

SCOTTISH TECHNICAL EDUCATION COUNCIL, 38 Queen Street, Glasgow G1 3DY (Tel 041-204 2271)

THE BREWERS' SOCIETY, 42 Portman Square, London W1H 0BB (Tel 01-486 4381)

THE ROYAL SOCIETY OF HEALTH, 13 Grosvenor Place, London SW1X 7EN (Tel 01-235 9961)

WINE AND SPIRIT EDUCATION TRUST LTD, Five Kings House, Kennet Wharf Lane, Upper Thames Street, London EC4V 3 AJ (Tel 01-236 3551/2)

YORKSHIRE AND HUMBERSIDE COUNCIL FOR FURTHER EDUCATION, Bowling Green Terrace, Leeds LS11 9SX (Tel 0532 40751)

6

Training for Supervisory and Management Posts

Four charts: full-time courses for school leaver with minimum 4 GCE/SCE 'O' levels; alternative routes, full-time and part-time with academic or craft qualifications and experience; TEC awards; SCOTEC awards. Ordinary National Diploma courses in Hotel, Catering and Institutional Operations, Hotel and Catering Operations, Institutional Housekeeping and Catering, Business Studies (Hotel Reception). Higher National Diploma courses in Hotel and Catering Administration, Hotel, Catering and Institutional Management, Institutional Management, Catering and Hotel Keeping. Industrial experience on courses. HCIMA Part A, Part B and Graduate-entry courses. Diploma in Hotel and Catering Administration, Hollings Faculty, Manchester Polytechnic. TEC awards in Hotel, Catering and Institutional Management. SCOTEC awards in Hotel, Catering and Institutional Management. Useful addresses.

THE opportunities for studying for supervisory and management qualifications are excellent for school leavers with three, four or more General Certificate of Education/Scottish Certificate of Education passes. The range of qualifications available is not quite as extensive as those for craft skills, but this is certainly not a disadvantage.

The opportunities are greater for full-time study than they are for part-time. It is nevertheless possible to acquire a management qualification while working full-time in the industry, either by part-time attendance at college, or by correspondence course.

It is also possible to proceed to a supervisory/management qualification as a mature student with substantial experience in the industry and craft qualifications.

Certain courses are more suitable for students wishing to work in one sector of the industry, rather than another, for example the welfare sector when a Degree or Diploma in Institutional Management would be more appropriate.

A previous chapter has outlined the changes that have taken place since 1946 in supervisory and management courses. The introduction of Technician Education Council (TEC) and Scottish Technical Education Council (SCOTEC) courses in 1980 and 1981, replacing Ordinary and Higher National Diplomas, will alter the picture for new students. The basic details of these changes have been well publicised and an explanation follows. At the time of going to press the Hotel, Catering and Institutional Management Association, the professional body for managers in the industry, had not yet determined the extent of recognition which it will accord the new Councils' awards. The charts which follow deal firstly therefore with those qualifications which can be related to professional recognition, and then with the new awards and opportunities offered by TEC and SCOTEC awards.

Degree courses are dealt with fully in the next chapter.

CHART 1

Full-time study: school leaver with minimum 4 GCE 'O' levels

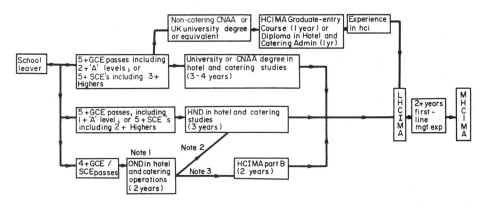

Notes

1 Many students will complete their studies at OND level
2 In Scotland it is sometimes possible for an OND student proceeding to an HND to be exempt from the first year of the HND
3 Those continuing via the HCIMA Part B course do so directly on a 2 year sandwich course (alternative routes are fully explained in the text)

Key

5+ = minimum of 5
GCE = General Certificate of Education
SCE = Scottish Certificate of Education
CNAA = Council for National Academic Awards
HND = Higher National Diploma
OND = Ordinary National Diploma
HCIMA = Hotel, Catering and Institutional Management Association
LHCIMA = Licentiate member of HCIMA
MHCIMA = Corporate member of HCIMA

CHART 2

Alternative routes, full-time and part-time with academic or craft qualifications and experience

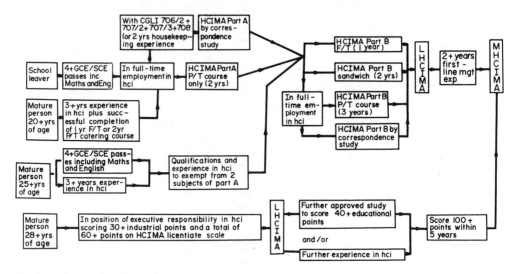

Key (see also key for Chart 1)

CGLI = City and Guilds of London Institute certificate
F/T = full-time course
P/T = part-time course
hci = hotel and catering industry

CHART 3

Via TEC awards: varying entry requirements, part-time and full-time study

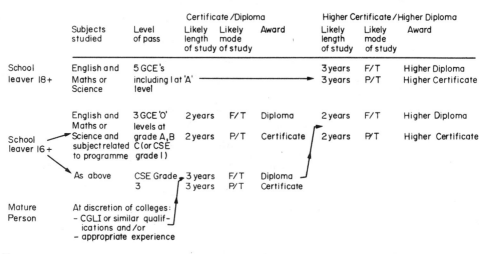

Key

See Charts 1 and 2
CSE = Certificate of Secondary Education

CHART 4

*Via SCOTEC Diploma and Higher Diploma courses in Hotel, Catering and
Institutional Operations / Management*

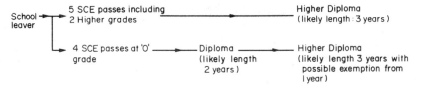

IMPORTANT NOTES

Whilst entry requirements will be recommended by SCOTEC (as above), students with alternative qualifications may be admitted at the discretion of the principal of the college.

SCOTEC puts no restriction on mode of attendance. The Diploma and Higher Diploma courses are likely to be offered on a full-time sandwich basis, two and three years in length respectively.

The variations to the normal entry routes that have been available on OND and HND courses in Scotland for those students with a mixture of SCE qualifications and City and Guilds of London Institute, SCOTBEC and SCOTEC qualifications are likely to be available under SCOTEC for the Diploma and Higher Diploma.

National Diplomas

From annual surveys conducted by the HCIMA it is possible to judge the scale of college enrolments of students on National Diploma courses. In 1978 almost 2900 students enrolled on an Ordinary National Diploma course in hotel and catering studies, a 52% increase on the 1972 figure of 1900. The number of students enrolling on the Higher National Diploma course increased by 30% from 1080 in 1972 to over 1400 in 1978.

In Scotland one Ordinary National Diploma (OND) course is offered: Hotel, Catering and Institutional Operations, and two Higher National Diploma (HND) courses: Catering and Hotel Keeping and Institutional Management.

Students studying at colleges in the remainder of the UK have a wider choice initially, but it is rare now for any one college to offer more than one course at OND or HND level. There are three OND courses: Hotel, Catering and Institutional Operations, Hotel and Catering Operations, Institutional Housekeeping and Catering.

There are also three HND courses: Hotel, Catering and Institutional Management, Hotel and Catering Administration, Institutional Management.

The new SCOTEC Diploma and Higher Diploma courses will replace the OND and HND from September 1980 in Scotland. South of the Scottish border, some colleges will be commencing new courses of study leading to TEC awards from September 1980. Information on TEC and SCOTEC awards is provided further on in this chapter.

In addition, some National Diploma courses in business studies are available, which specialise in reception.

Ordinary National Diploma

This is a two year full-time college course of around 2000 hours of tuition. Scottish colleges usually arrange for students to spend 12–16 weeks in industrial experience during the first summer vacation; two English colleges — South East London College, Lewisham and Thomas Danby College, Leeds — operate longer, sandwich OND courses of 2½ and 3 years respectively.

Entry requirements do vary in detail between Scotland and the rest of the UK, and minor adjustments to these details have been made from time to time by the Joint Committees. It is always advisable to check carefully with colleges.

The basic requirement is for four GCE passes (at grades A, B or C) at Ordinary level ('O'), or four SCE passes at Ordinary grade (band A, B or C). In Scotland one of these subjects must be English and two of the other subjects have to be from a specified range (Note A). In the rest of the UK, three of the subjects have to be "academic" (Note B). A Certificate of Secondary Education (CSE) Grade 1 pass in an approved subject is accepted as an alternative to a GCE 'O' level pass in that subject.

A pass in the CGLI 705 will be accepted in lieu of the fourth GCE (in England, Wales and Northern Ireland), while a credit pass in the two theory papers of the 705 examination, and an overall pass, may be accepted in addition to only two "academic" GCEs. It is important that candidates have attained an adequate standard of literacy and numeracy. The SCOTBEC Hotel Receptionist Certificate Stage II is an acceptable entry requirement for the Scottish OND course.

Equivalent qualifications, including those overseas examinations and certificates of similar standing to the GCE, are acceptable.

The aim of the OND course is to give a sound basic technical education to students who, with suitable post-college training and experience, will attain positions of supervisory responsibility in any sector of the industry, and normally be responsible for a specific function and immediate supervision of other people with no intervening levels.

The *Scottish* colleges all follow a detailed syllabus (about 1900 hours) and examinations are set centrally. The subjects studied include catering, professional cookery, food and beverage service, maintenance and housekeeping, applied science, business studies, general studies and elements of supervisory studies. In order to qualify for the award of a diploma it is necessary to have taken an approved course in consecutive sessions and sit all examinations at the appropriate stages (it is not therefore possible to complete one year of the course, leave college and return at a later time without repeating both years of the course). It is necessary to complete the first year of the course successfully before proceeding to the second, and in the final stage, in addition to attending for not less than 80% of the possible total attendance in each subject, each of the final examinations must be passed (40% pass mark).

Note A: One subject has to be from: Anatomy/Physiology and Health, Arithmetic, Biology, Botany, Chemistry, Mathematics, Physics, Zoology. A second subject has to be from: Economic Organisation, Geography, History, Modern Studies, Principles of Accounts, a modern language.

Note B: The following are "non-academic" subjects: Cookery Subjects, Needlework, Woodwork, Metalwork, Art, Drama, Crafts, Music, Design and Technology, Ballet, Building or Engineering.

Where a candidate fails in one or more subjects, he/she may, at the discretion of the Joint Committee, be allowed to re-sit the examination in the subject(s) on no more than two occasions within the period of the next two sessions, otherwise he/she will be deemed to have failed all the subjects.

A pass with "Special Mention" in any assessed subject is awarded to candidates who obtain 75% or higher in the final examination of that subject, and who simultaneously qualify for the award of the National Diploma concerned.

A National Diploma with "Distinction" is awarded to candidates who qualify for the award of a Diploma at first presentation with not less than 75% of the possible grand total of marks in the assessed examination of the final stage of the course.

In *England, Wales and Northern Ireland* colleges have more freedom to design courses according to the specific interests of the students, subject to the approval of the Joint Committee and within broad guidelines. Approximately 1000 hours will be spent on food and beverage preparation and service and accommodation operations (or institutional housekeeping), about 600 hours on related studies (i.e. applied science and business studies) and 400 hours on general studies (including liberal and social studies, English as a means of communication).

Colleges set their own examination papers in addition to assessing students' coursework, including practical work. The Joint Committee appoints assessors to monitor standards.

The final five assessed subjects on all three ONDs include Food and Beverage Preparation and Service I, Applied Science and Business Studies. On the Hotel and Catering Operations OND there is a second Business Studies subject (Economics, Law and Human Aspects, the first is Accounts), and either a second Food and Beverage Preparation and Service, or Accommodation Operations.

An OND in Hotel, Catering and Institutional Operations gives no alternative for the fifth subject, which is Accommodation Operations. An OND in Institutional Housekeeping and Catering includes Food and Beverage Preparation and Service II as the fourth subject, with Institutional Housekeeping as the fifth.

In the five assessed examinations, each of the written papers will be of $2\frac{1}{2}$ hours' duration.

The content, emphasis and application of the studies included on the different OND courses will differ rather more than it appears from a simple comparison of the outline syllabus.

In order to qualify for the award of a diploma it is necessary to have attended for not less than 75% of the prescribed time in each subject *each* stage of the course, and take all subjects as specified in the approved scheme. It is necessary to obtain a minimum of 50% of the total marks obtainable in the final year (of this total, the final examinations constitute 70%, coursework and practical work the balance of 30%), with not less than 40% in each of the final examinations, nor less than 40% in the continuous assessment of practical work, nor less than 40% of the possible marks obtainable for coursework.

The "final examination marks" constitute the sum of the marks awarded in the five theory papers plus the marks for continuous assessment of practical work in Food and Beverage Preparation and Service and Accommodation Operations/ Institutional Housekeeping.

A candidate may be referred in a subject or subjects, at the discretion of the Joint

Committee. In these circumstances the college will make arrangements for the candidate to re-sit the paper(s) — either by setting an examination at a special time, or by allowing the candidate to re-sit the paper the following year.

Progression within the course is at the discretion of the college principal; it is very exceptional for a student to be allowed to proceed to the second (or third) year of the course unless he/she has achieved satisfactory results in examinations and continuous assessment (in line with those stipulated for the final year).

A distinction is awarded to any candidate who qualifies to receive the Diploma with an overall mark of not less than 75% of the possible marks for the final examination and continuous assessment and the Diploma is specially endorsed to show the distinction.

Ordinary National Diploma in Business Studies
(Hotel Reception)

A Business Studies Ordinary National Diploma specialising in Hotel Reception is available at a few colleges including Ealing College of Higher Education in London. For entry to the OND course at Ealing a student must be at least 16 years of age (preferably 17 or 18) with five GCE passes at 'O' level including English Language and, desirably, French (it is essential to have studied French up to 'O' level); considerable importance is attached to the personal interview.

An Ealing College Diploma is also available for students who have qualified for the OND award. Course content includes: economics, accounting, English, French, hotel services and organisation — accommodation and restaurant operation, front office services. Additional subjects for college diploma students include practical housekeeping, floral art, practical restaurant and hotel reception operation, speech and deportment, typewriting and shorthand and either German or Spanish.

For two three week periods of industrial experience students are seconded first to the housekeeping department and secondly to the reception desk and front offices of a large hotel.

Higher National Diploma

In all cases, this is a three year college course including period(s) of industrial experience. The basic entry requirements are five GCE or SCE passes including, respectively, one at 'A' level, or two at Higher grade, or an OND in hotel and catering, or another qualification acceptable by the Joint Committees.

For Scotland the five subjects offered must include English and two subjects from the lists specified in Note A on page 110, and one of these three subjects has to be passed at Higher Grade. The same requirements regarding grades of GCE/SCE/CSE passes apply as for the OND.

In England, Wales and Northern Ireland the subject offered at 'A' level must be "academic" (see Note B on page 110). Only one other subject of the five may be "non-academic", and a credit pass in the two written papers of the CGLI 705 examination, an overall pass, will be accepted in lieu of both this "non-academic" 'O' level and one other 'O' level. A pass in CGLI 705 will be accepted in lieu of the fifth GCE. An OND in Business Studies is also acceptable. It is important that students have attained an adequate standard of literacy and numeracy, and a science subject is desirable.

The conditions regarding the award of a diploma, referrals, award of a diploma with distinction, are the same as those for the respective OND courses, and it is a requirement that the industrial training aspects of the course are satisfactorily completed.

The aim of the Higher National Diploma course is to give a sound technical education to students who, with suitable industrial experience, will attain positions of responsibility, normally responsible for the work of a number of section heads, supervisors or departmental heads.

Although there are three HND courses in England, Wales and Northern Ireland, it has become increasingly unusual for a college to operate more than one. Most colleges offer either the HND in Hotel and Catering Administration, or the HND in Hotel, Catering and Institutional Management. A few colleges offer an HND in Institutional Management.

In Scotland there are two HND courses, in 1978 two colleges enrolled students on the Institutional Management HND, two on the Catering and Hotel Keeping, and two operated both courses.

The content, emphasis and application of the studies included on the different HND courses will differ according to the HND. The commercial sectors of the industry, for example hotels, restaurants, industrial catering, will be emphasised on an HND in Hotel and Catering; the welfare sector, for example school meals, hospitals, halls of residence, will be emphasised on an HND in Institutional Management. Colleges will endeavour to relate all studies, and lecturers themselves will have different backgrounds of industrial experience.

Scottish colleges follow a detailed syllabus (about 2600 teaching hours) covering, on both courses: applied science — basic science, microbiology, and hygiene, food chemistry, nutrition, catering technology; general studies; business and management studies — book-keeping, accounting, office practice and control, economics, work study, management accounting, costing, legal aspects, introduction to management, personnel administration, statistics; principles and practice of food production; food service; administration of house services; basic design studies.

The HND in Catering and Hotel Keeping also includes beverage service, design studies, French, marketing, the planning of food and beverage operations.

The HND in Institutional Management includes communications, socio-economic background, planning of food services and a choice of design studies, marketing or a modern language.

As with the OND, the examinations are set centrally. Conditions for the award of a diploma, and for re-sitting failed subjects, are identical to the OND.

In *England, Wales and Northern Ireland* HND courses are based on about 1800 hours of teaching. One period of about thirty weeks of industrial experience, or two periods of twelve to fifteen weeks each, are included in the course, during the first two years.

The detail of each college's HND course varies, even between the same HND. All include about 600 hours of accommodation and house services, and food (and beverage) operations, about 650 hours of business studies and administration —

including economics, accounting, law, general studies, applied catering studies and catering technology.

All will include principles and practice of food production and service with topics like customers' requirements in all branches of catering, purchase and storage of food, menu planning, selection and maintenance of equipment.

Beverage aspects will be included in some depth on an HND course in Hotel and Catering Administration or Hotel, Catering and Institutional Management. An Institutional Management HND will include a greater proportion of time on house services and science of materials and building services with topics like location and functional planning; selection, working and running costs of all installations; selection, cost and maintenance of surface finishes, furniture and fittings; space heating, heat and sound insulation; lighting and ventilation.

Management studies will include topics like functions of management, leadership and methods, personnel management and welfare, salaries and wages, training, communication, employee service and amenities, trade unions and industrial relations, work study, ergonomics, industrial psychology, organisation and methods, problem and decision making, management exercises.

Examinations are set by the individual colleges; the final assessed subjects (which are moderated by Joint Committee assessors) are: Food and Beverage Operations, Accommodation and House Services, Business Studies, Management Studies and Applied Catering Studies.

Industrial experience is an important and integral part of all Higher National Diploma courses. Exact arrangements vary between colleges, sometimes one period of about thirty weeks is the practice, other colleges opt for two periods, each of twelve to fifteen weeks. The arrangements also vary regarding the timing of the industrial experience (the characteristics of the local industry is sometimes the determinant of timing, for example colleges in resort towns who wish to place many of their students in local hotels will plan the industrial experience to be during the summer season). In Scotland, the industrial experience will be during the vacation period, in the rest of the country it may be either then or in term time or a combination.

In the first phase of the industrial experience period(s) students will normally work as operatives in kitchens, restaurants, housekeeping or similar departments, depending on the sector of the industry and type of establishment. As they will only have had a limited opportunity to acquire expertise at practical skills at college, this phase will allow time to develop these skills, and the opportunity of working alongside operatives and craftsmen, and to gain additional experience of customer contact.

In the second phase, or the latter part of a single attachment, students will normally be given the opportunity of developing the administrative and managerial skills they have been taught at college. Typical placements include under-study to: assistant bursar in colleges/universities; assistant manager/manageress in industrial catering; assistant catering officer in hospitals; assistant manager/manageress in restaurants; head waiter/waitress in restaurants; duty management, receptionist, kitchen clerk, housekeeper in hotels.

Colleges will take account of the needs and interests of the individual student, and endeavour to find an establishment in a sector of the industry which will not only meet the immediate learning and development needs of the student, but help his/her future career.

Colleges normally agree training programmes with the student's employer for the period of industrial experience, often in close collaboration with the Hotel and Catering Industry Training Board. During the period in industry the student will be visited by one of the college lecturers and, depending on the sector of the industry, by an HCITB adviser.

It is not common for colleges to arrange industrial experience in Europe or further afield, because of the practical difficulties of making the arrangements, agreeing and undertaking a training programme, visiting the student and so forth. However, where these difficulties can be satisfactorily resolved, there is usually no barrier to such an arrangement.

Project work is often a part of the industrial experience element of the course. Companies and students can benefit from students being asked to examine a particular aspect of the operation in the form of a project.

Courses Leading to the HCIMA's Professional Qualification

The Hotel, Catering and Institutional Management Association (HCIMA) offers three courses: Part A and Part B of the HCIMA Professional Qualification and the HCIMA Professional Qualification Graduate-entry course.

In September 1978 the first one thousand plus students enrolled on the HCIMA's new Part A and B courses. Half this number enrolled on the Part A course, over four hundred on a two year sandwich course leading to Part B, 82 on a one year full-time Part B course and 75 on a three year part-time Part B course. In addition a small number of students enrolled on the new correspondence course.

By comparison, and these are levels of enrolments are expected to return to, in 1972 some 700 students enrolled on the Intermediate course (over 300 by correspondence) and about 800 on the Final (250 by correspondence, 130 on a part-time college course).

As Chart 2 indicates, the *Part A* course (two years' duration — 360 hours) is available at colleges on a part-time basis. This involves day release, afternoon or evening study at the college (about six hours per week for 30–36 weeks each year), the mode of attendance depending on the college. At present one college, the College of Business Studies in Belfast, offers the course on a block release basis (alternative periods in college — six weeks at a time — and in industry). The course may also be taken by means of correspondence study with Metropolitan College, Reading, for those students who are able to meet the additional entry requirements stipulated by the HCIMA. All students studying for Part A must be working full-time in the industry directly concerned with food preparation or service or with the provision or service of accommodation, or liquor. The Part A course concentrates on the technical skills and knowledge appropriate to all sectors of the industry.

It is divided into three subjects: *A1 Food Studies,* minimum 140 hours, which includes food as commodities (30%); preparation, cooking and service (50%); preparation and service plant and equipment (20%); *A2 Liquor Studies,* minimum 80 hours, which includes liquor as commodities (30%); liquor preparation (30%);

liquor outlets (20%) and legal aspects (20%); *A3 Accommodation Studies,* minimum 140 hours, which includes safety (10%), security (10%), servicing (20%), maintenance (20%), buildings and maintenance (15%), room interiors (15%), legal aspects (10%).

The entry requirements fall into three categories: students must either (a) be aged a minimum of 16 years and have four GCE or SCE 'O' level passes at grades A, B or C (or CSE grade 1), which includes an English subject, and mathematics subject (see Note C) and desirably a science subject; or (b) be aged a minimum of 20 years with not less than three years' full-time employment in the hotel and catering industry directly concerned with food preparation or service, or with the provision or service of accommodation or liquor, and have successfully completed a full-time catering course of one year's duration, or two years if part-time (Note D). In addition students wishing to study by correspondence course must have appropriate qualifications and experience to satisfy the HCIMA that they have the required standards of technical skills (Note E).

Examinations in the three Part A studies are set and marked by the HCIMA, and are usually held each June. There is only one component to each examination: a three hour written paper (which will often include an objective section). The pass mark is 50% and results are graded (see Note F). Students, who must be members of the Association, may only enter for examinations for which they have completed the appropriate course of study, and met the attendance requirement of 75%. Many colleges spread all three studies over both years of the course, others enter students for one examination at the end of one year, two at the end of the other year.

Students who fail a subject may re-sit another year; how often this is permitted and whether it is advisable to undertake further study depends on individual circumstances. Normally there is a time limit of four years from the date of the first attempt.

Part B

Students may not proceed to Part B unless they have successfully completed the whole of Part A or an equivalent qualification (notably an OND in hotel and catering studies, or the old HCIMA Intermediate Membership Examination).

Note C: Subjects which are acceptable as "English" are: English Language, English Literature, Economics, Geography, History, Sociology, a Modern Language; subjects which are acceptable as "Mathematics" are: Mathematics, Physics and Mathematics, Arithmetic, Pure Mathematics, Applied Mathematics, Mathematics (pure and applied), Statistics, Applied Mechanics, Commercial Mathematics, Engineering Science, Physics.

Note D: Appropriate catering studies is defined as success in one of the following City and Guilds of London Institute qualifications: 705, 706/1, 707/1, 708, 709, 764.

Note E: The additional requirements to study Part A subjects by means of a correspondence course are:

for A1 — a pass in CGLI 706/2 and 707/1

for A2 — a pass in CGLI 707/2 and 707/3

for A3 — either a pass in CGLI 708 or 764 or 2 years' housekeeping experience.

Note F: Results in the examinations of the HCIMA's Part A and B courses are graded as follows: marks of 80% and higher = Pass Grade A; 70–79% = Pass Grade B; 60–69% = Pass Grade C; 50–59% = Pass (unclassified); 40–49% = Fail Grade D; 30–39% = Fail Grade E; marks under 29% = Fail Grade F.

There are no additional requirements for study by correspondence course.

As Chart 2 indicates, the HCIMA does offer special opportunities for mature students. It is also possible for students to have received some exemption from Part A if they are initially able to meet the entry requirements for the course and have the qualifications and experience to justify subject exemption. Note G details the basic requirements.

A mature student aged 25 years or over who is able to meet the requirements for exemption from any two Part A studies (Note G) may be allowed direct entry to the Part B course.

Licentiate members of the Association are also eligible to study Part B, but will often only wish to take specific subjects in order to increase their educational point score (each Part B subject scores eight to ten points on the Licentiate scale).

Part B courses are available in four modes: a one year full-time course, a two year sandwich course (includes a minimum of six months' industrial experience), a three year part-time course (day release at college, eight to eleven hours per week), or by correspondence course with Metropolitan College, Reading. Students wishing to study on a part-time basis, or by correspondence course, must be working full-time in the industry. There is an additional entry requirement for the one year course for students without a Part A qualification: a minimum of twelve months' full-time experience in the industry, directly concerned with food preparation or service, the provision or service of accommodation or liquor. Hence a school leaver on successful completion of an OND course will normally proceed to a two year sandwich Part B course, alternatively, it is possible to work for a year or more in the industry before returning to college for a year to study Part B.

The Part B course (860 hours) comprises a compulsory common core of management-orientated subjects divided into Foundation and Major Studies with a third Elective Study area.

The three Foundation Studies are *B1 The Industry,* minimum 75 hours, which includes historical background (10%), structure and organisation (25%), significance (25%), supply and demand characteristics (15%), resources (25%); *B2 Management,* minimum 100 hours, which includes management environment (10%), objectives policy and planning (20%), organisation (25%), information and control (15%), specialist techniques (15%), legal framework (15%); and *B3 Marketing I,* minimum 75 hours, which includes consumer orientation (4%), marketing planning (33%), marketing research (40%), marketing control (10%), legal aspects (13%).

Each course also includes Compensatory Studies (minimum 60 hours), students given special entry to Part B will take Compensatory Studies in the third Part A study (i.e. A1 if exemption was granted from A2 and A3), otherwise programmes will be designed by colleges to meet individual students' needs as far as possible, taking account of different backgrounds, e.g. Part A, OND, Intermediate.

Note G: The qualifications which are accepted for credit exemptions (note it is also possible to take into account relevant experience gained in the industry where an applicant has some, but not all, of the required combination of certificates) are as follows:

for A1 — CGLI 706/2 + CGLI 707/2 + NEBBS or SCOTEC Certificate in Supervision
for A2 — CGLI 707/2 + CGLI 707/3 + NEBBS or SCOTEC Certificate in Supervision
for A3 — CGLI 708 or 764 + NEBBS or SCOTEC Certificate in Supervision.

The three Major Studies are *B4 Food and Beverage Management,* minimum 120 hours, which includes purchasing of foods and liquors (15%), production and service of foods and liquors (25%), outlets (5%), menus (5%), beverage lists (5%), cost and control concepts (25%), control cycle (10%), measurement of performance (10%); *B5 Financial Management I,* minimum 120 hours, which includes accounting concepts (10%), analysis and interpretation of accounting information (25%), cost-profit-volume relationships (20%), budgetary control (30%), pricing (15%); *B6 Manpower Studies,* minimum 120 hours, which includes human resources in the organisation (20%), training and development (20%), personnel administration (20%), industrial relations (20%), legal aspects (20%).

In addition students must study two Elective Studies (a few colleges on two year sandwich courses offer the opportunity for more than two to be studied). There are ten such studies, but colleges usually offer a shorter range: B7 Gastronomy, B8 Human Nutrition, B9 Food and Beverage Science and Technology, B10 Science and Technology of Accommodation, B11 Accommodation Management, B12 Financial Management II, B13 Business Statistics, B14 Information Processing, B15 Tourism and B16 Marketing II.

The Major Studies are examined externally by the HCIMA, usually each June. The Foundation and Elective Studies are examined internally by the colleges subject to moderation by HCIMA assessors, at the end of the appropriate terms. There is one common component to each of the eight examinations, a three hour written paper; most colleges must take into account students' coursework, project work etc., for the Foundation and Elective Studies when it will count for a maximum 25% or 30% of the final mark. The pass mark is 50% for each subject; the grades are as Note F on page 116. A pass in all eight subjects is required for the award of a certificate. Candidates for the examinations must be members of the HCIMA, have completed the appropriate course of study and met the attendance requirement of 75%.

There is no requirement to pass the examinations in any particular order, students who fail a subject may re-sit another year, how often this is permitted and whether it is necessary to undertake further study depend on individual circumstances. Normally there is a four year time limit starting from the date of the first attempt at the Major Studies.

HCIMA Professional Qualification Graduate-entry Course

The HCIMA Professional Qualification Graduate-entry course is a one year full-time college course including a short period of industrial experience. The course is suitable for graduates with non-catering UK university or CNAA degrees, or possessing qualifications of equivalent standing, who have developed a late interest in a career in hotel, catering and institutional management.

The course covers the three Part A Studies, the Part B Foundation and Major Studies. Students are assessed by examination and by continuous assessment (30%). The five examinations (papers set by each college and moderated by the HCIMA) are held at the conclusion of the course. Passes in all five are required for the award of a certificate. Students who marginally fail in no more than two of the

Students at Oxford Polytechnic cover gastronomy as an elective subject in their course.
Copyright: Peter Titmuss.

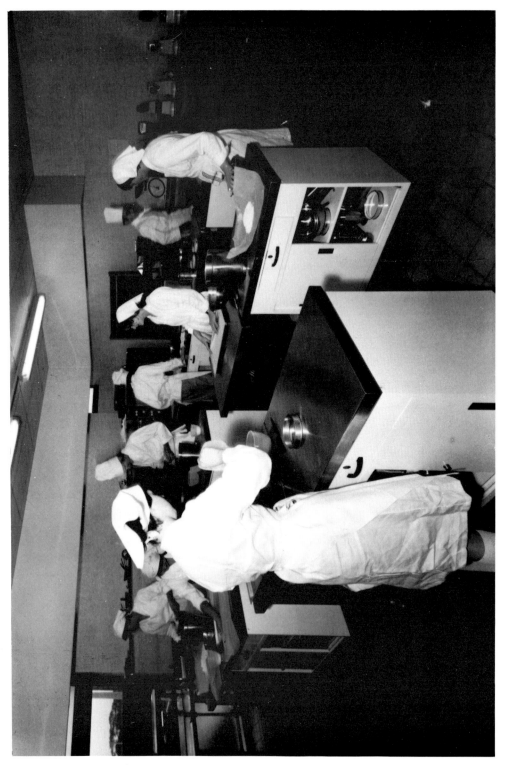

Pastry preparation in one of the training kitchens at the Dorset Institute of Higher Education, Poole. Copyright: Benham and Sons Ltd., London.

Tasting booths in the experimental kitchens at the Dorset Institute of Higher Education, Poole.

Operational situations are examined by simulation on the computer, University of Surrey.

examinations may be given the opportunity of a viva. A candidate who fails a maximum of two examinations will be allowed to re-sit the following year the failed papers. A candidate who fails three or more will be deemed to have failed all. There is a 75% attendance requirement and candidates for the examinations have to be registered as members of the HCIMA.

The four examination papers are Food and Beverage Management (A1, A2, B4), Management and Manpower Studies (B2, B6), The Industry and Financial Aspects (B1, B5), Marketing and Accommodation Management (B3, A3 and part of B11). The revealed case study counts as the fifth examination.

Successful completion of the course confers exemption from the examination requirements for membership of the HCIMA. On completion of one year's recognised industrial experience, candidates are eligible for upgrading from Student to Licentiate membership of the Association. Two colleges only offer this course at present: Queen Margaret College, Edinburgh, and Leeds Polytechnic. At Manchester Polytechnic a similar course, the Diploma in Hotel and Catering Administration, is available and is now described.

Diploma in Hotel and Catering Administration, Hollings Faculty, Manchester Polytechnic

This intensive one year course, which includes a short period of industrial experience, covers the technical and managerial aspects of the industry. There are two options available: Hotel and Catering, and Tourism. The entry requirements are a UK university or CNAA degree; and HND/C or equivalent, or an appropriate professional qualification.

Before 1977, the course was called "Advanced Diploma in Hotel and Catering Administration" (its name was changed when Hollings College merged with Manchester Polytechnic in January 1977).

The subjects studied in the Hotel and Catering Option include: provision of food and beverages, planning and organisation of accommodation, legal aspects of the hotel and catering industry, management, control systems and financial aspects, economic aspects and marketing systems.

Students' progress through the course is assessed in several ways including continuous assessment, in-course and final objective tests, a viva voce to complement the final objective tests and a thesis (6000 words minimum).

A review of this course is currently in progress and it is anticipated that the new, revised course will commence in September 1980.

TEC Awards in Hotel, Catering and Institutional Management

From September 1980 many colleges in England, Wales and Northern Ireland will no longer be offering Ordinary National Diploma courses in hotel and catering operations. In place of the OND these colleges will be offering new schemes of study leading to a Diploma or Certificate in Hotel, Catering and Institutional Management of the Technician Education Council. By September 1981 it is anticipated that no new students will be enrolled on OND courses.

Higher National Diploma courses in England, Wales and Northern Ireland will be phased out from September 1981, and in their place colleges will be offering new schemes of study leading to a Higher Diploma or Higher Certificate in Hotel, Catering and Institutional Management of the Technician Education Council.

These new awards mark the beginning of a new phase in the development of catering education. The Technician Education Council, TEC, was established in March 1973 with the task of developing a unified national system of technical education in the UK (except in Scotland, where the Scottish Technical Education Council, SCOTEC, has a similar function). TEC's aim is to provide a system of further education for technicians which is responsive to students' needs, to the requirements of industry, and which can be operated economically, efficiently and flexibly. Awards in hotel, catering and institutional management will only be a small part of the Council's work — indeed in 1979 three years after the first schemes of study leading to TEC awards started some 85 000 students were following over two thousand TEC schemes of study at around 400 colleges. In the 1980s it is anticipated that about 300 000 students will be studying for TEC awards each year.

The introduction of TEC awards in catering education brings a number of changes, and some unfamiliar expressions. The first of these is the use of the term "technician". While it is possible to relate specific occupations in the hotel and catering industry to "technician level", for example housekeeper, restaurant manager or kitchen superintendent, it is perhaps more meaningful to think of those who have previously qualified via the Ordinary and Higher National Diploma as being eligible in the future to qualify via TEC Diploma, Certificate, Higher Diploma and Higher Certificate awards.

The second, perhaps unfamiliar word in the TEC glossary is "programme". This expression is used in preference to "course". A programme is a scheme of study available to a student which leads to a TEC award. The title of the programme (for example Hotel, Catering and Institutional Management) is related to an occupational activity.

These schemes of study will in most cases be based on a unit system — in line with TEC policy of employing a credit system for its awards. A unit is a self-contained and significant component of a programme which may be separately assessed, and when successfully completed will count for credit towards a student's award.

This policy has a number of implications:

*The award document, in addition to stating the nature of the award (Diploma, Certificate, Higher Diploma, Higher Certificate), the title of the programme (for example Hotel, Catering and Institutional Management), the name of the student and the name of the college where he/she has studied, will state the title of the units the student has been exempted from, or passed (and the grade of success: Pass or Merit) and finally, it will state the level of the unit.

*TEC envisages that for design purposes, but not for timetabling, the average student will be able to acquire the knowledge and skills of a unit of study in 60-75 hours. These hours refer to college study but not necessarily to class contact or teaching time for they will usually include tutorials and directed private study, in fact whatever is necessary to achieve the objectives of the unit.

*The critical factor in the length of a programme is the number of units. Many colleges have chosen a unit length of 60 hours and the guidelines published by the TEC C4 Programme Committee (which has the task of overseeing awards in hotel, catering and institutional management) on Certificate, Diploma, Higher Certificate and Higher Diploma programmes in Hotel, Catering and Institutional Management are based on a unit length of 60 hours. The unit length adopted below is 60 hours.

*A CERTIFICATE programme will comprise 15 units and consist of approximately 900 hours of college-based study for students who do not receive credit for other attainment.

*A DIPLOMA programme will comprise 26 units and consist of approximately 1560 hours of studies for students who do not receive credit for any other attainment. The C4 Programme Committee has recommended an additional four practical units when a Diploma programme is offered on a full-time basis, bringing the total number of hours up to 1800.

*A HIGHER CERTIFICATE programme will normally comprise 10 units and consist of approximately 600 hours of college controlled study.

*A HIGHER DIPLOMA programme will normally comprise a minimum of 20 units and consist of approximately 1200–1500 hours of college controlled study.

*TEC awards can be obtained by any of the recognised modes of study — full-time, sandwich, block release, day release, evening study or by a combination of any of these. In practice a Certificate programme will usually involve a three year day-release programme for students with the minimum entry qualifications and no credit for previous study. A full-time Diploma programme will normally be operated over two years. A Higher Certificate programme will usually involve a two year day-release programme for students with the minimum entry qualifications; and similarly a Higher Diploma programme will usually involve a two year programme for a full-time student continuing his/her studies after satisfactorily completing a Certificate or Diploma programme, and a three year programme for those entering direct from school.

*A student who has gained a Certificate may qualify for a Diploma by completing the required additional units. In reverse, a student following a Diploma programme who does not qualify for this award may instead be awarded a Certificate if he/she has completed the required units for the award of this qualification. The same provision applies to the Higher Certificate and Higher Diploma.

*TEC has also made provision for individual unit awards where a student does not wish or need to undertake a complete programme. This provision is of particular interest to a mature student who wishes to return to further education for a short time in order to up-date his/her knowledge.

TEC programmes and awards cover a wide range of subjects and activities, nevertheless the amount of study for the same award will be broadly comparable over the whole spectrum. All Certificate programmes will therefore comprise approximately the same number of units, just as will all Diploma, Higher Diploma and Higher Certificate programmes from Structural Engineering to Hotel,

Catering and Institutional Management. This will help ensure that TEC awards have a national currency and facilitate movement between programmes and awards.

The unit structure of TEC programmes, the system of credit awards, the introduction for the first time of Certificate courses in catering education will do much to help those who cannot undertake full-time further education. Until now only the Hotel, Catering and Institutional Management Association has provided courses of study on a part-time basis leading to the Association's membership examinations. Other industries have had for many years Ordinary National Certificate and Higher National Certificate courses and indeed the number of students on these day release courses has been higher than those on full-time Diploma courses.

It is not possible to predict at this stage how many colleges will offer part-time courses leading to TEC awards, and if they do, how much support will be forthcoming from industry in releasing students. The success of Certificate programmes will depend on both.

Further explanation is now necessary of certain of the characteristics of TEC programmes.

Programme Structures

Units are classified as follows:

Essential units, to be taken by all students in a programme.

Optional units, which may be chosen by students in a programme, a fixed number of which will usually have to be taken to obtain an award (a unit which is essential in one programme may be optional in another).

Supplementary units, additional to the number and range required to qualify the student for the award.

A unit will be defined by the knowledge and skills to be attained by the student at its completion. Programmes may include half units, one and a half units, or double units, with the number of hours related proportionately to the standard period for a full unit.

It is a cornerstone of TEC policy that colleges or groups of colleges have the opportunity of devising schemes in close consultation with local industry, within the guidelines and subject to the approval of TEC. The approach of colleges to the designing of programmes is likely to fall into three categories: a number of colleges will design their own programmes entirely; in certain parts of the country consortiums of colleges have been formed to collaborate in the design of programmes for their common use; other colleges will rely largely on *Standard Units* that have been developed by the C4 Programme Committee for use on Certificate and Diploma programmes.

The guidelines issued by the C4 Programming Committee on Certificate and Diploma programmes indicate the need for a large common core in all programmes. The greatest differences are likely to be from those colleges which identify entire programmes common to all their students, compared to those which identify and can cater for optional vocational elements. In view of the importance TEC places on consultation with local industry, there will certainly be vocational overtones to the awards of some colleges. This is not a major departure from the OND/HND system, where certain colleges have a long tradition of serving the needs of one particular sector of the industry in their locality.

It has been well established that not only are their many common areas of skills and knowledge required by all sectors of the industry, but that considerable movement takes place between sectors and between different parts of the country — and world — so colleges will take account of national needs when designing programmes, as well as local needs. This is the reason for the guidelines "building-in" a large common core.

Mention was made earlier of *practical units* on full-time Diploma programmes. It is particularly important on hotel, catering and institutional management programmes that students are exposed to the working environment and to some of its pressures. In designing programmes colleges will naturally include practical work as part of the learning process specifically related to the achievements of the educational objectives of the programme. It will often be possible in the course of this practical work to simulate working conditions in the industry, for example in the training restaurant different types of food service and different eating environments can readily be created; in other cases colleges may use the facilities of industry to create a realistic situation, for example by collaborating in the operation of a local hotel for a short time, or a hospital or hall of residence Students on part-time and sandwich programmes will usually obtain a considerable amount of practical work outside the college environment. Students on a full-time programme are likely to have additional practical units built into their programmes to offset the lack of exposure outside their time at college, and successful completion of these would be a condition of the award.

Programmes will also include general and communication studies: at least 15% of the content of Certificate and Diploma programmes; Higher Certificate and Higher Diploma programmes will contain material related to supervisory or communication studies or studies complementary to the main theme of the programme. Such units are expected to contribute towards the development of the student's approach to, and skill in, oral and written communication. They will also help widen the student's further education. A Certificate or Diploma programme in Hotel, Catering and Institutional Management might include such topics as psychology, tourism, sociology, design, statistics, a foreign language.

Level of Units

The concept of levels is based on prerequisites. In any particular field of study the minimum entry requirements will describe the attainment expected of the student at the start of a programme and the aims of the programme will describe his or her expected achievement when the programme is completed. The content can then be divided into a number of units with stated prerequisites, from which it is possible to ascribe a level to a particular unit.

Levels thus provide for a logical progression upwards in a programme, from elementary to advanced. TEC recognises five different levels of units, I to V.

Level I units are designed to progress from a minimum attainment of five years of secondary education; the C4 Programme Committee has defined this minimum level as CSE Grade 3. Therefore, an appropriate GCE 'O' level pass at grades A, B or C, or CSE Grade 1, may merit a credit exemption from the associated Level I unit — this would only occur on a subject for subject basis, for example GCE 'O' level Mathematics exempting from a Level I unit in Mathematics.

Level II units will reflect an academic progression in depth from one or more Level I units; an example of a prerequisite for Level II might be an appropriate GCE 'O' or CSE Grade 1 qualification.

Level III units will reflect an academic progression in depth from one or more Level II units. An appropriate GCE 'A' level pass may merit a credit exemption from the associated Level III unit (if indeed the programme has such a unit). Level IV and Level V units follow the same pattern.

Units may be sequential: thus, Food Sales and Service I, Food Sales and Service II, Food Sales and Service III. Equally, Accommodation and Cleaning Science I and Human Relations I may be a prerequisite for Organisation and Provision of Rooms Services II. General Science I may be a prerequisite for Premises and Plant II.

Certificate and Diploma programmes will normally contain units at Levels I, II and III, and TEC specify a maximum number of units at Level I, and a minimum number of units at Level III. On a Certificate programme of 15 units, for example, the maximum number of units at Level I is 7, the minimum number of units at Level III is 2. On a Diploma programme of 26 units, the maximum number of units at Level I is 12, the minimum number of units at Level III is 6.

Higher Certificate and Higher Diploma programmes will have units at levels ranging from II to V, a minimum number of which must be at Levels IV and V. On a Higher Certificate programme of 10 units, the minimum number of units at Levels IV and V is 6; on a Higher Diploma programme of 20 units, the minimum number of units at Levels IV and V is 12.

The TEC concept of level has to be clearly distinguished from that of year of study. Higher Certificate and Higher Diploma programmes designed for GCE 'A' level entry will contain material which students entering direct from school will meet for the first time; such material could well be at Level II or III (and not Level IV simply because it is part of a higher award programme).

Aim of Programmes

Certificate and *Diploma* programmes will normally be designed to cater for a wide student entry, including those students who intend to be or are being trained to occupy a position between that of craftsman or operative on the one hand, and that of the professional manager on the other hand, and including those progressing from craft routes.

Some students will complete their studies at this level, others may proceed to higher awards — to Higher Certificates or Higher Diplomas, to degree courses, to the membership examinations of the Hotel, Catering and Institutional Management Association. Yet other students may choose to work in the industry for a while, before returning to full- or part-time study to continue their education. Colleges will design programmes according to the industrial needs which they have identified, and the students' personal and vocational needs. Further general aims of these programmes are as follows:

1. To provide the student with knowledge and skills he/she will require to operate effectively on the job, and in particular to enable the student to:
   (a) know the characteristics of the materials used and their costs;
   (b) understand and be able to select and apply the basic techniques and processes required;
   (c) operate relevant equipment efficiently, safely and with regard to its maintenance and economy;
   (d) identify and analyse specific problems and propose solutions;
   (e) understand and apply relevant legal requirements;
   (f) use and communicate information;
   (g) identify the constraints of the industrial situation and the needs of the consumer;
   (h) understand the commercial and economic framework of the industry;
   (i) appreciate the financial implications of any operation undertaken.
2. To stimulate the personal development of the students and, in particular:
   (a) increase the confidence of students in their own intellectual abilities and encourage them to think for themselves;
   (b) enable students to appreciate the social relevance of the knowledge and skills obtained;
   (c) prepare students to adapt to change;
   (d) where appropriate, lead students to appreciate the possibilities of further study and progression.

Higher Certificate and *Higher Diploma* programmes will normally be designed for students who intend to be or are being trained as supervisors or managers; they will aim to achieve a progression to an acceptable standard beyond the related Certificate or Diploma programme.

The higher awards will be terminal qualifications for most students, for others they are likely to give exemption from part of a degree course.

The overall aims of the higher award programmes include:

1. To provide the appropriate managerial and technical skills to: plan, organise and be responsible for the work of others at the early professional stages of a career in the industry and further to provide an appreciation of the skills required for more senior management. In particular to enable the student to:
   (a) appreciate the structure, organisation and resources of business in the various sectors of the industry and the importance of the criteria for selection, the operational characteristics, and the care of those resources;
   (b) select appropriate materials, processes and services for given situations;
   (c) identify, investigate and analyse objectively technical and managerial problems and prepare and present solutions;
   (d) develop an awareness of the changing nature of business and the factors which affect change;
   (e) understand the factors which determine the standards in the industry;
   (f) understand the principles of marketing and their application to the industry;

(g) understand the characteristics of various occupations in the industry and attributes of people who can best fulfil them;

(h) understand the role of individuals and groups at work and how they are motivated and their skills and attitudes developed;

(i) be aware of the importance and means of achieving sound industrial relations and consultative processes;

(j) understand the nature and effects of conflicts within an organisation and how to deal with them;

(k) be aware of current legislation which affects the provision and sale of food, liquor, accommodation and other associated services, and to understand the relationships which should exist between the consumer, producer and supplier;

(l) recognise factors affecting employees, consumers and the public related to work and the requirements of current legislation on employment, health, safety and welfare and in particular the responsibility of the various parties;

(m) be aware of the essential nature of profit in commercial operations and the means of achieving it;

(n) understand the means by which financial and other resources are obtained and controlled within and between companies/organisations and the economic implications of these transactions;

(o) understand the principles of financial management and their application and importance in the pursuit of economic operation and goals.

2. To stimulate the personal development of the student and in particular to:

(a) increase the confidence of students in their own intellectual abilities and encourage them to reason;

(b) develop a desire and skill to work with others;

(c) develop a sense of self discipline and commitment to work and accept responsibilities;

(d) communicate effectively, orally and in writing, including the choice of the appropriate methods and media;

(e) develop an appreciation of their social responsibilities; and identify their attitudes and aptitudes to aid them in their selection of a satisfactory career;

(f) enable them to appreciate the relevance of their knowledge and skills in their working life;

(g) encourage them to appreciate the possibility of further self development, study and progression;

(h) enable them to practise and develop their social skills.

Entry Requirements

The ultimate justification of entry to a TEC programme is evidence that the student is likely to complete the programme successfully.

Certificate and *Diploma* programmes in Hotel, Catering and Institutional Management: school leavers should have studied Mathematics, a physical or biological science subject, English Language or a subject requiring a facility in English, and achieved at least CSE Grade 3 or a comparable standard in these subjects.

If students expect to complete the Diploma programme in two years of full-time study, or a Certificate programme in two years with appropriate day release, colleges will seek enhanced qualifications such as passes at least at GCE 'O' level Grade C or CSE Grade 1. These enhanced qualifications should be sufficiently related to the content of the programme to provide a broad, relevant educational background which would enable students to assimilate elements of the programme more quickly than those with the minimum admission requirements. The following subjects would provide such an educational background:

(a) English (or a subject testing facility in English); and
(b) either Mathematics (or a subject testing numeracy) or a physical or biological science; and
(c) another subject related directly to some element(s) of the programme (for example a foreign language, psychology, food and nutrition, economics etc.) which does not significantly overlap with the subjects listed under (a) and (b).

Higher Certificate and *Higher Diploma* programmes: for some students a TEC Certificate or Diploma will be the usual admission route.

For students entering a higher award programme straight from school the requirements are likely to be:

Four GCE passes in different academic subjects (but not subjects like those regarded as "non-academic" of the OND or HND, see page 110), one of which must be at 'A' level and include passes at least at 'O' level in:

(a) English (or a subject testing facility in English);
(b) either Mathematics (or a subject testing numeracy) or a physical or biological science.

Exceptional Cases of Admission

In exceptional cases students without CSE or 'O' level qualifications but with an equivalent attainment (City and Guilds Certificates, similar qualifications, mature students with appropriate experience) might be accepted on to a Certificate or Diploma programme. In such cases special selection and assessment procedures will usually be employed by the college (the admission of students without CSE or GCE qualifications is at the discretion of the college) and the college will have consulted with the TEC external moderator in these instances.

Unit Exemption: allied to this system of more flexible entry criteria, TEC policy allows for a system of unit exemption. The basic criteria for gaining exemption for a particular unit is an ability (which must be demonstrated with appropriate experience and qualifications) in sufficient of the objectives of that unit to be able to succeed in the units following. Students may not normally be exempted from more than half of the units in any programme by virtue of previous study.

Assessment/Examination Structure

The simple two point grading system of indicating success in individual units of a programme has already been described: Pass or Merit. Awards will not be graded overall.

Each unit will be assessed by whatever means is most appropriate for it. The design of the assessment system is decided by the college, and its detailed proposals have to be approved at the time the programme is validated. In practice the assessment procedures are likely to follow the pattern established on OND and HND courses, written examinations, continuous assessment, project work, assessed practical work, case studies and so forth.

The purpose of assessment is for TEC to be satisfied that a student on an approved programme merits the grades given for the individual units. The assessment system could also give students a target towards which they can work, providing feedback to the student, to the teacher and ultimately to the college, on performance.

Each college's regulations will specify the assessment arrangements for each unit, state what the student should do to achieve success in each grade, what the procedure will be in the event of border-line failure, outright failure, and the requirements for proceeding on to other units of the programme.

An *external moderator* will be involved in all programmes leading to a TEC award. Where a college undertakes its own assessment and colleges will normally do so, the moderator is responsible for monitoring the programme (to check that the programme is meeting the requirements of the students and industry, to check that the college is keeping to the approved programme specification); for endorsing students' grades; for assisting colleges to identify and rectify failings in the programme; for discussing with colleges proposed changes in programmes as well as for giving the college general advice on the interpretation of the policy of TEC Council and for providing relevant information back to Council through the C4 Programme Committee.

Moderators will be selected for subject expertise relevant to the programmes and will have preferably both educational and industrial experience. Normally moderators are appointed to a group of colleges for one or more closely related programmes but arrangements may vary depending on circumstances.

SCOTEC Awards in Hotel, Catering and Institutional Management

From the autumn of 1980 colleges in Scotland will be offering two new courses in place of the Ordinary National Diploma in Hotel, Catering and Institutional Operations, and the two Higher National Diplomas (Catering and Hotel Keeping, and Institutional Management).

These new courses will lead to the Diploma in Hotel, Catering and Institutional Operations, and the Higher Diploma in Hotel, Catering and Institutional Management, of the Scottish Technical Educational Council (SCOTEC).

SCOTEC was established in June 1973; the Council's objects include "to devise, prepare, organise, develop and review technician courses with respect to the technical and related sectors of employment".

Philosophy of the New Courses

Whilst it is true that much of the material contained in any educational course has already been incorporated in previous courses, SCOTEC, in producing the new courses, has attempted a fundamental re-think on what is actually needed by students intending to make a career in the industry. The courses are not, however, occupation-orientated in the narrowest sense, that is they are industry based rather than job based.

It is intended that the new Diploma and Higher Diploma courses in Hotel, Catering and Institutional Operations/Management will provide a good basis for students to obtain employment in all sectors of the hotel and catering industry, and for them to proceed to more senior positions in the industry. The courses do not claim to provide the industry with instant managing directors!

SCOTEC do not at present have proposals for the introduction of a Certificate or Higher Certificate course in Hotel, Catering and Institutional Operations/Management.

Aims and Objectives

The general aims and objectives of SCOTEC's courses are:
—to provide a general preparation for industrial employment in terms of technical knowledge and skills which have validity for a variety of jobs within a broad occupational area;
—to provide a course of general educational value recognised in its own right and providing a base for more advanced studies;
—to develop the student as an individual and member of the community.

Entry Requirements

SCOTEC provides guidance on entry requirements appropriate for each course. The final decision on entry requirements is at the discretion of the principal of the college. It is possible, within certain constraints, for exemptions to be granted from parts of a course.

The recommended entry requirements for the Diploma in Hotel, Catering and Institutional Management are four appropriate SCE 'O' grades.

Most students will enter a Higher Diploma course with either a Diploma or a number of SCE Higher grade passes. The recommended entry requirements for the Higher Diploma in Hotel, Catering and Institutional Management are either a Diploma in Hotel, Catering and Institutional Operations, or five appropriate SCE subjects, of which two must be passed at Higher grade, the balance at 'O' grade.

The variations to the normal entry routes that have been available on OND and HND courses in Scotland for those students with a mixture of SCE qualifications and City and Guilds of London Institute, SCOTBEC and SCOTEC qualifications are likely to be available under SCOTEC, for the Diploma and Higher Diploma.

Industrial Experience

Although SCOTEC policy does not demand it, it is almost certain that both the Diploma and Higher Diploma courses will include an element of industrial experience — on a similar basis to the previous OND and HND courses in Scotland.

Syllabus Development

All the colleges in Scotland likely to offer these Diploma and Higher Diploma courses have been involved in the syllabus development through representatives on the E4 Hotel, Catering and Institutional Management Course Committee and Syllabus Panel. The syllabuses have been drawn up in objective terms in great detail and will be common to all Scottish colleges. They state the expected learning outcome of all aspects of the course.

The syllabus development work was done in three stages: identification of areas of knowledge required by practising managers in the industry (surveys were conducted and the HCIMA's Corpus of Knowledge taken into account); detailed work on the content of the Diploma and Higher Diploma (seen as one entity at this stage), and finally, division of the syllabus into the two courses — horizontally — the Higher Diploma course taking the subjects to greater depth.

Diploma in Hotel, Catering and Institutional Operations

Although SCOTEC does not stipulate a mode of attendance, the likely duration of the Diploma course will be two years where the course is offered on a full-time sandwich basis. The number of hours is slightly lower than the previous OND (nevertheless well in excess of the Council's minimum requirement of 1320 hours for an 'O' grade entry qualification).

The subjects studied in the Diploma course are:

Systems of Production and of Service (about 730 hours) with two themes, food and beverage production and service, and accommodation service (including reception); and including types of unit, skills and technical knowledge involved, equipment, social skills and public relations.

Catering Technology (about 320 hours) with topics including properties of matter, the cell, carbon chemistry, food handling and hygiene, constituents, commodity groups, preservation and processing, quality control, food packaging, nutrition, building science, electricity, cleaning science, pests and pest control.

Financial and Business Systems (about 220 hours) which includes economics, book-keeping and accounting, costing, record keeping and office practice.

Supervisory Studies (about 130 hours) which includes functions of management, work study and data-handling, human relations and personal administration, marketing.

Industrial and Commercial Legislation: the general concepts will be taught as general studies, the operational law (i.e. licensing law, consumer law, food hygiene and food standards, hotel and catering law, law of employment and safety at work) will be fully integrated into the relevant sections of the subjects above.

General Studies (about 120 hours): this is likely to include, *inter alia*, communications in all its forms, and a number of other topics are likely to be considered, for example tourism, economics, background to the industry, the EEC.

**Higher Diploma in Hotel, Catering and
Institutional Management**

The mode of attendance for the Higher Diploma is not laid down by SCOTEC. The duration of the course is likely to be three years for students with 'H' grade qualifications when offered on a full-time sandwich basis. It is possible that students with a Diploma may be given some exemption from the course (at the discretion of SCOTEC).

The number of hours for the course will be of the order of 1980 (the Council's minimum requirements), slightly lower than the previous HND courses.

For the Higher Diploma the subjects are similar to the Diploma, but taken to a greater depth, with less teaching time devoted to more elementary aspects and more to evaluation and application.

In *Systems of Production and of Service* (about 760 hours), for example, and within the section covering skills and technical knowledge involved in accommodation services: systems of re-decoration are evaluated as are systems of refurbishing, replacement, re-use and cannibalisation and students are expected to be able to compile programmes for varying circumstances. Students are expected to apply knowledge from other sections of the syllabus to accommodation administration, for example purchasing and acquisition procedures, control of stocks procedures; methods of collection of laundry, valet service, laundry operation for linen will be evaluated. In addition to evaluating machines with regard to design, function, durability, ease of operation, cost of operation, safety, user skill required, repair and replacement aspects, the students will be expected to evaluate systems of maintenance and demonstrate an ability to instruct staff in the use and care of machines.

This subject also includes additional topics: physical planning of accommodation, catering facilities planning and operations management.

Topics of *Catering Technology* on which more time is spent (total about 350 hours) and the treatment taken to a greater depth include constituents, commodity groups and building science.

The treatment of economics in *Financial and Business Systems* (total about 430 hours) is considerably deeper, so is that of costing and accounting, and an additional topic is included, management accounting.

Practice of Management (about 220 hours) is substantially different from Supervisory Studies, with topics: nature and functions of management, techniques of management, organisation behaviour, personnel management and marketing.

The treatment of *Industrial and Commercial Law* follows the pattern with additional topics: law of contract, law of property and of insurance, and almost four times the figure of hours for law of employment in comparison with the Diploma course.

General Studies (about 170 hours) are also included on the Higher Diploma course.

The Award Document

The SCOTEC award document will include information on: the nature of the award (Diploma, Higher Diploma), the subject (Hotel, Catering and Institutional

Operations/Management), the name of the student, the college studied at, and the achievement of the student in the individual examinable subjects, for example:

Subject	Grade	Date passed
Catering Technology	2	July 1981

The grades awarded by SCOTEC are as follows. Grades 1 to 7 are pass grades, the pass mark is 40%.

Pass grades	Mark range (%)	Fail grades	Mark range (%)
1	80–100	8	35–39
2	70–79	9	30–34
3	60–69	10	0–29
4	55–59		
5	50–54		
6	45–49		
7	40–44		

Students who fail subject(s) on their course may re-take the failed subject(s) in following year(s). The award will be made when all the examinable subjects have been passed. Practical problems, for example future changes in syllabus, re-structuring of the course, may limit the number of times that a student can re-take subject(s). The grade achieved and the advisability of undertaking further study, as well as the possibility, are important factors. The nature of the components of the examination will also have an effect on the arrangements for re-taking, for example if laboratory, practical work, or coursework assessment is included in addition to, or in place of, a written examination.

Student Assessment

SCOTEC operates a central assessment scheme for all the Council's courses. Examination papers are set by SCOTEC examiners, and the marking of the scripts is undertaken by them. All forms of continuous assessment which contribute to success in an examination, including project work, is subject to Council scrutiny.

Useful Addresses

HOTEL, CATERING AND INSTITUTIONAL MANAGEMENT ASSOCIA-TION, 191 Trinity Road, London SW17 7HN (Tel 01-672 4251)
JOINT COMMITTEE FOR NATIONAL DIPLOMAS IN HOTEL CATERING AND INSTITUTIONAL MANAGEMENT:
England, Wales and Northern Ireland, 46 Britannia Street, London WC1X 9RG (Tel 01-278 2468)
Scotland: Scottish Technical Education Council, 38 Queen Street, Glasgow G1 3DY (Tel 041-204 2271)
SCOTTISH TECHNICAL EDUCATION COUNCIL, 38 Queen Street, Glasgow G1 3DY (Tel 041-204 2271)

TECHNICIAN EDUCATION COUNCIL, 76 Portland Place, London WIN 4AA (Tel 01-580 3050)

(For addresses of colleges see Chapter 9.)

7

Degree, Postgraduate and Post Experience Courses in Hotel and Catering Studies

The Diplomas of Battersea College of Technology and the Scottish Hotel School become degrees. The formation of the Council for National Academic Awards, and new degrees in hotel and catering studies. A description of DipHE, Postgraduate and Post Experience Awards. A detailed description of the degree courses of: University of Surrey; University of Strathclyde; University College, Cardiff; Napier College of Commerce and Technology, Edinburgh; The Polytechnic, Huddersfield; Leeds Polytechnic; The Polytechnic of North London; Manchester Polytechnic; Oxford Polytechnic; Sheffield City Polytechnic; Ulster Polytechnic. Useful addresses.

THE opportunity to study for a degree in hotel and catering studies has been available in the United Kingdom since 1964.

The Associateship Diploma of the old Battersea College of Technology was converted into a BSc degree course in 1964, once the college had been assured of university status as the proposed University of Surrey. The move from Battersea Park to the new campus at Guildford took place in 1968.

The Scottish Hotel School at Ross Hall in Glasgow, the second hotel school to be established in the UK (September 1944), had extended its diploma course to three years from 1959. It was converted into a degree course six years later with the formation of the University of Strathclyde.

For some years before the creation of these two "technological" universities, their diploma courses had been recognised as degree equivalent. The entry requirements demanded were set at a similar level. Demand for the courses has consistently been high; in the 1970s each university received several hundred enquiries annually.

After the formation of the Council for National Academic Awards (CNAA) it became possible for establishments outside the university sector to offer degree courses leading to CNAA awards. The first such course in the hotel and catering field began at The Polytechnic, Huddersfield in 1971 leading to a BSc degree in Catering Studies. Subsequently other CNAA degree courses have commenced and in 1977 a BSc degree course in Institutional Management began at University College, Cardiff.

This chapter also describes the Diploma in Higher Education and various postgraduate and post experience awards. The degree courses are each described in detail.

Summary of Degree, Postgraduate and Post Experience Courses

University Degrees

University of Surrey, Guildford: BSc(Hons) Hotel and Catering Administration (4 years).

University of Strathclyde, Glasgow: BA and BA(Hons) Hotel and Catering Management (Pass degree course 3 years, Honours degree 4 years).

University College, Cardiff: BSc(Hons) Institutional Management (3 years).

Council for National Academic Awards (CNAA) degrees

Napier College of Commerce and Technology, Edinburgh: BA Catering and Accommodation Studies (4 years).

The Polytechnic, Huddersfield: BSc(Hons) Catering Science and Applied Nutrition (4 years) *and* BA Hotel and Catering Administration (4 years).

Leeds Polytechnic: BA Food and Accommodation Studies (4 years).

The Polytechnic of North London: BSc Institutional Management (4 years).

Hollings Faculty, Manchester Polytechnic: BSc Hotel and Catering Studies (4 years).

Oxford Polytechnic: BA and BSc degrees, Honours degree (modular course 3-4 years).

Sheffield City Polytechnic: BSc(Hons) Catering Systems (4 years).

Ulster Polytechnic, Newtownabbey: BA Catering Administration (4 years).

Diploma in Higher Education

Oxford Polytechnic modular course.

Diploma in Management Studies
(hotel and catering bias)

Plymouth Polytechnic/South Devon Technical College.

Brighton Polytechnic.

Looking ahead, a number of other CNAA degree courses are in the development stage, including:

— at Portsmouth Polytechnic, a BA degree in Hotel and Catering Administration,

— at Dorset Institute of Higher Education, Poole, a BSc degree in Catering Administration;

— at Middlesex Polytechnic, London, a BSc degree in Hotel and Catering Administration;

  —at Queen Margaret College, Edinburgh, a BA degree in Institutional Management;
  —at Robert Gordon's Institute of Technology, Aberdeen, a BA degree in Hotel, Catering and Institutional Management.

Each of the degree courses available in the UK in hotel and catering studies is described further on in this chapter.

DipHE, Postgraduate and
Post Experience Awards

From September 1976 the CNAA assumed responsibility for courses leading to the nationally recognised Diploma in Management Studies (DMS), previously administered by two Joint Committees. The DMS is an advanced course of study in management for students who are well qualified by education, and by experience. Courses are designed to provide students with a basic knowledge of the background to industry, to raise their general level of understanding of management processes, and to acquaint them with the tools and techniques and to meet the needs of industry.

Generally DMS courses are available on a full-time basis (minimum 25 weeks), on a part-time basis (usually spread over two years) or by block release. Entry requirements are a UK university or CNAA degree, an HND or HNC or the agreed equivalent awards of BEC, TEC, SCOTBEC or SCOTEC, an appropriate grade of membership of a professional body approved by the CNAA, or the equivalent. Exceptionally candidates with relevant experience and proven ability to profit from and contribute to the course may be admitted.

Two DMS courses are of particular relevance to this book. Since September 1977 a *DMS in Hotel and Tourism* has been offered jointly by Plymouth Polytechnic and South Devon Technical College, Torquay, on a full-time basis over three terms.

Stage 1 of the course (ten weeks at Plymouth Polytechnic) examines the purpose, problems and circumstances in which business functions together with the human aspects involved. Subjects studied include economics, law, statistical methods, work study, financial control, industrial sociology and psychology, with emphasis placed on analytical techniques appropriate to management and integrative hotel and tourism studies.

Stage 2 (sixteen weeks at South Devon Technical College) examines the principles and practice of management in the hotel and tourism industries. Subjects studied include finance, operation planning and control, marketing, manpower studies, business policy and organisations. During this stage students prepare, under guidance, a fully researched project to illustrate their capacity to communicate in a convincing way, to apply management principles to a practical situation, to analyse problems and make considered judgement on them.

Brighton Polytechnic from September 1979 has offered a special DMS for *managers in the hotel and catering industry.* Two modes of study are available, one year of full-time study, or two years of part-time study (afternoon and evening).

The *Diploma of Higher Education* (DipHE) is a relatively new award (since 1972) made on successful completion of a two year full-time (or three year part-time) course of study equivalent in standard to that of the first two years of a degree course. The standard of entry is essentially the same as for a degree course, and Diploma courses may be free-standing or form the first part of a course leading to the award of a degree. At Oxford Polytechnic a DipHE programme is available as part of the modular degree course, see page 149.

Postgraduate Diploma courses designed for students with a wide range of academic backgrounds or experience are not new to catering education. Hollings Faculty, Manchester Polytechnic have offered a similar course leading to the award of a Polytechnic certificate since 1972. The HCIMA Professional Qualification Graduate-entry course is a newer example, the Association awarding the certificate. (Both are described in detail in the previous chapter.)

Entry requirements to the CNAA's Postgraduate Diploma (normal duration, minimum 25 weeks of full-time study) are essentially the same as those demanded by the universities, viz., a degree of the CNAA or a UK university, or a qualification which meets the academic requirements for full or corporate membership of one of the major professional bodies, or a Certificate in Education with appropriate experience, or, where appropriate, substantial experience of employment in an area related to the subject matter of the course.

Postgraduate diploma courses have different objectives to those of Masters courses leading to a *MA, MEd or MSc.* Schemes leading to a master degree in order to be approved by the CNAA must recognisably and considerably expand a student's knowledge in one of the following two ways, or in a combination of them:

(a) by an analytical treatment of a subject beyond that attempted at first degree level, or in greater depth than is possible at first degree level;
(b) by an approach which synthesises and integrates a number of disciplines which can be found in undergraduate studies but which involves a treatment which is appropriate to a programme of postgraduate studies.

Courses are designed to achieve specific objectives with particular types of applicants in mind. It will normally include the presentation of a substantial dissertation. Students should normally possess an Honours degree of the CNAA or a UK university.

The Universities of Surrey and Strathclyde have offered MSc courses in Tourism since 1972. No CNAA masters courses are currently approved in the Food, Accommodation and Related Studies field.

The CNAA awards its degrees of *Master of Philosophy* (MPhil) and *Doctor of Philosophy* (PhD) to candidates who successfully complete approved programmes of work carried out under supervision in environments approved as suitable (e.g. educational, industrial, commercial or professional establishments). The normal minimum duration of programmes of work for a MPhil is twenty-one months for full-time students, thirty-three months for part-time, and for a PhD an additional twelve months (either mode of study). For admission to an approved programme of supervised research a first or second class Honours degree of the CNAA or a UK university is normally required. The regulations for the control of these awards — both by the CNAA and the universities — are rigorous and great care is taken in considering all proposals.

The CNAA has recently introduced a new award called the *Diploma in Professional Studies* (DPS) — so far approved in the areas of education and nursing. The award is intended to recognise specifically the needs of experienced mature students, with a minimum of two years' relevant practical experience, who are not necessarily graduates, but who should hold an initial qualification. Courses are designed to provide further academic development, advancing professional skills and understanding by building on previous educational attainments, training and experience.

**University Degrees in Hotel
and Catering Studies**

It is important to note that the possession of qualifications specified for admission to degree courses merely affords eligibility for consideration! The Scottish Hotel School and Department of Hotel, Catering and Tourism Management are responsible for the admission of students within the confines of the regulations of the Universities of Strathclyde and Surrey respectively. Both establishments look for high academic ability and motivation.

Competition for places is keen: applicants are advised to place either the University of Surrey or the University of Strathclyde as their first choice. The majority of candidates are interviewed.

It is sometimes possible to transfer from the hotel and catering management degree course at the University of Strathclyde to another degree course offered by the University. This alternative exists because, in addition to specialist hotel and catering subjects at the Scottish Hotel School, the curriculum includes basic subjects from the Schools of Business and Administration, and of Arts and Social Studies. It is not possible to make a transfer to another course at the University of Surrey.

**University of Surrey:
Department of Hotel,
Catering and Tourism Management,
Guildford**

*BSc(Hons) Hotel and
Catering Administration*

The course aims to provide a combination of business, technical and general education with a particular orientation to accommodation, catering and related services.

Entry requirements: 5 GCEs of which at least 2 must be at 'A' level, or 4 GCEs of which at least 3 are at 'A' level, or equivalent qualification. A great majority of admitted students have 3 or more 'A' levels, candidates with only 2 have a very limited prospect of admission. Holders of certain qualifications in hotel and catering subjects (e.g. HCIMA Final/Part B, National Diploma in Hotel Keeping and Catering, HND in Hotel and Catering Management) may be considered for direct admission into the second year of the degree course and if they have had adequate industrial training and experience, to complete the course in two years. About sixty students in total are admitted annually. Applications for admission are made through UCCA.

The course is of four years' duration: three years of full-time study and an industrial stage of 48 weeks' supervised practical training in selected organisations (arrangements are made by the university). In addition it is a requirement of the course that all students undertake to work in the industry for not less than 6 weeks during the first long vacation.

A broad distinction is drawn between studies which are considered essential for all students (the common core of the course) and those which are desirable or possible (options). Thus each student has a certain amount of freedom in selecting subjects, but the course is maintained as a coherent whole, with a high degree of horizontal and vertical integration.

The stages of the course cut across academic years. Subjects studied are:

Stage 1 (term 1)
Business mathematics and statistics, social framework, introduction to industry, introduction to law, foods, beverages, food preparation I.

Stage 1 (terms 2 and 3)
Accounting I, economics I, law I, food preparation II, food and beverage operation I, food science I and one option (gastronomy, or applied statistics, or languages — beginners, intermediate or advanced).

Stage 2 (terms 4 and 5)
Accounting II, economics II, law II, food and beverage operation II, introduction to management, food science II, industrial orientation (one week) and one option (choice as for terms 2 and 3).

Industrial Stage (48 weeks)

Stage 3 (terms 6, 7, 8)
Human resource management, marketing, and three options (catering management,* hotel management,* economics and finance, food technology, nutrition, tourism; note at least one of the two options asterisked must be taken).

Stage 3 (term 9)
Project.

**University of Strathclyde,
Scottish Hotel School, Glasgow**

*BA and BA(Hons) Hotel and
Catering Management*
The Scottish Hotel School offers a three year full-time course leading to a Pass Degree, and, since 1978, an additional fourth year of study for an Honours Degree.

The course is designed for those who are primarily interested in hotel and catering management, tourism and industries associated with leisure and recreation. It is based on the concept that the first purpose of a university education is to provide intellectual stimulus but it is also recognised that modern society depends increasingly on the special skills brought to it by graduates.

Applicants have in addition to meeting the general entrance requirements of the University, to meet the course requirements. These are 4 Higher grade SCE passes at grades B,B,B,C, or 5 at grades B,B,C,C,C; or 3 GCE 'A' level passes at grades C,C,D, or 2 at grades B,B. About 75 students are admitted annually. Applications for admission are made through UCCA, or direct to the University if the student is resident in the UK and only applying to one or more of the Universities of Aberdeen, Glasgow and Strathclyde.

The Pass Degree course, which consists of 13 classes taken over the 3 years, covers a wide range of learning giving the student a breadth of knowledge and a general understanding of business practice as a whole and of hotel and catering management in particular. Students are required to participate in laboratory work and to study practical problems in hotel operations and quantity food preparation and service.

Industrial experience is arranged in two required 12 week periods during the two summer vacations. Students must submit their proposals to the School's industrial liaison officer for approval. In their first summer stage students are required to operate in the food production side of an hotel or catering unit.

The arrangement of classes is as follows:

First year	Second year	Third year
Hotel Operations I, Catering I, 2 subjects from list A, 1 subject from list C.	Hotel Operations II, Catering II, 1 subject from list A or B, 1 subject from list C.	Hotel Operations III, Any 2 subjects from lists A, B, C or D, 1 subject from list C.

List A: economics, accountancy I, administration I, British legal systems, operational research I, marketing I (not to be taken in first year), industrial relations I.

List B: statistics, economic history, geography, sociology, French IA, German IA, Spanish and Latin American studies IA, Italian IA, Russian IA, German IB, Spanish IB, Italian IB, information processing.

List C: catering III, planning and development, services planning, tourism I, tourism II, catering technology I, catering technology II, international cuisine, catering facilities planning.

List D: personnel administration I, and additional classes in accountancy, administration, economics, marketing, labour law, business law and a modern language.

Admission to Honours is dependent upon the level of performance during the Pass Degree course and entails a fourth year of study with 4 Honours classes from: advanced hotel operations, catering systems design, comparative catering, hotel and catering comptrol,* hotel and catering legislative control,* manpower in the hotel and catering industry,* property management.* The classes asterisked count as half-classes only. A dissertation of 10 000 words is also required.

University College, Cardiff, School of Home Economics

BSc(Hons) Institutional Management

The course is designed for students who will later hold responsible positions in catering and residential establishments in the education, health and welfare services, commerce and industry, such as hospitals, schools, factories and hotels. Openings also exist in product development, and in testing and control.

The course is of three years' duration with industrial experience arranged mainly in the summer vacations.

Entry requirements: students must be at least 17 years of age and have matriculated in accordance with the regulations of the University of Wales. Holders of the GCE will be eligible for matriculation provided they have passed either English Language, or Welsh Language (or Use of English) at 'O' level, and either 4 other approved subjects including 2 at 'A' level, or 3 approved subjects at 'A' level. In addition to satisfying matriculation requirements, students must have passed Mathematics and a science subject, preferably Chemistry. A good OND/HND in Institutional Management/Hotel and Catering is also an acceptable entry qualification.

The course is divided into two parts, each part consisting of three component courses and industrial experience. In Part I, the first year, the subjects studied include introduction to accounting, to law and to general economics theory and practice; building materials and maintenance; furnishings and interior design; introduction to work study; theory of catering; food production and service; basic physics and chemistry; introduction to biological science, microbiology, polymers and fibres.

In Part I students spend 2 weeks in the Schools Meals Service during term 2, and 12 weeks in the summer vacation in this or another sector of the industry.

Part II of the course covers the second and third years. Students spend 5 weeks at the end of the summer term plus a minimum of 5 weeks of the vacation in an industrial placement (that is between the second and third years of the course). The first two terms of year 3 include 4 weeks' field work.

The subjects studied in Part II include: organisation behaviour, personnel management, industrial relations, management accounting, decision making process, policy formulation and administration; institutional management, accommodation services, ergonomics, catering production technology, catering and accommodation technology; nutrition, food science, microbiology, food legislation standards and storage, textile science, materials science, environmental physics, energy, heating, illumination and acoustics.

Council for National Academic Awards (CNAA) Degrees

The CNAA's normal minimum requirements for entry to first degree courses are essentially the same as those demanded by universities:

(a) A General Certificate of Education (GCE) with passes in five subjects, including two subjects at Advanced ('A') level; or

(b) GCE passes in four subjects, including three at 'A' level; or

(c) A Scottish Certificate of Education (SCE) with passes in five subjects of which three are at the Higher Grade; or

(d) SCE passes in four subjects all at the Higher Grade; or

(e) An Ordinary National Certificate or Diploma (ONC/D) at a good standard, in an appropriate subject, or its agreed equivalent of BEC, SCOTBEC or SCOTEC; or

(f) Students holding TEC awards may be accepted on the following interim basis: a TEC Certificate or Diploma which includes passes with Merit at Level III in three units. Additionally, in appropriate cases, the CNAA will accept either a TEC C/D with a minimum of four unit passes at Level III including two with Merit, or a TEC C/D with Merit passes at Level III in two units provided these are underpinned by passes with Merit at Level II in appropriate units.

GCE 'O' level passes must be at Grade C or above: CSE passes at a sufficiently high standard will be accepted in lieu of 'O' level passes. SCE 'O' grade passes must be at Grade C or above. Additionally the CNAA has resolved that the International Baccalaureate and the European Baccalaureate should be deemed equivalent to these qualifications listed above, provided they have been attained at the appropriate level.

Overseas qualifications will be evaluated by the individual institutions in relation to the course for which application is being made.

In addition to the Council's minimum requirements, the colleges may specify the subjects that must be passed in order to help ensure the suitability of applicants for the particular course. These requirements are specified in the information which follows on each degree course.

The CNAA does not insist upon 'O' and 'A' levels for mature students (that is those aged over 21), but colleges will not only restrict the percentage of students without qualifications that are admitted to any course, but they will vet such applications with the greatest care seeking evidence of some kind of the candidates' capacity to meet successfully the demands of the course.

The CNAA does not provide a standard application form for its approved courses, although polytechnics have introduced standard forms. Enquiries and applications should be made directly to the individual polytechnic or college. There is no official closing date for applications, nevertheless they should be made as early as possible during the preceding academic year. There is no limit to the number of applications that may be made.

Napier College of Commerce and Technology,
Department of Catering and Hotel Studies,
Edinburgh

BA Catering and Accommodation
Studies (CNAA)

The course is based on a broad foundation of the principles of catering and accommodation technology and aims to give an insight into the complexities of commercial catering and accommodation organisations. The course leads to careers in hotels, restaurants, industrial catering, outdoor catering, catering for the services, airlines, marine organisations and university halls of residence.

The subjects offered to meet the entry requirements (see page 141) should include English Language and Mathematics.

The course is of four years' duration; between the end of the second year in college and the commencement of the fourth year, students undertake a 52 week period of planned industrial training in an establishment designated by the college.

The curriculum covers the areas of technological studies and industrial studies.

Year One: catering, accommodation, psychology, sociology, economics, accounting, quantitative methods; the lecture programme in catering and accommodation studies is supported by laboratory work of an investigative nature.

Year Two: catering, accommodation, manpower studies, marketing, economics, accounting, quantitative methods. Students expand and consolidate the knowledge gained in the first year study of food production and service procedure and evaluate this information in operational laboratories. In accommodation, the programme in house services and front office operation is broadened by lectures and seminars in ergonomics, design, work study and building services.

Psychology and sociology aim to give students the necessary background to handle the social aspects of working in the hotel and catering industry successfully. Economics and quantitative methods link with accounting to provide the business management knowledge required. Management aspects are contained in manpower studies.

Year Three: apart from gaining experience and training during the industrial training period, students are given check lists and projects to complete to be used in catering and accommodation development.

Year Four: catering and accommodation development, manpower studies, marketing, financial management.

Catering and accommodation development provides a focus for the disciplines of marketing, financial management and manpower by studying different situations, problems and opportunities; it is designed to extend students' capability in assessing relevant commercial situations and problems and in selecting appropriate solutions.

The Polytechnic, Huddersfield,
Department of Catering Studies

BSc(Hons) Catering Science
and Applied Nutrition (CNAA)

This is a four year sandwich course (before 1977 the title was BSc Catering Studies), which aims to produce science-based caterers whose education will be concerned with the principles and practices of volume catering and with the principles of nutrition, together with their applications to the feeding of people, notably in welfare contexts.

The subjects offered to meet the entry requirements (see page 141) should include Mathematics and a science subject.

The first period of industrial training (in the first term of year two) generally involves an attachment to a welfare catering situation. The second period (terms two and three of year three) may be spent either in a catering situation or in the food manufacturing industry or allied areas.

Content:

Year One: catering (scope and range of catering operations, basic techniques of catering and food processing, hygiene regulations), natural and physical science, social sciences (introduction to psychology, sociology and organisation theory), quantitative analysis.

Years Two and Three: catering (chemical composition, structure and nutrient content in various stages, methods of large-scale catering, taste-panel techniques for food evaluation), nutrition, natural and physical sciences, social sciences, quantitative analysis.

Year Four: catering (the scientific and technological basis of catering systems and applied nutrition).

BA Hotel and Catering Administration (CNAA)

The aim of the BA degree course is to produce graduates who understand the complexities of the hotel and catering industry and who are able to make judgements on administrative issues with which hotels, restaurants and bars are faced.

The subjects offered to meet the entry requirements (see page 141) should include Mathematics and a subject showing competence in written English.

The third year of this four year sandwich course is spent by students on supervised industrial training in the industry (arrangements made by the Polytechnic).

The course is structured around three elements: technology, human behaviour and business. The technology element is concerned with the study of the products, equipment, processes and services of hotels, restaurants and bars. The human behaviour element is the main feature of the course because of the centrality of people to hotels, restaurants and bars. The business element is included because hotels, restaurants and bars are businesses.

Content:

Year One: hotel studies I, catering studies I, quantitative analysis, social science, accounting I, structure of business.

Year Two: hotel studies II, catering studies II, organisation and behaviour I, labour studies I, accounting II, marketing.

Year Four: administration and the hotel and catering industry, organisation and behaviour II, labour studies II, business and business policy.

Leeds Polytechnic, School of
Home and Institutional Studies

BA Food and Accommodation
Studies (CNAA)

This four year sandwich course is designed to provide an education and training which will enable graduates, after appropriate induction training and experience, to discharge executive responsibilities in the food and accommodation industry.

The subjects or qualifications offered to meet the entry requirements (see page 141) should include English Language and Mathematics.

The third year of the course consists of 48 weeks' industrial experience, normally with one organisation. Arrangements are made by the Polytechnic.

As food and accommodation administration is a complex activity the course draws on a number of disciplines and is broadly based.

Technical subjects concerned with the provision of food and accommodation form an important section of the course. Food materials, design maintenance and hygiene have been selected to provide a logical approach to the control of technical processes. The course also includes finance, law, quantitative and behavioural subjects which develop administrative skills. To help develop a thorough understanding of what the manager is trying to achieve and thereby a professional approach, seminars in food production and service and accommodation concentrate on allowing the student to use technical and administrative knowledge in practical situations; a project and the industrial training period assist in this process.

The *first year* concentrates on the principles of several subjects: basic science, microbiology and hygiene, food materials and equipment, food production and service, the history of food and accommodation studies, the financial system, introduction to English law, introduction to sociology and psychology, quantitative studies.

In the other years the emphasis is on the analysis and solution of problems. Subjects studied in the *second year* include: building materials and the control of accommodation, nutrition, food production and service, marketing, financial decisions and control, food and accommodation law, industrial psychology and sociology, quantitative studies.

In the *fourth year*, which includes a dissertation and general seminar, the subjects are accommodation control and the design of buildings, studies in catering technology, industrial relations and quantitative studies.

The Polytechnic of North London,
Department of Food Sciences

BSc Institutional Management (CNAA)

The aim of this four year sandwich course is to enable students to apply the latest developments in management science to the conditions arising from rapid technological developments in food, building planning and maintenance so that they are equipped to take full administrative responsibility for the food and accommodation services of an establishment.

The subjects offered to meet the entry requirements (see page 141 should include English Language, Mathematics and a science subject.

Students spend two six month periods in industrial training (arrangements made by the Polytechnic). The first period includes the first two terms of the second year of the course; the second period includes the third term of the third year and a proportion of the summer vacation between the third and fourth years of the course.

Throughout the course field studies are undertaken in order that subjects may relate to the industrial situation and provide a realistic platform for decision making exercises.

Course content:

Basic disciplines: economics and behavioural sciences are designed to enable students to understand and appreciate the economic and behavioural factors which influence management decisions.

Core studies: half of the course is given to the study of food and accommodation; of this time, half is in practical work.

Food studies: include food processing, production and service, food science, microbiology and nutrition, financial planning, control of catering systems.

Accommodation studies: include the planning and design of buildings to meet customer needs and management objectives. Science of materials and services, environmental science, ergonomics. The development and control of planned maintenance programmes, financial planning, control of building services.

The final year of the course is the synthesis of previous study into an integral approach to *institutional management.* The subject is divided into five modules:

Organisation and control
Staff management
Marketing and communication
Purchasing and distribution
Forward planning

Related Studies: contextual science (designed to give students a sound knowledge of the basic science relevant to the course), accounting and quantitative methods (designed to put the core studies onto a firm base).

**Hollings Faculty, Manchester Polytechnic,
Department of Hotel, Catering
and Institutional Management**

BSc Hotel and Catering Studies (CNAA)

A four year sandwich course designed to prepare students for managerial and executive responsibility across the whole spectrum of the catering and accommodation industries, industrial, commercial and welfare.

The subjects offered to meet the entry requirements (see page 141) should desirably include Mathematics and a science subject.

The third year of the course is spent in guided industrial experience. Areas of placement (arranged by the Faculty) include hotels, large scale industrial catering organisations, hospital catering units, schools and other institutional catering units, restaurants, licensed houses and flight catering units.

Course content:

The first year commences with a series of visits to establishments and concentrates on the fundamental principles of the different subjects. The second year emphasises the practical application of these principles and their integration within functioning systems. The subjects studied are:

Food studies: the nature of food materials and the way these are modified by processes and equipment to satisfy varying consumer requirements for food and beverages.

Accommodation studies: design, planning and construction of accommodation in all sectors of the industry, its marketing, the operational management of housekeeping, front office and maintenance departments.

Accounting
Economics
Law
Behavioural studies: Covers elements of psychology and sociology and looks particularly at organisation behaviour with hotel and catering operations.

In the fourth year three main subjects are studied:

Food and accommodation studies: explores the inter-relationships between the various operations involved in food production and accommodation operations in a wide range of situations with a view to establishing concepts and principles.

Catering and accommodation administration: develops the marketing theme running through the course, deals with the processes of planning, organising and controlling, the management of human resources.

Comparative studies in catering organisation: drawing on previous studies and experience, compares a wide variety of establishments in marketing, organisational and human terms, introduces problem solving techniques (including computer modelling), culminating in an extended major case study.

**Oxford Polytechnic, Department of
Catering Management**

*BA and BSc Degrees, Honours Degree
and DipHE, Modular Course (CNAA)*

The Department offers over thirty modules as part of the BA, BEd, BSc and DipHE modular course. Modules are grouped together into fields and the student specialises in one double field or a combination of two single fields. A degree and honours degree course involves three years of full-time study, plus, if it is a field requirement, a year's industrial experience, or a year abroad, or the equivalent on a part-time basis (this unusual alternative should be noted).

The Department offers a Catering Double Field; alternatively a student may combine the Catering Single Field with Food and Nutrition or one of these single fields with many of the other fields offered in the Polytechnic, for example Geography, French Language and Contemporary Studies, Mathematical and Computer Studies.

Entry requirements are as above (page 141); certain fields (but not Catering) specify passes in appropriate subjects. Students with an HNC, HND, successful completion of an adequate part of an appropriate degree course, or an equivalent qualification may be able to complete the degree or diploma course with the equivalent of one year's exemption from full-time study. To be allowed to complete the course in this way, the student will have to be granted exemption from not fewer than eight modules; exemption will not normally be granted for more than twelve modules.

The individual student has considerable freedom to choose "his" own course and to change the programme as his knowledge increases and interests develop, and is given the opportunity of spending a part of the time working outside his chosen disciplines and appropriate credit is given for this in the final assessment. The modular structure allows students to broaden their studies so that they learn some of the principles and methods of several disciplines and to concentrate more deeply in areas of special interest. A counselling system gives the student advice on the choice of modules in the light of his desires and attainments in pursuing particular areas of study, and will ensure that the student is fully aware of the possibilities and implications of his choice of modules as he progresses through the course.

Outline of the BA, BSc, DipHE Requirements

	DipHE	Degree	Honours
Stage I	Take 12+ (that is minimum of 12) basic modules. Pass either 10+ basic modules or 8+ basic modules with an average of 40% on 12 taken, Including 3 basic modules required for field A and 3 basic modules required for field B		
Stage II	Pass 9+ further modules including 7+ acceptable for fields A and B of which 5+ must be acceptable for one of these fields.	Pass 18+ further modules, including 7+ acceptable for field A, 7+ acceptable for field B.	Pass 21+ further modules including 9+ acceptable for field A, 9+ acceptable for field B. (Classification based on the best 18 modules taken in Stage II.)

The Catering Double Field aims to provide the student with an education to Honours Degree level and with a vocational knowledge which embraces a range of skills considered to be of importance to the industry. Between Stages I and II (that is after the first year) students spend one full year gaining practical experience in selected catering and accommodation organisations (arrangements made by the Polytechnic).

A core of studies for food and accommodation service forms a compulsory element of the course (in Stage I: introduction to catering skills, a 3-term single module, introduction to catering studies, a 2-term double module, accommodation studies I). The student may vary the pattern and content of his/her other studies to suit interests and career aspirations. In order to ensure structural cohesion and progression to more advanced work, a student is obliged to take one of the advanced modules: catering and accommodation industry, industrial relations in the catering industry and financial administration in the catering industry.

A DipHE programme is available.

The Catering Single Field through practical studies places emphasis on management and technological subjects. Time in the third year is spent analysing, discussing and searching for solutions in real situations in catering. It is a field requirement that students spend two periods of at least eight weeks each in appropriate, approved industrial training, normally arranged during the long vacation.

Two modules are compulsory in the first year — introduction to catering skills and introduction to catering studies; in addition there is a compulsory single module in the second year which develops food production and service (catering methods) and a compulsory triple module in the third year (catering operations) which advances student opportunities for participating in problem solving.

DipHE programmes are not available.

The Food and Nutrition Single Field is designed to allow students in catering and science subjects to develop their interest in the scientific and industrial aspects of food, and is suitable as an entry qualification for the food industries and its related professions. When combined with the Catering Single Field, the programme is suitable as a basis for entry into the large scale sector of the catering industry.

A DipHE programme is available.

The Diploma of Higher Education (DipHE) award is made on successful completion of a two year full-time course of study, equivalent in standard to that of the first two years of study of a degree course. The Diploma is both a terminal qualification and also an award designed to facilitate transfer without loss in time to programmes of further study. At Oxford Polytechnic the DipHE course forms the first part of the course leading to the award of a degree.

Sheffield City Polytechnic,
Department of Hotel and Catering Studies
and Home Economics

BSc(Hons) Catering Systems (CNAA)

A four year sandwich course which aims to enable students, by means of a broadly based study of management and operational subjects, to prepare for senior executive positions, including those of consultant and adviser.

The subjects offered to meet the entry requirements (see page 141) should include Mathematics and a science subject.

The course is in three parts, separated by two periods of supervised training within the hotel and catering industry totalling 52 weeks.

There are five main areas of study:

Food studies, which includes food preparation and formulation and food science. This area examines food materials and investigates how they may be processed to produce customer satisfaction.

Food production, which includes work design, equipment studies, planning of catering production systems and operational research.

Economics and financial studies, the latter emphasising cost and management accounting.

Behavioural studies which considers people both as customers and as members of the work-force. This area covers:

— the principles of marketing, consumer behaviour and the psychology of food choice
— human behaviour at work, with a focus on the effects of introducing change into an organisation.

Systems studies: to understand the interaction of the component parts of hotel and catering organisations, and appreciate the realities of this industry.

The first year includes lectures from practising managers, followed by visits and critical report writing. At the end of this year students spend twenty weeks in industry.

In the second academic year, further visits and talks on the industry take place, followed by an eight month practical training where students focus on planning and management activities.

In the final year, small groups of students study various actual operations in detail and propose plans for improvement. The course ends with an individual project, which is normally a real-life problem of an hotel or other catering operation and draws on previous studies from all parts of the course.

**Ulster Polytechnic, School of Hotel,
Catering and Tourism Studies,
Newtownabbey**

BA Catering Administration (CNAA)

The aim of this four year sandwich course is to provide a relevant professional education for a management career in hotels, restaurants, industrial caterers, hospitals and other appropriate institutions of the catering industry.

The subjects offered to meet the entry requirements (see page 141) should include English, Mathematics and a science subject. A rather unusual arrangement is the possibility for transfer between the degree course and the Higher National Diploma in Hotel, Catering and Institutional Management which the Polytechnic offers. There is sufficient commonality in subject matter in the first year of both courses to enable students to transfer between the courses at or before the end of this year when the ability, interests and performance of the students show it to be desirable.

The third year of the course is spent in the industry; arrangements for the 48 week long period of industrial experience are made by the Polytechnic. The training programme will normally be in two halves, the first period in production areas, the second within the management of the organisation.

The course takes a multi-product, non-sector based approach, and is designed to provide a thorough education in the principles and practices of adminstration in the catering industry, with emphasis on the managerial and technical aspects of food, accommodation and beverage production.

Year One of the course is an introductory year and subjects studied include food studies — food, food formulation, equipment; catering environments; science; quantitative analysis; behavioural science — a study of key psychological and sociological aspects; economics.

Year Two: includes catering operations — which will aid the development of skills in the analysis of production systems and in the operation of catering systems; catering science, catering law, organisation studies — which will examine organisation variables and structures in catering and provide a theoretical preparation for personnel management; accounting and marketing. During the industrial placement year each student undertakes a project on an in-firm problem.

Year Four of the course includes the following subjects: developments in catering; catering administration; personnel management; financial management and marketing management. A major project is undertaken in this year to provide an integrative focus by student participation in a major replanning exercise within a catering facility.

Useful Addresses

COUNCIL FOR NATIONAL ACADEMIC AWARDS, 344–354 Gray's Inn Road, London WC1X 8BP (Tel 01-278 4411)

(For addresses of universities, polytechnics, colleges see Chapter 9, where they are listed by location. Thus for University of Surrey, see Guildford; for Napier College of Commerce and Technology, see Edinburgh.)

UNIVERSITIES CENTRAL COUNCIL ON ADMISSIONS (UCCA), P.O. Box 28, Cheltenham GL50 1HY

8

Catching Up

A description of the opportunities in further and higher education, of short courses for mature people wishing to enter the industry, of short courses aimed at those who have experience in the industry and wish to up-date or develop their knowledge in specialist subjects. Introduction to the opportunities provided by the HCITB, LGTB, the professional bodies, management centres and private enterprise. Description of the University of Surrey and University of Strathclyde short courses, the "Norwich scheme", courses for the licensed trade, and other initiatives. Useful addresses.

OPPORTUNITIES abound! Broadly they fall into four categories:
* *short intensive courses for mature people wishing to enter the industry;
* *short courses and seminars aimed at those who have experience in the industry wishing to up-date or develop their knowledge of a specialist subject;
* *short courses and seminars offered by a wide variety of management centres, professional bodies and private enterprise, on topics and techniques that are relevant for the hotel and catering industry; and
* *full-time and part-time courses in further and higher education.

The courses in *further and higher education* have been described in Chapters 5, 6, and 7. There are opportunities for mature people with experience in the hotel and catering industry and some craft qualifications to study for a management qualification via the HCIMA's courses, on a full-time or part-time basis, or by correspondence.

The Diploma in Management Studies is offered by various modes of study at a large number of colleges. The DMS courses particularly appropriate for this industry were briefly decribed in Chapter 7. It is possible for candidates aged 27 or over who do not possess the necessary academic qualifications to be admitted to a DMS course. This special and exceptional entry route is restricted to those who can produce evidence of at least four years' experience in a post of professional or administrative responsibility and can satisfy the college's selection committee that they are capable of profiting from and contributing to the course.

The special arrangement available at the University of Surrey for direct entry on to the BSc degree course in Hotel and Catering Administration has been described. A similar arrangement is available at Oxford Polytechnic on the modular degree course, with the possibility of one year's exemption from full-time study for holders of certain qualifications (for example an appropriate HND/HNC). On CNAA degree courses special exemption to the normal entry requirements may be made for mature students with other qualifications, provided that they can produce evidence of their ability to undertake the programme of studies for which they wish to obtain admission.

There is a facility at Oxford Polytechnic for mature students to study for a degree or Diploma in Higher Education on a part-time basis, or by a combination of part-time and full-time study. The modular structure of the course provides an enormous range of possibilities.

It is also possible at Oxford Polytechnic to study particular modules of interest on a part-time basis without commitment to a qualification-orientated programme.

Looking slightly ahead to the future, the new Technician Education Council awards in hotel, catering and institutional management will provide additional opportunities for mature students — not only to gain special entry to the programmes, but to return to college for a short time at a later stage in their careers, to study additional units. It is possible for Licentiate and Corporate members of the HCIMA to study for individual subjects of the new Professional Qualification, and many Licentiates will choose this route in order to gain additional points for upgrading to Corporate membership.

The Diploma in Professional Studies award of the CNAA may at some time in the future be offered in the catering field.

Courses described in Chapter 5 (Craft Skills Training) include many that are suitable for, as well as some that are specifically intended for, mature students. One of the principal objectives of the City and Guilds of London Institute's pattern of awards is to provide a progression through career stages.

The Associate Student programme of the Open University provides for certain courses to be taken on a one-off basis.

Short Courses of Direct Relevance

Short courses offered by the Department of Hotel, Catering and Tourism Management at the University of Surrey have a history which dates back to the 1960s. In 1970, after the Department had moved from London to Guildford, the first comprehensive *Management Development Programme* was formulated. It consists of a systematic series of courses available individually or in combination.

The courses are of five day, three day and two day lengths. A five day course (one week) includes about 25 hours of tuition, a three day course 15 hours, and a two day course 12 hours.

The programme is designed in such a way that participants can select either single courses, appropriate to their needs at the time, or a collection to suit their developing needs over a period of years. Each course is normally offered at least once every two years, but some are available more frequently. In addition to the standard repertoire each year one or two other courses are offered in response to particular needs and demands at the time.

The courses in *catering management* include: Marketing in Catering (5 days), which aims to provide a basic understanding of the application of the marketing concept to catering situations; Food and Beverage Control in Hotels and Restaurants (5 days), which covers the food and beverage control cycle from purchasing to sales; Catering Technology (5 days); Food Cost Control in Industrial and Welfare Catering (3 days); Purchasing in Catering (3 days); Catering Planning and Design (2 days).

The courses in *hotel and accommodation management* include Marketing Accommodation (3 days) which aims to examine marketing prospects and problems of hotels and related units and the role of marketing in accommodation generally; The Future of Accommodation (3 days), which includes trends in financing, planning and design, management and organisation, and in substitution between different forms of accommodation; Sales Promotion (2 days) which aims to provide an understanding of the techniques which may be used in accommodation and catering operations to increase sales and promote consumer satisfaction.

The *common courses in management* include: Introduction to Management (5 days) which examines, from a behavioural point of view, the functions of planning, organising, directing and controlling, and how they are applied in a management context; Business Management (5 days) which aims to examine the process of management in commercial and other organisations in accommodation, catering and tourism; Financial Management (5 days), which aims to develop an understanding of accounting and finance in the conduct of business; Work Study (3 days) which covers the principal techniques available and ways in which they can be used to improve the planning and staffing of new or modernised facilities.

Participants who complete an integrated programme of courses are eligible for the *Award of the University Certificate* in Catering Management or Hotel and Accommodation Management. A programme of courses and University Certificate in Tourism are also offered.

Those wishing to enrol for the Certificate Award should either have a degree or completed the membership examinations of the HCIMA, or hold an equivalent qualification, or be not less than thirty years of age and have achieved a recognised management position, and normally have attended a satisfactory interview at the University. In order to qualify for the award of the Certificate a candidate must:

(a)   Acquire a total of 120 credits of which no less than 40 must be from the catering management or hotel and accommodation management courses and no less than 40 from the common courses in management. The credits for the courses are 5 days, 20 credits; 3 days, 12 credits and 2 days, 8 credits.

(b)   Complete a dissertation or project report. All candidates are required in the first instance to agree an outline of their proposed study with the programme tutor and it may be necessary for the candidate to be formally interviewed by the head or another member of the Department. A supervisor is then appointed who is responsible for advising the candidate throughout — the frequency of contact between the student and supervisor will vary, usually at least four discussions are appropriate. Detailed requirements for the presentation of the study are laid down, the equivalent of 6–10 weeks' full-time work is normally necessary to reach the required standard, and the length will be in the region of 8000 to 10 000 words. The study is assessed by an external moderator and is subject to approval by University Senate.

(c)   Completed these requirements within a period of five years from the date of enrolment on the first course in the programme.

(d)   Paid a registration and examination fee to the University.

The Scottish Hotel School has a long record of close liaison with local industry; three early initiatives were reported in the HCI Journal of Spring 1961: "Plans are now in hand . . . to provide part-time training from next session:

(a)   in an attempt to ease the urgent need for more and better culinary craftsmen, an advanced course in hotel and restaurant cookery is planned suitable for chefs de partie and those with experience which it is hoped will enable selected participants to be entered for the City and Guilds of London Institute 152 examination;

(b)   intended for those aspiring to or already in executive positions, and would prepare them for Associate Membership Examination of the HCI to satisfy a demand from many who had been unable to take full-time training and who wished to secure a professional qualification;

(c)   shorter course for executive and managerial grades, on subjects such as work study, accounting, personnel management, recruitment selection and similar aspects of management."

The activities of the School in this field have continued since the formation of the University of Strathclyde with the emphasis on the third category above, on new developments — technical and legal — affecting the industry, on management workshops, and on short intensive courses for aspiring entrants to the industry with capital available or who have recently taken over their own operation.

The five day course operated in autumn 1979 is a typical example. This course, "Introduction to Hotel and Catering Operations", was intended for proprietors and prospective proprietors of small hotels who have no previous experience of hotel and catering operations, and managers of small units whose knowledge is limited and who seek a refresher course in operational aspects. The course aimed to provide an introduction to the basic requirements of hotel and catering operations. The content included: the unit and its departments, their functions; marketing; establishing and maintaining standards; essential legal requirements; catering sales and production; selling food and beverages; menu planning; food production methods; commodities; purchasing; kitchen equipment; convenience foods; meat cuts; cost and control aspects; simplified system of accounts and control for small units; staffing; training staff.

Licensed Trade

Training courses suitable for the licensed trade fall into three categories: part-time courses available at technical colleges in England and Wales leading to awards of the Licensed Trade Education and Training Committee (details from colleges, the Brewers' Society, or the regional offices of the Licensed Trade Development Association); residential courses operated by the Brewers' Society Training Centres Limited at two training centres in England, and occasional courses organised by the HCITB in conjunction with colleges and the industry. In the first category falls:

The *Licensed House Training Course*, designed for licensees, their staff and aspiring entrants to the trade; the minimum total period of instruction is 60 hours, usually arranged in classes of three hours' duration in the afternoon or evening, twice a week. Courses start in January, April and September.

The syllabus covers brewing and preparing beers for sale, cellar management, bar dispense, wines, spirits, services and salesmanship, the licensee and the law, financial and stock records, housekeeping, principles of catering in licensed premises, the licensee and his staff, hygiene and safety, and the structure of the licensed trade.

Candidates successful in the examination are awarded the Licensed Trade Diploma.

The *Licensed Trade Catering Course* is designed for licensees and their wives in order to give them the knowledge essential for successful catering in the average licensed house. Weekly instruction is arranged either on one afternoon for six months, or two afternoons for three months. Courses start in February and September; a slightly shorter version of the course is that of the North Western Regional Advisory Council described in Chapter 5.

The course is divided into two parts. The aim of the first part (30 hours) is to demonstrate how a catering service, varying from hot and cold snacks to more substantial dishes, can be established and successfully marketed. The second part of the course (48 hours) aims to reinforce what has been taught in the earlier part of the course and to extend the student's knowledge to formal meals, and the organising of wedding receptions, club suppers and other functions. There is an emphasis throughout the course on hygiene, portion control and costing.

Successful candidates in the examination are awarded the Licensed Trade Catering Diploma.

The *residential* courses are offered at different times throughout the year at the Brewers' Society's two residential training centres: in Buxton, Derbyshire and in Donhead St Andrew, Wiltshire. There are currently five different courses:

Public House Operational Management Course: this is a ten day (two week) residential course (60 hours) for licensees and prospective licensees. The minimum age for students is 18. The object of the course is to give students a sound grounding in the essential knowledge required in the operational management of a profitable public house. The syllabus includes cellar management (13 hours) and bar dispense (13 hours) — including the tasks involved in bar and cellar work, as well as the management of both; the law, both as it affects customers and as it affects staff, the management of staff, including recruitment and selection, induction and training, supervision and motivation of staff; financial and control aspects; hygiene, safety and security; and the role of the licensee, including responsibility to customers, the community and the brewery, trade organisations.

Profitable Bar Catering Course: a five day course aimed at adding catering management knowledge and commercial concepts to students' domestic culinary skills and knowledge in order that they may make the bar catering side of their business profitable in its own right. This 30 hour course is intended for licensees and prospective licensees and their wives. The syllabus includes kitchen hygiene and safety; marketing; costing and control aspects; the fast food concept; the principles of purchasing, of storage and of quality control; equipment and service arrangements; and some 12 hours on the preparation, service and presentation of hot and cold snacks and simple cold buffets in which students are asked to participate.

Advanced Course for Tenants and Managers: a five day course suitable for practising . licensees, with 30 hours of teaching, which aims to develop the management skills of students by up-dating their knowledge and skills in those areas of public house management which have been the subject of recent change. These include: marketing and selling in the context of the modern public house, management of staff, motivation of staff — in particular how their new legal responsibilities may be explained to them and why they must be willing to adopt new practices; involvement of staff in the necessary steps to improve their own knowledge and performance.

Business Management Course for Licensees: a five day course for tenants of at least one year's experience to develop their management skills in the areas of marketing, financial planning and control and effective use of staff. The syllabus includes the marketing concept, assessing the market, reaching the market, the craft of selling, recruitment and selection of staff, training and motivating staff, labour turnover, financial planning and control, and costing.

Advanced Catering Course: a ten day (two week) course intended for existing licensees, their wives and staff, who are already actively engaged in catering on a small scale, who intend to extend their catering operations or are moving to another establishment with full restaurant facilities. The main subject headings of the course include special aspects of function catering, simple economics for successful catering, legal topics, food purchasing and control aspects; appetisers and starters, soups, egg dishes, farinaceous dishes, fish dishes, grills and poultry dishes, vegetable and garnishes, salads and salad dressing, sweets and desserts, coffee; as well as suggestions for lamp cookery for the luxury trade.

The Norwich Scheme

For mature people who wish to enter the hotel and catering industry, there is also "The Norwich Scheme". The aim of this six week intensive course is to provide a good grounding in the basic skills and administrative techniques necessary for success in the industry.

The course is normally offered three times each academic year at the Department of Hotel Keeping and Catering of Norwich City College of Further and Higher Education. The syllabus is comprehensive and the length of the sessions gives an indication of the intensiveness: morning 9 am to 12 noon; afternoon 1 pm to 5 pm; evening 5 pm to 6 pm and 7 pm to 9 pm. Over 180 hours are devoted to the technical aspects, and over 100 to the administrative aspects.

The syllabus includes:

Preparation and service of food and beverages (153 hours): design and planning; purchase and control of materials, menu planning; service of food and beverages; wines, spirits and beers; food production and service.

Provision of accommodation (9 hours): planning of room interiors; floors, flooring and floor coverings; wall coverings and wall surfaces; cleaning premises; linen room management; safety and security.

Financial management control (57 hours): basic accounting principles; final accounts; taxation; profit planning and measurements; finance for business; control of the use of capital; development of management accounting concepts; *and the following:*

Applied science (12 hours); sales systems (3 hours); building — structural requirements (6 hours); economics and the industry (15 hours); law for the industry (15 hours); human aspects — organisation theories and personnel practices (30 hours).

To qualify for the award of the Certificate the candidate must normally be not less than 25 years of age, attend not less than 90% of the prescribed time in each subject (unless qualified in a particular subject to a higher standard), receive not more than two unsatisfactory subject ratings on assessment and receive not less than 50% of the marks in any end of course written test or project.

Sheffield City Polytechnic

At Sheffield City Polytechnic two five day intensive courses were offered in autumn 1979, and may become a regular feature, called "Starting Your Own Business in the Hotel and Catering Industry".

The course covered the major practical aspects of the planning process required before starting a new business. Topics included: market research; sources and control of finance; tax planning; legal aspects — contracts, obtaining licences, employing staff; budgeting and forecasting; selection and use of foods and production and service techniques; equipment selection and layout; public health, fire and planning requirements.

Other Initiatives

The Sheffield City Polytechnic intensive course is an example of a recent initiative taken by a further or higher educational establishment, publicised well in advance in the catering press, and likely to be offered in future years if there is an indication of demand. Similar initiatives will no doubt be taken in the future by other establishments, some of which will be publicised nationally, others in the local press.

Careful study of college prospectuses may also reveal such opportunities. For example in the 1979/80 prospectus of North Devon College, Barnstaple, information is included on a college "Certificate Course in Catering". This is intended for small hotel keepers and is offered on an evening basis with weekly attendances. The course is designed in four self contained units, each covering a different aspect of the catering and domestic work of a small hotel, so it is possible to study one unit only, or indeed all four.

Hotel and Catering Industry Training Board

The Hotel and Catering Industry Training Board (HCITB) offers an extremely comprehensive range of short courses via its regional offices and a number of colleges. These include 10 day Instructor Courses, 5 day On-job Trainer Courses, and a wide range of shorter courses some appropriate for managers, others for supervisors, others are for specific skills and on particular themes. Some courses are more suitable for large businesses, others for the smaller.

The titles of some of the HCITB courses is an indication of their range: Supervisory Skills for Managers, Legal Obligations of Management, Health and Safety at Work for Managers, Managing the Marketing Effort, Personnel Skills, Industrial Relations, Trade Union Recognition, Legislation in the Small Business, Financial Aspects of Management, Costing and Control, Costing for Small Businesses, Customer Relations, Interview and Selection, Coaching Skills, Appraisal Interviewing, and Inter-active Skills.

Recently the HCITB has operated a pilot part-time executive development programme at the Manchester Business School, spread over a period of eight months. The phasing of the programme was designed to reduce to a minimum the periods over which students would be away from their job. Project work played an important part of the programme.

Local Government Training Board

The Local Government Training Board is very active in those areas of the industry out of scope with the Hotel and Catering Industry Training Board. These include catering in schools, colleges, polytechnics and the social services.

Regular five day courses for School Meals Organisers are held at Leicester in co-operation with Leicester Polytechnic; seminars have been held on the use of computers in the School Meals Service; Health and Safety Courses have been held; the LGTB grant aids instructors taking the HCITB Instructor Course; special five day management courses have been held for Catering Advisers/Officers/Home economists in the Social Service.

Courses have been operated for some years by the senior catering adviser at the Department of Education and Science for catering officers, domestic bursars, residential and financial managers. Many local authorities organise in-service courses for those working in the social services.

Professional Bodies, Trade Associations and Interest Groups

An important part of the work of the different professional bodies, trade associations and interest groups described in Chapter 10 is the organisation of short courses, conferences and seminars on topics of special interest to their members.

Larger Employers

The larger employers in the hotel and catering industry run regular courses for their employees — to teach them specific skills and techniques, to bring up to date their knowledge on new technology and legislation, to introduce them to and train them in the operation of company systems.

Short Courses of Indirect Relevance

Management centres, business schools, business studies departments of polytechnics and colleges throughout the country; establishments funded largely by government and local authorities, as well as privately; a wide variety of professional bodies . . . . all offer opportunities for an enthusiastic and highly motivated person to develop himself or herself. The profiles of people working in the industry contained in Chapter 3 illustrate the variety of opportunities, and indicate their value and relevance.

The professional bodies which offer short courses and seminars of interest include those in the field of personnel management, for example the Institute of Personnel Management, those in the more general field of management, for example the British Institute of Management, the Institution of Works Managers, The Industrial Society, and more specialist bodies, for example the Institute of Marketing and the Institute of Purchasing and Supply.

Obtaining Further Information

Up to date information on the availability of these courses may be obtained directly from the organiser. The HCIMA publishes information on short courses and conferences regularly in *Hospitality* and the *Mid-Month News*. Information on the HCITB courses is published regularly in the Board's monthly newsheet *Service*.

The Journals of the professional bodies, as well as their information departments, usually carry news of forthcoming conferences, short courses and seminars, which they and other organisations are planning. The national and local press will frequently carry advertisements of courses offered by various educational and privately run establishments. The trade papers are another valuable source of information.

Useful Addresses

HOTEL AND CATERING INDUSTRY TRAINING BOARD, PO Box 18, Ramsey House, Central Square, Wembley, Middlesex HA9 7AP (Tel 01-902 8865)

HOTEL, CATERING AND INSTITUTIONAL MANAGEMENT ASSOCIATION, 191 Trinity Road, London SW17 7HN (Tel 01-672 4251)

LOCAL GOVERNMENT TRAINING BOARD, 8 The Arndale Centre, Luton LU1 2TS (Tel 0582 21111)

MANAGEMENT DEVELOPMENT PROGRAMME, Short Course Tutor, University of Surrey, Guildford, Surrey GU2 5XH (Tel 0483 71281, ext 584)

NORWICH CITY COLLEGE OF FURTHER AND HIGHER EDUCATION, Department of Hotel Keeping and Catering, Ipswich Road, Norwich NR2 2LJ (Tel 0603 60011)

SCOTTISH HOTEL SCHOOL, University of Strathclyde, Ross Hall, Crookston Road, Glasgow G52 3NQ (Tel 041-882 1717)

SHEFFIELD CITY POLYTECHNIC, Department of Hotel and Catering Studies and Home Economics, Pond Street, Sheffield S1 1WB (Tel 0742 20911)

THE BREWERS' SOCIETY, 42 Portman Square, London W1H 0BB (Tel 01-486 4831)

THE OPEN UNIVERSITY, P.O. Box 76, Milton Keynes MK7 6AN (Tel 0908 63248)

9

Finding a College

Application for places. Fees and grants. TOPS awards. Enrolment. Residential accommodation. Guide to colleges: the names and addresses of over 260 colleges offering craft, management and degree courses in catering, in England, Wales, Scotland, Northern Ireland, the Channel Islands, Isle of Man. Colleges listed by location, with county check list for cross referencing. Addresses and telephone numbers of local education authorities in England, Wales, Scotland and the Education and Library Boards in Northern Ireland.

Application for Places

Applications for places on courses should be made direct to the colleges concerned, except for the degree courses of the University of Surrey, University College, Cardiff and, in some instances, the University of Strathclyde (see entries in Chapter 7). Except for the universities there are no compulsory closing dates for applications. It is important to remember that the number of places available is usually limited and prospective students are advised to contact the colleges as soon as possible.

For those applicants who find themselves late in the summer without a place on a full-time course, up to date information on course vacancies throughout England and Wales may be obtained from the Local Advisory Officer of the Further Education Information Services which operates during August and September. The name and address of the Local Advisory Officer may be obtained from Chief Education Officers (see page 182).

Fees and Grants

Full-time students up to the age of 18, like their contemporaries still attending school, are not normally required to pay tuition fees; for part-time students up to 18 the position is more complicated. While many LEAs pay expenses and fees for all part-time vocational courses, others do not.

For students undertaking full-time advanced courses after the age of 18 the fees vary considerably from authority to authority. However, the great majority of students on full-time advanced courses qualify for LEA grants similar to those awarded for university degree courses and many courses carry grants which are mandatory upon the LEAs to pay.

For some students, however, like those on vocational courses in art and design, a discretionary award system operates which allows local authorities to pay as much or as little as they choose.

Mandatory awards are those which a local authority is required by Government to bestow on persons with the necessary educational qualifications for certain full-time courses. First degree courses, the diploma of higher education and higher national diploma awards are included in this category.

Discretionary awards are those which a local authority is enabled to bestow on students over compulsory school age attending full-time or part-time courses of further education.

College based students taking a sandwich course will be financed on a similar basis to a university student while at college and can expect to receive an industrial salary while at work — although not always a very high one.

Students taking non-advanced full-time courses may qualify for a maintenance grant and for assistance towards travelling expenses. Part-time students on day release will be paid by their employers while in attendance at the college (usually), and the more progressive employers will also make a contribution towards the enrolment fee, the examination fees, and the cost of books and equipment. Part-time students may qualify for assistance towards their travelling expenses.

Grants — England and Wales

The grants system is complex so it is only possible to give general guidance. Any enquiries about eligibility for or assessment of grant should be addressed to the Chief Education Officer of the area in which the student lives. A list of addresses and telephone numbers of the Local Education Authorities is given on pages 182–187.

The designated courses, that is those which qualify for mandatory awards, include: full-time or sandwich courses leading to university or CNAA first degrees, the Diploma of Higher Education, Higher National Diplomas, Higher Diplomas of the Technician Education Council and the Business Education Council. Other courses which are specifically prescribed as being comparable to first degree courses qualify for mandatory awards; an up-to-date list of these may be obtained from local education authorities or from the Department of Education and Science.

Courses which do not meet the above criteria qualify for discretionary awards. Grants for such courses are made entirely at the discretion of each local education authority.

Students are advised to apply in writing for an award as soon as possible. Do not wait until acceptance on the course is confirmed, for example if this is dependent on examination results. Late applications may mean a delay in the first payment and if a written application fails to reach the local education authority concerned before the end of the first term of the course, the student will no longer be eligible for a mandatory award.

A student's "home" local education authority is the one in whose area he or she is normally resident on 30 June preceding the start of the course.

The conditions of eligibility for a mandatory award also include the following:

(a)   the student must have been ordinarily resident in the United Kingdom for the three years immediately preceding the academic year in which the course begins (or would have been so resident if student, spouse or either parent had not been temporarily employed outside the UK);

(b)   have not previously attended any one of certain courses of further education (a period of up to one term's attendance on one such course is disregarded);

(c)   the student must provide a written undertaking to the local education authority to repay any sum which has, for whatever reason, been paid in excess of his or her entitlement to grant;

(d)   the student must not have shown himself or herself to be unfitted to receive an award in the opinion of the local authority.

Grants are usually paid termly, to arrive at or near the beginning of term and nearly always through the college office. Maintenance grant covers periods of term-time attendance and the Christmas and Easter vacations, but not the long summer vacation.

The starting point for calculating the amount of grant to be paid for the academic year is an assessment of the student's "maintenance requirements". These consist of a basic maintenance grant and any additional maintenance grant appropriate to the student's circumstances. From the total maintenance requirements are deducted the student's "resources", that is the student's own income and, where appropriate, a contribution based on parental income. There is a minimum payment.

Grants — Scotland

The system of Student's Allowances to enable students to take full-time courses at universities and advanced full-time or sandwich courses at other further education establishments is administered by the Scottish Education Department. The maximum Student's Allowance, for which a substantial number of students qualify, consists of the amount of approved fees payable for the course plus a standard maintenance allowance and, in some cases, additional special allowances for dependants etc. The allowance can be reduced by the amount of a parental contribution, or a contribution from a spouse, assessed on a prescribed income scale, and by the amount by which a student's personal income exceeds a certain figure.

A minimum allowance consisting of payment of fees for the course plus a cash allowance is payable to all eligible students, irrespective of the level of their own income or the income of their parents or spouse. A copy of the "Guide to Students' Allowances" may be obtained free of charge from education authority offices or from the Scottish Education Department Awards Branch (page 186 for address).

Bursaries may be available from education authorities for students taking less advanced full-time courses and for part-time courses of further education. Enquiries and applications should be addressed to the education authority of the area in which the student is normally resident. Addresses and telephone numbers on page 186.

TOPS Awards and Courses

Following the passage of the Employment and Training Act 1973 the government set up a new Manpower Services Commission with two executive arms, the Employment Services Agency (broadly speaking embracing the job-finding activities formerly carried out by the Department of Employment) and the Training Services Agency. The Training Services Agency (TSA) is organised in three operating divisions and three support branches.

The *Training Services Division* (TSD) of the TSA embraces the regional offices and skill centres (formerly known as Government Training Centres) and administers awards to individual trainees.

The *Training Opportunities Scheme* (TOPS) is for people who want to brighten up their job prospects and to provide industry and commerce with people who are trained in the skills they require. The scheme offers the opportunity of training with pay for up to a year on one of over 500 courses, including hotel and catering.

The range of courses falls into two categories: TOPS "exclusive" courses, that is all places are reserved for TOPS sponsored students, and other courses which fulfil TOPS criteria, on which students are sponsored. The latter arrangement is called "infilling", and the TSD pay the fees and personal training allowances on exactly the same basis as for exclusive TOPS courses.

The conditions for applying for a TOPS course are as follows (August 1979): the applicants must:

(a) be aged a minimum of 19 years and been away from full-time education for a total period of more than two years;

(b) have the intention to take up employment using the skill for which training is given;

(c) be either unemployed or willing to give up present employment to take the full-time training course;

(d) normally not have had a government training course during the past three years;

(e) be suited to the course chosen (which must not exceed one year in length).

TOPS trainees are paid a weekly allowance during training which varies according to age and family responsibilities, travelling expenses (if the training centre or college is more than two miles away from the trainee's home or lodgings), and free midday meals (or an allowance in lieu if they are not available). In addition if residential accommodation is not provided and the trainee is not living at home, a lodging allowance is paid. An earnings related supplement is also paid in certain circumstances, as are the trainee's National Insurance contributions. Information on TOPS is available from any Employment Service Division Jobcentre or Employment Office (ask for the Employment Adviser who deals with TOPS).

Enrolment

Courses normally begin at the start of the academic year — usually September but in Scotland it is usually October in the case of Central Institutions and August in the case of Further Education Colleges. The prospectus of the college concerned will usually give the dates for enrolments, as well as other information.

Residential Accommodation

A number of colleges do have halls of residence in which a proportion of their full-time students are accommodated. Lists of approved lodgings and help in finding accommodation are available from college accommodation or welfare officers.

Guide to Colleges

The purpose of this guide is to provide a list of all universities, polytechnics, central institutions, colleges of further education, technical colleges, institutes of higher education . . . that is all major educational establishments . . . offering courses in hotel and catering studies, with an *indication* of their level.

The courses offered by a particular establishment depend on a number of factors. These include the purpose and nature of the establishment, its geographical location, the availability or otherwise of courses offered by other accessible establishments, student demand, physical resources, availability of lecturing staff, and approval by the necessary authorities to offer courses at a particular level — which may include the Local Education Authority (in terms of resource commitments), the Department of Education and Science/Scottish Education Department/Department of Education, Northern Ireland, the Regional Advisory Council, and the validating body.

Generally the higher the level of the course, the more strenuous the control on its availability. The great majority of colleges listed in this guide offer courses at "craft level", indicated by the letter "C". For the purpose of this guide, the "C" category encompasses all those courses described in Chapter 5 — including those of the City and Guilds of London Institute, the Regional Examining Bodies, the supervisory courses of the National Examinations Board for Supervisory Studies and the Scottish Technical Education Council, nautical cookery courses, courses in hotel reception, including those of the Scottish Business Education Council, Wine and Spirit Education Trust courses, courses leading to examinations of the Royal Society of Health and the Royal Institute of Public Health and Hygiene, Licensed Trade Catering courses, and some of the National Council for Home Economics Education courses. No college offers all these, some offer one or two of these only.

Colleges (there are about one hundred) offering courses at Diploma/Certificate level are indicated by the letters "MD". Colleges require the approval of the Joint Committee to offer Ordinary National Diploma courses (included in this level), and will require the approval of the Technician Education Council to offer the new TEC programmes leading to the Diploma and Certificate awards of the Council. A number of colleges will be offering TEC programmes from September 1980. In Scotland the colleges presently offering Ordinary National Diploma courses will be replacing them from September 1980 by Scottish Technical Education Council Diploma courses. Colleges offering the HCIMA's Part A course (for which the Association's approval is required) are also included in this category.

About thirty colleges (the expression "college" is used to cover all major educational establishments) are offering courses at Higher Diploma/Higher Certificate level, and they are indicated by the letters "MHD". Higher National Diplomas, as well as their replacement in Scotland, the Higher Diploma of the

Scottish Technical Education Council, are included in this category. It is expected that the new programmes leading to the Higher Diploma and Higher Certificate awards of the Technician Education Council, for which the Council's approval is required, will replace HNDs in England, Wales and Northern Ireland from September 1981. Colleges offering the HCIMA's Part B course, whether on a full-time, sandwich or part-time basis, are included in this category. So are colleges offering a Diploma in Management Studies of special interest to hotel and catering students.

The three universities offering degree courses are indicated by the letter "D". The polytechnics and central institutions with approval to offer a Council for National Academic Awards degree course in hotel and catering studies as at September 1979 are included in this category.

Sources of Information

Many organisations provide lists of colleges offering particular courses; these include the Scottish Education Department, the City and Guilds of London Institute, the Hotel and Catering Industry Training Board, many of the Regional Advisory Councils, the Hotel, Catering and Institutional Management Association, the Joint Committees, the National Examinations Board for Supervisory Studies, and the Council for National Academic Awards. A number of directories (including the "Compendium of Advanced Courses in Technical Colleges" produced annually as a combined publication by the Regional Advisory Councils) and year books also include this information.

This list has been carefully compiled from all the above sources, and every possible care taken to ensure its accuracy. As many inconsistencies have appeared in the different sources used, it is unfortunately inevitable that some remain!

For details of the exact courses offered by a particular establishment, it is best to write for the college prospectus, indicating the sort of course(s) you are interested in studying.

Using this Guide

The list below is arranged in alphabetical order, by town or city — not by the name of the college, which in many cases does not indicate its location — with separate lists for England, Wales, Northern Ireland, Scotland, the Channel Islands, the Isle of Man. After each of these lists a shorter guide is provided, grouping the locations of the colleges listed by their local education authority area. Therefore, it is possible to ascertain quickly the colleges offering catering courses in a particular area, as well as those in a specific city or town.

A list of the addresses and telephone numbers of the chief education officers of each local education authority is given separately (to obtain information on grants).

Colleges in England

ABINGDON — C — Abingdon College of Further Education, Northcourt Road, Abingdon OX14 1NW

ACCRINGTON — C — Accrington and Rossendale College, Sandy Lane, Accrington BB5 2AW

ALTRINCHAM — MD,C — South Trafford College of Further Education, Manchester Road, West Timperley, Altrincham WA14 5PQ

ANDOVER — C — Cricklade College, Charlton Road, Andover SP10 1EJ

ASHINGTON — C — Northumberland Technical College, College Road, Ashington NE63 9RG

ASHTON-UNDER-LYNE — MD,C — Tameside College of Technology, Beaufort Road, Ashton-under-Lyne OL6 6NX

AYLESBURY — C — Aylesbury College of Further Education, Oxford Road, Aylesbury HP21 8PD

BANBURY — C — North Oxfordshire Technical College and School of Art, Broughton Road, Banbury OX16 9QA

BARNSTAPLE — MD,C — North Devon College, Old Sticklepath Hill, Barnstaple

BASINGSTOKE — MD,C — Basingstoke Technical College, Worting Road, Basingstoke RG21 1TN

BATH — MD,C — City of Bath Technical College, Avon Street, Bath BA1 1UP

BEDFORD — C — Bedford College of Higher Education, Cauldwell Street, Bedford MK42 9AH

BIRKENHEAD — C — North Wirral College of Technology, Borough Road, Birkenhead L42 9QD

BIRMINGHAM — MHD,MD,C — Birmingham College of Food and Domestic Arts, Summer Row, Birmingham B3 1JB

BIRMINGHAM — C — Garretts Green Technical College, Garretts Green Lane, Birmingham B33 0TS

BLACKBURN — C — Blackburn College of Technology and Design, Fieldon Street, Blackburn

BLACKPOOL — MHD,MD,C — Blackpool and Fylde College of Further and Higher Education, Ashfield Road, Bispham, Blackpool FY2 0HB

BLETCHLEY — C — Bletchley College of Further Education, Sherwood Drive, Bletchley MK3 6DR

BOLTON — MD,C — Bolton Technical College, Manchester Road, Bolton BL2 1ER

BOSTON — MD,C — Boston College of Further Education, Rowley Road, Boston PE21 6JF

BOURNEMOUTH — MD,C — Bournemouth and Poole College of Further Education, Lansdowne, Bournemouth BH1 3JJ

BRACKNELL — C — Bracknell College of Further Education, Church Road, Bracknell RG12 1DJ

BRADFORD — MD,C — Bradford College, Great Horton Road, Bradford BD7 1AY

BRAINTREE — C — Braintree College of Further Education, Church Lane, Braintree CM7 5SN

BRIGHTON — MHD — Brighton Polytechnic, Moulsecoomb, Brighton BN2 4AT

BRIGHTON — MHD,MD,C — Brighton Technical College, Pelham Street, Brighton BN1 4FA

BRISTOL — MHD,MD,C — Brunel Technical College, Ashley Down, Bristol BS7 9BU

BROADSTAIRS — MHD,MD,C — Thanet Technical College, Ramsgate Road, Broadstairs CT10 1PN

BROXBOURNE — C — East Herts College, Turnford, Broxbourne EN10 6AF

BURTON UPON TRENT — MD,C — Burton upon Trent Technical College, Lichfield Street, Burton upon Trent BE14 3RL

BURY — C — Bury Metropolitan College of Further Education, Market Street, Bury BL9 0BG

BUXTON — MD,C — High Peak College of Further Education, Harpur Hill, Buxton SK17 9JZ

CAMBRIDGE — MD,C — Cambridgeshire College of Arts and Technology, Collier Road, Cambridge CB1 2AJ

CANTERBURY — C — Canterbury College of Technology, New Dover Road, Canterbury CT1 3AJ

CARLISLE — MD,C — Carlisle Technical College, Victoria Place, Carlisle CA1 1HS

CHELMSFORD — MD,C — Chelmer Institute of Higher Education, Victoria Road South, Chelmsford CM1 1LL

CHELTENHAM — MHD,MD,C — North Gloucestershire College of Technology, The Park, Cheltenham GL50 2RR

CHESTERFIELD — C — Chesterfield College of Technology, Infirmary Road, Chesterfield S41 7NG

CHICHESTER — MD,C — Chichester College of Technology, Westgate Fields, Chichester PO19 1SB

CHIPPENHAM — C — Chippenham Technical College, Cocklebury Road, Chippenham SN15 3QD

CINDERFORD — C — West Gloucestershire College of Further Education, College Road, Cinderford GL14 2JY

COALVILLE — C — Coalville Technical College, Bridge Road, Coalville

COLCHESTER — MHD,MD,C — The Colchester Institute, Sheepen Road, Colchester CO3 3LL

CONSETT — C — Consett Technical College, Park Road, Consett

CORBY — C — Tresham College, George Street, Corby NN17 1QA

COVENTRY — MHD,MD,C — Henley College of Further Education, Henley Road, Bell Green, Coventry CV2 1ED

CRAWLEY — MD,C — Crawley College of Technology, College Road, Crawley RH10 1NR

CREWE — MD,C — South Cheshire College, Dane Bank Avenue, Crewe CW2 8AB

CROYDON — See London Boroughs

DARLINGTON — MD,C — Darlington College of Technology, Cleveland Avenue, Darlington DL3 7BB

DARTFORD — C — North-West Kent College of Technology, Miskin Road, Dartford DA1 2LU

DERBY — C — Derby College of Further Education, Wilmorton, Derby DE2 8UG

DEWSBURY — C — Dewsbury and Batley Technical and Art College, Halifax Road, Dewsbury WF13 2AS

DONCASTER — C — Doncaster Metropolitan Institute of Higher Education, Waterdale, Doncaster DN1 3EX

DURHAM — MD,C — New College, Durham, Framwellgate Moor, Durham DH1 5ES

EASTBOURNE — C — Eastbourne College of Further Education, St Anne's Road, Eastbourne BN21 2HS

EASTLEIGH — C — Eastleigh College of Further Education, Chestnut Avenue, Eastleigh SO5 5HT

EXETER — MD,C — Exeter College, Hele Road, Exeter ED4 4JS

FAREHAM — C — Fareham Technical College, Bishopfield Road, Fareham PO14 1NH

FARNBOROUGH — C — Farnborough College of Technology, Boundary Road, Farnborough GU14 6SB

FOLKESTONE — C — South Kent College of Technology, Shorncliffe Road, Folkestone CT20 2NA

GAINSBOROUGH — C — Gainsborough College of Further Education, Morton Terrace, Gainsborough DN21 2SU

GRANTHAM — C — Grantham College for Further Education, Stonebridge Road, Grantham NG31 9AP

GRAYS — MD,C — Thurrock Technical College, Woodview, Grays RM16 4YR

GREAT YARMOUTH — C — Great Yarmouth College of Further Education, Southtown, Great Yarmouth NR31 0JU

GRIMSBY — MD,C — Grimsby College of Technology, Nuns Corner, Grimsby DN34 5BQ

GUILDFORD — MD,C — Guildford County College of Technology, Stoke Park, Guildford GU1 1EZ

GUILDFORD — D — University of Surrey, Guildford GU2 5XH

HALESOWEN — MD,C — Halesowen College of Further Education, Whittingham Road, Halesowen B63 3NA

HALIFAX — C — The Percival Whiteley College of Further Education, Francis Street, Halifax HX1 3UZ

HARLOW — C — Harlow Technical College, College Gate, The High, Harlow CM20 1LT

HARROGATE — C — Harrogate College of Further Education, Haywra Crescent, Harrogate HG1 5BE

HASTINGS — MD,C — Hastings College of Further Education, Archery Road, St Leonards-on-Sea TN38 0HX

HAVANT — C — South Downs College of Further Education, College Road, Purbrook Way, Havant

HEREFORD — MD,C — Herefordshire Technical College, Folly Lane, Hereford HR1 1LS

HIGH WYCOMBE — C — Buckinghamshire College of Higher Education, Queen Alexandra Road, High Wycombe HP11 2JZ

HUDDERSFIELD — MD,C — Huddersfield Technical College, New North Road, Huddersfield HD1 5NN

HUDDERSFIELD — D,MHD — The Polytechnic, Queensgate, Huddersfield HD1 3DH

HULL — MD,C — Hull College of Further Education, Queen's Gardens, Hull HU1 3DG

HULL — C — Hull College of Higher Education, Cottingham Road, Hull HU6 7RT

IPSWICH — MD,C — Suffolk College of Higher and Further Education, Rope Walk, Ipswich IP4 1LT

KENDAL — C — Kendal College of Further Education, Milnthorpe Road, Kendal LA9 5AY

KING'S LYNN — C — Norfolk College of Arts and Technology, King's Lynn PE30 2QW

LANCASTER — MD,C — Lancaster and Morecambe College of Further Education, Morecambe Road, Lancaster L1 2TY

LEEDS — D,MHD — Leeds Polytechnic, Calverley Street, Leeds LS1 3HE

LEEDS — MD,C — Thomas Danby College, Roundhay Road, Sheepscar, Leeds LS7 3BG

LEICESTER — MD,C — South Fields College of Further Education, Aylestone Road, Leicester LE2 7LW

LEIGH — C — Leigh College, Marshall Street, Leigh WN7 4HX

LETCHWORTH — MD,C — North Herts College, Broadway, Letchworth SG6 3PB

LINCOLN — C — Lincoln College of Technology, Cathedral Street, Lincoln LN2 5QH

LIVERPOOL — MD,C —Colquitt Technical and Nautical Catering College, Colquitt Street, Liverpool L1 4DB

LONDON — See p. 172

LOUGHBOROUGH — C — Loughborough Technical College, Radmoor, Loughborough LE11 3BT

LOUGHTON — C — Loughton College of Further Education, Borders Lane, Loughton IG10 3SA

LUTON — MD,C — Barnfield College (Luton), New Bedford Road, Luton LU3 2AX

LONDON
Polytechnics
Middlesex Polytechnic — MHD,MD — Middlesex Polytechnic, The Burroughs, Hendon, London NW4 4BT

The Polytechnic of North London — D,MHD — The Polytechnic of North London, Holloway Road, London N7 8DB

Inner London Education Authority
C — London School of Nautical Cookery, 202 Lambeth Road, London SE1 7JW

MD,C — South East London College, Breakspears Road, Lewisham Way, London SE4 1UT

MHD,MD,C — Westminster College, Vincent Square, London SW1P 2PD

London Boroughs
Brent — C — Kilburn Polytechnic, 373 Edgware Road, Colindale, London NW9 6NH

Croydon — MD,C — Croydon College, Fairfield, Croydon CR9 1DX

Ealing — MHD,MD,C — Ealing College of Higher Education, St Mary's Road, Ealing, London W5 5RF

Enfield — C — Southgate Technical College, High Street, London N14 6BS

Hounslow — C — Hounslow Borough College, London Road, Isleworth, Middlesex TW7 4HS

Merton — MD,C — Merton Technical College, Gladstone Road, London SW19

Newham — C — West Ham College, Welfare Road, Stratford, London E15 4HT

Redbridge — C — Redbridge Technical College, Little Heath, Romford RM6 4XT

Sutton — C — Carshalton College of Further Education, Nightingale Road, Carshalton, Surrey SM5 2EJ

Waltham Forest — MD,C — Waltham Forest College, Forest Road, Walthamstow, London E17 4JB

MACCLESFIELD — C — Macclesfield College of Further Education, Park Lane, Macclesfield SK11 8LF

MAIDSTONE — C — Mid Kent College of Further and Higher Education, Westree Road, Maidstone

MALVERN — C — Malvern Hills College, Albert Road North, Malvern WR14 2TW

MANCHESTER — D,MHD — Manchester Polytechnic, Hollings Faculty, Old Hall Lane, Manchester M14 6HR

MANSFIELD — C — West Nottinghamshire College of Further Education, Derby Road, Mansfield NG18 5BH

MIDDLESBROUGH — C — Kirby College of Further Education, Roman Road, Middlesbrough TS5 5PJ

NELSON — MD,C — Nelson and Colne College, Scotland Road, Nelson BB9 7YT

NEWBURY — C — Newbury College of Further Education, Oxford Road, Newbury RG13 1PQ

NEWCASTLE — MD,C — College of Arts and Technology, Maple Terrace, Newcastle upon Tyne NE4 7SA

NEWPORT — MD,C — Isle of Wight College of Arts and Technology, Newport PO30 5TA

NORTHAMPTON — MD,C — Northampton College of Further Education, St Gregory's Road, Booth Lane South, Northampton NN3 3RF

NORTHWICH — C — Mid-Cheshire College of Further Education, Hartford Campus, Northwich CW8 1LJ

NORWICH — MHD,MD,C — Norwich City College of Further and Higher Education, Ipswich Road, Norwich NR2 2LJ

NOTTINGHAM — MD,C — Clarendon College of Further Education, Pelham Avenue, Mansfield Road, Nottingham NG5 1AL

NUNEATON — C — North Warwickshire College of Technology and Art, Hinckley Road, Nuneaton CV11 6BH

OLDHAM — C — Oldham Centre for Community Education, Chaucer Street, Oldham OL1 1BA

OXFORD — MD,C — Oxford College of Further Education, Oxpens Road, Oxford OX1 1SA

OXFORD — D,MHD — Oxford Polytechnic, Gipsy Lane, Headington, Oxford OX3 0BP

PETERBOROUGH — MD,C — Peterborough Technical College, Park Crescent, Peterborough PE1 4DZ

PLYMOUTH — MD,C — Plymouth College of Further Education, 40 Portland Square, Plymouth, PL4 6DN

PLYMOUTH — MHD — Plymouth Polytechnic, Drake Circus, Plymouth PL4 8AA

POOLE — MHD — Dorset Institute of Higher Education, Wallisdown Road, Poole BH12 5BB

PORTSMOUTH — MHD,MD,C — Highbury College of Technology, Cosham, Portsmouth PO6 2SA

PORTSMOUTH — MHD — Portsmouth Polytechnic, Mercantile House, Hampshire Terrace, Portsmouth PO1 2QQ

PRESTON — C — W. R. Tuson College, St Vincent's Road, Fulwood, Preston PR2 4UR

READING — Correspondence Course — Metropolitan College, Aldermaston Court, Reading RG7 4PW

READING — MD,C — Reading College of Technology, King's Road, Reading RG1 4HJ

REDHILL — C — Redhill Technical College, Redstone Hill, Redhill RH1 4AW

REDRUTH — MD,C — Cornwall Technical College, Redruth TR15 3RD

ROCHDALE — C — Rochdale Technical College, St Mary's Gate, Rochdale OL12 6RY

ROTHERHAM — C — Rotherham College of Technology, Howard Street, Rotherham S65 1JJ

ST HELENS — C — St Helens College of Technology, St Helens WA10 1PZ

ST LEONARDS-ON-SEA — See Hastings

SALFORD — MD,C — Salford College of Technology, Frederick Road, Salford M6 6PU

SALISBURY — MD,C — Salisbury College of Technology, Southampton Road, Salisbury SP1 2LW

SCARBOROUGH — MD,C — Scarborough Technical College, Lady Edith's Drive, Scalby Road, Scarborough YO12 5RN

SCUNTHORPE — C — North Lindsey College of Technology, Kingsway, Scunthorpe DN17 1AJ

SHEFFIELD — MD,C — Granville College, Granville Road, Sheffield S2 2RL

SHEFFIELD — D,MHD — Sheffield City Polytechnic, Pond Street, Sheffield S1 1WB

SHREWSBURY — MD,C — Shrewsbury Technical College, Radbrook Road, Shrewsbury SY3 9BL

SKIPTON — C — Craven College of Adult Education, High Street, Skipton BD23 6SD

SLOUGH — MHD,MD,C — Slough College of Higher Education, Wellington Street, Slough SL1 1YG

SOLIHULL — C — Solihull College of Technology, Blossomfield Road, Solihull B91 1SB

SOUTH SHIELDS — C — South Shields Marine and Technical College, St George's Avenue, South Shields NE34 6ET

SOUTHAMPTON — MD,C — Southampton Technical College, St Mary Street, Southampton SO9 4WX

SOUTHEND — MD,C — Southend College of Technology, Carnarvon Road, Southend-on-Sea SS2 6LS

SOUTHPORT — C — Southport College of Art, Mornington Road, Southport PR9 0TS

STAFFORD — MHD,MD,C — Stafford College of Further Education, Earl Street, Stafford ST16 2QR

STAMFORD — C — Stamford College for Further Education, Drift Road, Stamford PE9 1XA

STOKE-ON-TRENT — MD,C — Stoke-on-Trent Cauldon College of Further Education, Stoke Road, Shelton, Stoke-on-Trent ST4 2DG

STRATFORD-UPON-AVON — MD,C — South Warwickshire College of Further Education, The Willows North, Stratford-upon-Avon CV37 9QR

SUNDERLAND — C — Monkwearmouth College of Further Education, Swan Street, Sunderland SR1 1EP

SUTTON COLDFIELD — C — Sutton Coldfield College of Further Education, Lichfield Road, Sutton Coldfield B74 2NW

SWINDON — C — The College, Regent Circus, Swindon SN1 1PT

TAMWORTH — C — Tamworth College of Further Education, Croft Street, Upper Gungate, Tamworth B79 8AE

TAUNTON — MD,C — Somerset College of Arts and Technology, Wellington Road, Taunton TA1 5AX

TONBRIDGE — C — West Kent College of Further Education, Brook Street, Tonbridge TN9 2PW

TORQUAY — MHD,MD,C — South Devon Technical College, Newton Road, Torquay TQ2 5BY

WAKEFIELD — C — Wakefield College of Technology and Arts, Margaret Street, Wakefield WF1 2DH

WALLSEND — C — North Tyneside College of Further Education, Embleton Avenue, Wallsend NE28 9NL

WALSALL — C — Walsall College of Technology, St Paul's Street, Walsall WS1 1XN

WARE — C — Ware College, Scotts Road, Ware SG12 9JF

WATFORD — MD,C — Cassio College, Langley Road, Watford WD1 3RH

WEDNESBURY — C — West Bromwich College of Commerce and Technology, Woden Road South, Wednesbury WS10 0PE

WESTON-SUPER-MARE — MD,C — Weston-super-Mare Technical College, Knightstone Road, Weston-super-Mare BS23 2AL

WEYBRIDGE — MD,C — Brooklands Technical College, Heath Road, Weybridge KT13 8TT

WEYMOUTH — MD,C — South Dorset Technical College, Newstead Road, Weymouth DT4 0DX

WIDNES — C — Halton College of Further Education, Kingsway, Widnes WA8 7QQ

WIRRAL — C — Carlett Park College of Technology, Eastham, Wirral L62 0AY

WISBECH — C — Isle of Ely College of Further Education and Horticulture, Ramnoth Road, Wisbech PE13 2JE

WOLVERHAMPTON — C — Bilston College of Further Education, Westfield Road, Bilston, Wolverhampton WV14 6ER

WORCESTER — MD,C — Worcester Technical College, Deansway, Worcester WR1 2JF

WORKINGTON — MD,C — West Cumbria College, Park Lane, Workington CA14 2RW

WORKSOP — C — North Nottinghamshire College of Further Education, Carlton Road, Worksop S81 7HP

WORTHING — C — Worthing College of Technology, Broadwater Road, Worthing BN14 8HJ

YORK — C — York College of Arts and Technology, Dringhouses, York YO2 1UA

**Locations of Colleges by Their Local Authority Area
— England**

Key: LOCAL AUTHORITY AREA — Location(s) of College(s)

Greater London
Includes: ILEA and London Boroughs of Brent, Croydon, Ealing, Enfield, Hounslow, Merton, Newham, Redbridge, Sutton and Waltham Forest. (Colleges in this area are to be found under *London.*)

Metropolitan Districts

Greater Manchester
BOLTON — Bolton
BURY — Bury
MANCHESTER — Manchester
OLDHAM — Oldham
ROCHDALE — Rochdale
SALFORD — Salford
STOCKPORT — Stockport
TAMESIDE — Ashton-under-Lyne
TRAFFORD — Altrincham
WIGAN — Leigh

Tyne and Wear
NEWCASTLE UPON TYNE —
  Newcastle upon Tyne
NORTH TYNESIDE — Wallsend
SOUTH TYNESIDE — South Shields
SUNDERLAND — Sunderland

West Yorkshire
BRADFORD — Bradford
CALDERDALE — Halifax
KIRKLEES — Dewsbury,
  Huddersfield
LEEDS — Leeds
WAKEFIELD — Wakefield

Merseyside
LIVERPOOL — Liverpool
ST HELENS — St Helens
SEFTON — Southport
WIRRAL — Wirral, Birkenhead

South Yorkshire
DONCASTER — Doncaster
ROTHERHAM — Rotherham
SHEFFIELD — Sheffield

West Midlands
BIRMINGHAM — Birmingham,
  Sutton Coldfield
COVENTRY — Coventry
DUDLEY — Halesowen
SANDWELL — Wednesbury
SOLIHULL — Solihull
WALSALL — Walsall
WOLVERHAMPTON —
  Wolverhampton

Non-Metropolitan Counties
AVON — Bath, Bristol, Weston-super-Mare
BEDFORDSHIRE — Bedford, Luton
BERKSHIRE — Bracknell, Newbury, Reading, Slough
BUCKINGHAMSHIRE — Aylesbury, Bletchley, High Wycombe
CAMBRIDGESHIRE — Cambridge, Peterborough, Wisbech
CHESHIRE — Crewe, Macclesfield, Northwich, Widnes
CLEVELAND — Middlesbrough
CORNWALL — Redruth

CUMBRIA — Carlisle, Kendal, Workington
DERBYSHIRE — Buxton, Chesterfield, Derby
DEVON — Barnstaple, Exeter, Plymouth, Torquay
DORSET — Bournemouth, Poole, Weymouth
DURHAM — Consett, Darlington, Durham
EAST SUSSEX — Brighton, Eastbourne, Hastings, St Leonards-on-Sea
ESSEX — Braintree, Chelmsford, Colchester, Grays, Harlow, Loughton, Southend
GLOUCESTERSHIRE — Cheltenham, Cinderford
HAMPSHIRE — Andover, Basingstoke, Eastleigh, Fareham, Farnborough, Havant, Portsmouth, Southampton
HEREFORD AND WORCESTER — Hereford, Malvern, Worcester
HERTFORDSHIRE — Broxbourne, Letchworth, Ware, Watford
HUMBERSIDE — Grimsby, Hull, Scunthorpe
ISLE OF WIGHT — Newport
KENT — Broadstairs, Canterbury, Dartford, Folkestone, Maidstone, Tonbridge
LANCASHIRE — Accrington, Blackburn, Blackpool, Lancaster, Nelson, Preston
LEICESTERSHIRE — Coalville, Leicester, Loughborough
LINCOLNSHIRE — Boston, Gainsborough, Grantham, Lincoln, Stamford
NORFOLK — Great Yarmouth, King's Lynn, Norwich
NORTH YORKSHIRE — Harrogate, Scarborough, Skipton, York
NORTHAMPTONSHIRE — Corby, Northampton
NORTHUMBERLAND — Ashington
NOTTINGHAMSHIRE — Mansfield, Nottingham, Worksop
OXFORDSHIRE — Abingdon, Banbury, Oxford
SALOP — Shrewsbury
SOMERSET — Taunton
STAFFORDSHIRE — Burton upon Trent, Stafford, Stoke-on-Trent, Tamworth
SUFFOLK — Ipswich
SURREY — Guildford, Redhill, Weybridge
SUSSEX — See East Sussex, West Sussex
WARWICKSHIRE — Nuneaton, Stratford-upon-Avon
WEST SUSSEX — Chichester, Crawley, Worthing
WILTSHIRE — Chippenham, Salisbury, Swindon

Colleges in Wales
ABERDARE — C — Aberdare College of Further Education, Cwmdare Hill, Aberdare CF44 8ST
BARRY — C — Barry College of Further Education, Colcot Road, Barry CF6 8JY
BRECON — C — Coleg Howell Harris (Brecon College of Further Education), Penlan, Brecon LD3 9SR
BRIDGEND — C — Bridgend College of Technology, Cowbridge Road, Bridgend CF31 3DF
CARDIFF — MHD,MD,C — South Glamorgan Institute of Higher Education, Colchester Avenue, Cardiff CF3 7XR

CARDIFF — D — School of Home Economics, University College Cardiff, Llantrisant Road, Llandaff, Cardiff CF5 2YT

CARDIGAN — C — Cardigan College of Further Education, Cardigan SA43 1AB

CARMARTHEN — C — Carmarthen Technical and Agricultural College, Pibwrlwyd, Carmarthen SA31 2NH

COLWYN BAY — MHD,MD,C — Llandrillo Technical College, Llandudno Road, Colwyn Bay LL28 4HZ

CROSSKEYS — C — Crosskeys College of Further Education, Crosskeys NP1 7ZA

DEESIDE — C — North East Wales Institute of Higher Education, Kelsterton College, Connah's Quay, Deeside CH5 4BB

DOLGELLAU — C — Coleg Meirionnydd, Barmouth Road, Dolgellau LL40 2YF

EBBW VALE — C — North Gwent College of Further Education, Ebbw Vale NP3 6LE

HAVERFORDWEST — MD,C — Pembrokeshire Technical College, College Campus, Haverfordwest SA61 1TG

HENGOED — C — Ystrad Mynach College of Further Education, Twyn Road, Ystrad Mynach, Hengoed CF8 7XR

MERTHYR TYDFIL — C — Merthyr Tydfil Technical College, Ynsfach, Merthyr Tydfil CF48 1AR

NEATH — C — Neath Technical College, Dwryfelin Road, Neath SA10 7RF

NEWPORT — MD,C — South Gwent College of Further Education, Nash Road, Newport NP6 2BR

NEWTOWN — C — Montgomery College of Further Education, New Road, Newtown SY16 1BE

RHYDYFELIN — C — Pontypridd Technical College, Yns Terrace, Rhydyfelin CF37 5RN

SWANSEA — C — Gorseinon College of Further Education, Belgrage Road, Gorseinon, Swansea SA4 2RD

SWANSEA — C — Swansea College of Further Education, Tycoch, Swansea SA2 9EB

TONYPANDY — C — Rhondda College of Further Education, Llwnpia, Tonypandy CF40 2TQ

WREXHAM — C — North East Wales Institute of Higher Education, Cartrefle College, Cefn Road, Wrexham LL13 9NL

Location of Colleges by Their Local Education Authority — Wales

CLWYD — Colwyn Bay, Deeside, Wrexham

DYFED — Cardigan, Carmarthen, Haverfordwest

GWENT — Crosskeys, Ebbw Vale, Newport

GWYNEDD — Dolgellau

MID GLAMORGAN — Aberdare, Bridgend, Hengoed, Merthyr Tydfil, Rhydyfelin, Tonypandy

POWYS — Brecon, Newtown
SOUTH GLAMORGAN — Barry, Cardiff
WEST GLAMORGAN — Neath, Swansea

Colleges in Scotland

ABERDEEN — MD,C — Aberdeen Technical College, Gallowgate, Aberdeen AB9 1DN

ABERDEEN — MHD — Robert Gordon's Institute of Technology, Kepplestone Premises, Queen's Road, Aberdeen AB9 2PG

ALLOA — C — Clackmannan College of Further Education, Branshill Road, Alloa FK10 3BT

AYR — MD,C — Ayr Technical College, Dam Park, Ayr KA8 0EU

BATHGATE — C — West Lothian College of Further Education, Marjoribanks Street, Bathgate, West Lothian EH48 1QJ

CLYDEBANK — MD,C — Clydebank Technical College, Kilbowie Road, Clydebank G81 2AA

CUPAR — C — Elmwood Agricultural and Technical College, Carslogie Road, Cupar KY15 4JB

DALKEITH — C — Esk Valley College, Newbattle Road, Dalkeith, Midlothian EH22 3AE

DUMFRIES — MD,C — Dumfries and Galloway College of Technology, Heathhall, Dumfries DG1 3QZ

DUNDEE — MHD — Duncan of Jordanstone College of Art, Perth Road, Dundee DD1 4HT

DUNDEE — MD,C — Kingsway Technical College, Old Glamis Road, Dundee DD3 8LE

DUNFERMLINE — C — Lauder Technical College, Halbeath, Dunfermline KY11 5DY

EDINBURGH — D,MHD — Napier College of Commerce and Technology, Colinton Road, Edinburgh EH10 5DT

EDINBURGH — MHD — Queen Margaret College, 36 Clerwood Terrace, Edinburgh EH12 8TS

EDINBURGH — MD,C — Telford College of Further Education, Crewe Toll, Edinburgh EH4 2NZ

ELGIN — MD,C — Moray College of Further Education, Hay Street, Elgin IV30 2NN

FALKIRK — MD,C — Falkirk College of Technology, Grangemouth Road, Falkirk FK2 9AD

GLASGOW — C — Cumbernauld Technical College, Town Centre, Cumbernauld, Glasgow G67 1HU

GLASGOW — MHD,MD,C — Glasgow College of Food Technology, 230 Cathedral Street, Glasgow G1 2TG

GLASGOW — MHD,MD — The Queen's College Glasgow, 1 Park Drive, Glasgow G3 6LP

GLASGOW — D — University of Strathclyde, Scottish Hotel School, Ross Hall, Crookston Road, Glasgow G52 3NQ

GLENROTHES — C — Glenrothes and Buckhaven Technical College, Stenton Road, Glenrothes KY6 2RA

GREENOCK — C —James Watt College, Finnart Street, Greenock, Renfrewshire PA16 8HF

HAWICK — C — Henderson Technical College, Commercial Road, Hawick TD9 7AW

INVERNESS — MD,C — Inverness Technical College, Langman Road, Inverness IV1 1SA

KIRKCALDY — MD,C — Kirkcaldy Technical College, St Brycedale Avenue, Kirkcaldy KY1 1EX

KIRKWALL — C — Kirkwall Grammar School Further Education Centre, Kirkwall, Orkney

LERWICK — C — Anderson High School Further Education Department, Twageos, Lerwick, Shetland ZE1 0BA

MOTHERWELL — MD,C — Motherwell Technical College, Dalzell Drive, Motherwell ML1 2DD

PAISLEY — C — Reid Kerr College, Renfrew Road, Paisley, Renfrewshire PA3 4DR

PERTH — MD,C — Perth Technical College, Brahan Estate, Crieff Road, Perth PH1 2NX

PLOCKTON — C — Duncraig Castle College, Plockton, Ross-shire IV52 8UA

STORNOWAY — C — Lews Castle College, Stornoway, Isle of Lewis PA86 0XR

Location of Colleges by their Local Education Authority — Scotland

BORDERS — Hawick

CENTRAL — Alloa, Falkirk

DUMFRIES AND GALLOWAY — Dumfries

FIFE — Cupar, Dunfermline, Glenrothes, Kirkcaldy

GRAMPIAN — Aberdeen, Elgin

HIGHLAND — Inverness, Plockton

LOTHIAN — Bathgate, Dalkeith, Edinburgh

STRATHCLYDE — Ayr, Clydebank, Glasgow, Greenock, Motherwell, Paisley

TAYSIDE — Dundee, Perth

Islands

ORKNEY — Kirkwall

SHETLAND — Lerwick

WESTERN ISLES — Stornoway

Colleges in Northern Ireland

ANTRIM — C — Antrim Technical College, Antrim BT41 4AL

ARMAGH — C — Armagh Technical College, Lonsdale Street, Armagh BT61 7HN

BALLYMENA — C — Ballymena Technical College, Trostan Avenue, Ballymena, Co Antrim BT43 7BN

BANGOR — C — North Down Technical College, Castle Park Road, Bangor

BELFAST — MHD,MD,C — The College of Business Studies, Brunswick Street, Belfast BT2 7GX

DOWNPATRICK — C — Downpatrick Technical College, Market Street, Downpatrick, Co Down

DUNGANNON — C — Dungannon Technical College, Circular Road, Dungannon, Co Tyrone BT71 6BQ

ENNISKILLEN — C — Fermanagh College of Further Education, Fairview Avenue, Enniskillen, Co Fermanagh

LARNE — C — Larne Technical College, 32-34 Pound Street, Larne, Co Antrim BT40 1SQ

LIMAVADY — C — Limavady Technical College, Limavady, Co Londonderry BT49 0EX

LISBURN — C — Lisburn Technical College, Lisburn, Co Antrim

LURGAN — C — Lurgan Technical College, Kitchen Hill, Lurgan, Co Armagh BT66 6AZ

MAGHERAFELT — C — Magherafelt Technical College, Moneymore Road, Magherafelt, Co Londonderry BT32 6AE

NEWRY — C — Newry Catering College, Newry, Co Down BT35 8DN

NEWTOWNABBEY — D,MHD — Ulster Polytechnic, Shore Road, Newtownabbey, Co Antrim BT37 0QB

OMAGH — C — Omagh Technical College, Omagh, Co Tyrone BT79 7AH

PORTRUSH — MD,C — Portrush Hotel and Catering College, Ballywillan Road, Portrush, Co Antrim BT56 8EB

STRABANE — C — Strabane Technical College, Derry Road, Strabane, Co Tyrone BT82 8DX

Location of Colleges in Northern Ireland by
Education and Library Board

BELFAST — Belfast

NORTH EASTERN — Antrim, Ballymena, Larne, Magherafelt, Newtownabbey, Portrush

SOUTH EASTERN — Bangor, Downpatrick, Lisburn

SOUTHERN AREA — Armagh, Dungannon, Lurgan, Newry

WESTERN AREA — Enniskillen, Limavady, Omagh, Strabane

Colleges in the Channel Islands

GUERNSEY — C — College of Further Education, Route des Coutanchez, St Peter Port, Guernsey

JERSEY — MD,C — Highlands College, St Saviour, Jersey

College in the Isle of Man

DOUGLAS — C — Isle of Man College of Further Education, Homefield Road, Douglas, Isle of Man

Local Education Authorities: Chief Education Officers

England

AVON — Education Department, PO Box 57, Avon House North, St James Barton, Bristol BS99 7EB (Tel 0272 290777)

BARKING — Education Offices, Town Hall, Barking IG11 7LU (Tel 01-594 3880)

BARNET — Education Offices, Town Hall, Friern Barnet, London N11 3DL (Tel 01-368 1255)

BARNSLEY — District Education Offices, 50 Huddersfield Road, Barnsley S75 1DP (Tel 0226 87621)

BEDFORDSHIRE — Education Offices, County Hall, Cauldwell Street, Bedford MK42 9AP (Tel 0234 63222)

BERKSHIRE — Kennet House, 80-82 Kings Road, Reading RG1 3BL (Tel 0734 55981)

BEXLEY — Education Offices, Town Hall, Crayford, Kent DA1 4EN (Tel 01-303 7777)

BIRMINGHAM — Education Office, Margaret Street, Birmingham B3 3BU (Tel 021-235 9944)

BOLTON — Education Offices, PO Box 53, Paderborn House, Civic Centre, Bolton BL1 1JW (Tel 0204 22311)

BRADFORD — District Education Offices, Provincial House, Tyrrel Street, Bradford BD1 1NP (Tel 0274 29577)

BRENT — Education Offices, Chesterfield House, 9 Park Lane, Wembley HA9 7RW (Tel 01-903 1400)

BROMLEY — Education Offices, Sunnymead, Bromley Lane, Chislehurst BR7 6LH (Tel 01-467 5561)

BUCKINGHAMSHIRE — Education Offices, County Hall, Aylesbury HP20 1UZ (Tel 0296 5000)

BURY — Athenaeum House, Market Street, Bury BL9 0BN (Tel 061 761 5121)

CALDERDALE — District Education Offices, Alexandra Buildings, King Edward Street, Halifax HX1 1EB (Tel 0422 57133)

CAMBRIDGESHIRE — Shire Hall, Castle Hill, Cambridge CB3 0AP (Tel 0223 58811)

CHESHIRE — County Hall, Chester CH1 1SQ (Tel 0244 602424)

CLEVELAND — Woodlands Road, Middlesbrough TS1 3BN (Tel 0642 248155)

CORNWALL — County Hall, Truro TR1 3BA (Tel 0872 4282)

COVENTRY — Council Offices, Earl Street, Coventry CV1 5RS (Tel 0203 25555)

CROYDON — Education Offices, Taberner House, Park Lane, Croydon CR9 1TP (Tel 01-686 4433)

CUMBRIA — Education Offices, 5 Portland Square, Carlisle CA1 1PU (Tel 0228 32161)

DERBYSHIRE — Education Offices, County Offices, Matlock DE4 3AG (Tel 0629 3411)

DEVON — Education Department, County Hall, Exeter EX2 4QG (Tel 0392 77977)

DONCASTER — District Education Offices, Princegate, Doncaster DN1 3EP (Tel 0302 4041)

DORSET — County Hall, Dorchester DT1 1XJ (Tel 0305 3131)

DUDLEY — Education Offices, 2 St James's Road, Dudley DY1 3JQ (Tel 0384 214311)

DURHAM — County Hall, Durham DH1 5UJ (Tel 0385 64411)

EALING — Education Offices, Hadley House, 79-81 Uxbridge Road, Ealing, London W5 5SU (Tel 01-579 2424)

ENFIELD — Education Department, PO Box 56, Civic Centre, Enfield EN1 3XQ (Tel 01-366 6565)

ESSEX — Education Department, PO Box 47, Threadneedle House, Market Road, Chelmsford CM1 1LD (Tel 0245 67222)

GATESHEAD — Education Offices, Prince Consort Road South, Gateshead NE8 4LP (Tel 0632 783031)

GLOUCESTERSHIRE — Shire Hall, Gloucester GL1 2TP (Tel 0452 21444)

HAMPSHIRE — The Castle, Winchester SO23 8UG (Tel 0962 4411)

HARINGEY — Education Offices, Somerset Road, Tottenham, London N17 9EH (Tel 01-808 4500)

HARROW — Education Offices, Civic Centre, Harrow, Middlesex HA1 2UW (Tel 01-863 5611)

HAVERING — Education Offices, Mercury House, Mercury Gardens, Romford RM1 3DR (Tel 70 66999)

HEREFORD AND WORCESTER — County Offices, Castle Street, Worcester WR1 3AG (Tel 0905 23400)

HERTFORDSHIRE — Education Department, County Hall, Hertford SG13 8DF (Tel 32 54242)

HILLINGDON — Education Department, Civic Centre, Uxbridge, Middlesex UB8 1UW (Tel 01-895 0111)

HOUNSLOW — Education Offices, Civic Centre, Hounslow, Middlesex TW3 4DN (Tel 01-570 7728)

HUMBERSIDE — County Hall, Beverley HU17 9BA (Tel 0482 887131)

INNER LONDON — The County Hall, Westminster Bridge, London SE1 7PB (Tel 01-633 5000)

ISLE OF WIGHT — County Hall, Newport, Isle of Wight PO30 1UD (Tel 098 381 4031)

ISLES OF SCILLY — Town Hall, St Mary's, Isles of Scilly TR21 0LW (Tel 072 04 537)

KENT — Education Offices, Springfield, Maidstone ME14 2LJ (Tel 0622 671411)

KINGSTON UPON THAMES (ROYAL) — Education Offices, Tolworth Tower, Surbiton, Surrey KT6 7EE (Tel 01-399 5111)

KIRKLEES — District Education Offices, Oldgate House, Oldgate, Huddersfield HD1 6QW (Tel 0484 37399)

KNOWSLEY — Education Offices, Huyton Hey Road, Huyton, Merseyside L36 5YH (Tel 051-480 5111)

LANCASHIRE — Education Department, PO Box 61, County Hall, Preston PR1 8RJ (Tel 0772 54868)

LEEDS — Department of Education, Great George Street, Leeds LS1 3AE (Tel 0532 463000)

LEICESTER — County Hall, Glenfield, Leicester LE3 8RF (Tel 0533 871313)

LINCOLNSHIRE — County Offices, Lincoln LN1 1YQ (Tel 0522 29931)

LIVERPOOL — Education Offices, 14 Sir Thomas Street, Liverpool L1 6BJ (Tel 051-236 5480)

LONDON — See Inner London

MANCHESTER — Education Offices, Crown Square, Manchester M60 3BB (Tel 061-228 2191)

MERTON — Education Offices, Station House, London Road, Morden, Surrey SM4 5DR (Tel 01-542 8101)

NEWCASTLE UPON TYNE — Education Department, Civic Centre, Barras Bridge, Newcastle upon Tyne NE1 8PU (Tel 0632 28520)

NEWHAM — Education Offices, Broadway, Stratford, London E15 4BH (Tel 01-534 4545)

NORFOLK — County Education Office, County Hall, Norwich NR1 2DL (Tel 0603 611122)

NORTHAMPTONSHIRE — County Education Offices, Northampton House, Northampton NN1 2HX (Tel 0604 34833)

NORTHUMBERLAND — Eldon House, Regent Centre, Newcastle upon Tyne NE3 3HZ (Tel 0632 850181)

NOTTINGHAMSHIRE — County Hall, West Bridgford, Nottingham NG2 7QP (Tel 0602 863366)

OLDHAM — Education Offices, Old Town Hall, Middleton Road, Chadderton, Oldham OL9 6PP (Tel 061-624 0505)

OXFORDSHIRE — Education Offices, Macclesfield House, New Road, Oxford OX1 1NA (Tel 0865 722422)

REDBRIDGE — Education Offices, Lynton House, 255/259 High Road, Ilford IG1 1NN (Tel 01-478 3020)

RICHMOND UPON THAMES — Education Offices, Regal House, London Road, Twickenham, Middlesex TW1 3QB (Tel 01-892 4466)

ROCHDALE — Municipal Offices, Manchester Old Road, Middleton, Manchester M24 4EA (Tel 061-643 6291)

ROTHERHAM — Municipal Offices, Howard Street, Rotherham S60 1QR (Tel 0709 2121)

ST HELENS — Education Department, Century House, Hardshaw Street, St Helens WA10 1RN (Tel 0744 24061)

SALFORD — Education Office, Chapel Street, Salford M3 5LT (Tel 061-832 9751/8)

SALOP — Shirehall, Abbey Foregate, Shrewsbury SY2 6ND (Tel 0743 222100)

SANDWELL — Education Offices, PO Box 41, High Street, West Bromwich B70 8RG (Tel 021-553 6541)

SEFTON — Education Offices, Burlington House, Crosby Road North, Liverpool L22 0LG (Tel 051-928 6677)

SHEFFIELD — District Education Offices, PO Box 67, Leopold Street, Sheffield S1 1RJ (Tel 0742 26341)

SOLIHULL — PO Box 20, Council House, Solihull B91 3QU (Tel 021-705 6789)

SOMERSET — County Hall, Taunton TA1 4DY (Tel 0823 3451)

STAFFORDSHIRE — County Education Offices, Tipping Street, Stafford ST16 2LP (Tel 0785 3121)

STOCKPORT — Education Division, Stopford House, Stockport SK1 3XE (Tel 061-480 4949)

SUFFOLK — Education Department, Grimwade Street, Ipswich IP4 1LJ (Tel 0473 55801)

SUNDERLAND — Town Hall and Civic Centre, Sunderland SR2 7DN (Tel 0783 76161)

SURREY — Education Department, County Hall, Kingston upon Thames KT1 2DJ (Tel 01-546 1050)

SUSSEX (EAST) — Education Department, PO Box No 4, County Hall, Lewes BN7 1SG (Tel 079 16 5400)

SUSSEX (WEST) — County Education Office, County Hall, West Street, Chichester PO19 1RF (Tel 0243 85100)

SUTTON — Education Offices, The Grove, Carshalton, Surrey SM5 3AL (Tel 01-661 5000)

TAMESIDE — Education Department, Town Hall, Dukinfield, Cheshire SK16 4LA (Tel 061-330 8300)

TRAFFORD — Education Department, Town Hall, Sale M33 1ZF (Tel 061-973 2253)

TYNESIDE (NORTH) — Education Offices, The Chase, North Shields NE29 0HW (Tel 089 45 76621)

TYNESIDE (SOUTH) — Education Office, Town Hall, Jarrow NE32 3EL (Tel 0632 891141)

WAKEFIELD — District Education Offices, 8 Bond Street, Wakefield WF1 2QL (Tel 0924 70211)

WALSALL — Civic Centre, Darwall Street, Walsall WS1 1DQ (Tel 0922 21244)

WALTHAM FOREST — Education Offices, Municipal Offices, Leyton High Road, Leyton E10 5QJ (Tel 01-539 3650)

WARWICKSHIRE — 22 Northgate Street, Warwick CV34 4SR (Tel 0926 43431)

WIGAN — Education Offices, Civic Centre, Millgate, Wigan WN1 1YD (Tel 0942 44991)

WILTSHIRE — County Hall, Trowbridge BA14 8JB (Tel 022 14 3641)

WIRRAL — Education Department, Municipal Offices, Cleveland Street, Birkenhead L41 6NH (Tel 051-647 7020)

WOLVERHAMPTON — Education Department, Civic Centre, St Peter's Square, Wolverhampton WV1 1RR (Tel 0902 27811)

YORKSHIRE (NORTH) — Education Offices, County Hall, Northallerton D17 8AE (Tel 0609 3123)

Wales

CLWYD — County Education Offices, Shire Hall, Mold CH7 6ND (Tel 0352 2121)

DYFED — Education Department, Pibwrlwyd, Carmarthen SA31 2NH (Tel 0267 4591)

GLAMORGAN (MID-) — Education Offices, County Hall, Cathays Park, Cardiff CF1 3NF (Tel 0222 28033)

GLAMORGAN (SOUTH) — City Education Department, Municipal Offices, Kingsway, Cardiff CF1 4JG (Tel 0222 31033)

GLAMORGAN (WEST) — Princess House, Princess Way, Swansea SA1 4PD (Tel 0792 42024)

GWENT — Education Department, County Hall, Cwmbran NP4 2XG (Tel 063 33 67711)

GWYNEDD — Education Offices, Castle Street, Caernarfon LL55 1SD (Tel 0286 4121)

POWYS — Education Department, County Hall, Llandrindod Wells LD1 5LE (Tel 0597 3711)

Scotland

BORDERS — Education Department, Regional Headquarters, Newtown St Boswells, Roxburghshire TD6 0SA (Tel 083 52 3301)

CENTRAL — Education Offices, Central Region Offices, Viewforth, Stirling FK8 2ET (Tel 0786 3111)

DUMFRIES AND GALLOWAY — Education Offices, 30 Edinburgh Road, Dumfries DG1 1JQ (Tel 0387 63822)

FIFE — Education Department, Regional Offices, Wemyssfield, Kircaldy, Fife KY1 1XS (Tel 0592 62351)

GRAMPIAN — Department of Education, Woodhill House, Ashgrove Road West, Aberdeen AB9 2LU (Tel 0224 23401)

HIGHLAND — Education Offices, Regional Buildings, Glenurquhart Road, Inverness IV3 5NX (Tel 0463 34121)

ISLE OF LEWIS — Education Offices, Stornoway, Isle of Lewis PA87 2BW (Tel 0851 3992)

LOTHIAN — Education Office, 40 Torphichen Street, Edinburgh EH3 8JJ (Tel 031-229 9292)

ORKNEY — Education Offices, Council Offices, Kirkwall, Orkney KW15 1NY (Tel 0856 3535)

SHETLAND — Education Office, 1 Harbour Street, Lerwick, Shetland ZE1 0LS (Tel 0595 3535)

STRATHCLYDE — Department of Education, 25 Bothwell Street, Glasgow G2 6NR (Tel 041-204 2900)

TAYSIDE — Education Department, Tayside House, Dundee DD1 3RJ (Tel 0382 23281)

Other Useful Addresses

SCOTTISH EDUCATION DEPARTMENT AWARDS BRANCH, Haymarket House, Clifton Terrace, Edinburgh EH12 5DT

SED "DIRECTORY OF DAY COURSES", Room 410, 8 George Street, Edinburgh EH2 2PF (Tel 031-226 3521, ext 7)

Northern Ireland

BELFAST — Education and Library Board, 40 Academy Street, Belfast BT1 2NQ (Tel 0232 29211)

NORTH-EASTERN AREA — Education and Library Board, County Hall, 182 Galgorm Road, Ballymena, Co Antrim BT42 1HN (Tel 0266 3333)

SOUTH-EASTERN AREA — Education and Library Board, 18 Windsor Avenue, Belfast BT9 6EF (Tel 0232 661188)

WESTERN AREA — Education and Library Board, Headquarters Office, 1 Hospital Road, Omagh BT79 0AW (Tel 9662 44931)

Channel Islands

GUERNSEY — Education Department, PO Box No 32, La Couperderie, St Peter Port, Guernsey (Tel 0481 23535)

JERSEY — Education Department, PO Box 142, Highlands Street, St Saviour, Jersey (Tel 0534 71065)

Isle of Man

ISLE OF MAN — Education Department, Government Buildings, Bucks Road, Douglas (Tel 0624 26262)

10

The Agencies

The professional bodies and trade associations that have a visible link with catering education, as well as those that have a direct link with working on the job in different sectors of the industry. Useful addresses.

THROUGHOUT the history of catering education in the UK, various professional bodies and trade associations have played a key role. They have aided the development of training courses in hotel and catering subjects by working with award-making bodies, as well as by becoming examining bodies in their own right.

The role has been a constantly evolving one. With their interest in upholding standards and their commitment to maintaining and enhancing the prestige and standing of the occupation, professional bodies as well as trade associations will always maintain an active interest in catering education. The need for providing examinations has, however, diminished over time. Technical education has become more and more closely integrated for all industries and catering plays an ever more important part in the activities of national award-making bodies.

Agencies actively involved in catering education today include those involved from the start: the Cookery and Food Association, the City and Guilds of London Institute, the British Hotels Restaurants and Caterers Association (formed by the amalgamation in 1972 of the British Hotels and Restaurants Association with the Caterers' Association of Great Britain), Catering and Institutional Management Association (formed by the merger in 1971 of the Institutional Management Association and the Hotel and Catering Institute).

There have been many subsequent additions: the Joint Committees for National Diplomas in Hotel, Catering and Institutional Management, the Hotel and Catering Industry Training Board, the Catering Teachers Association, the various Regional Examining Bodies, the Guild of Sommeliers, the Brewers' Society, the Local Government Training Board, the Wine and Spirit Education Trust, the National Council for Home Economics Education, the Royal Society of Health, the Royal Institute of Public Health and Hygiene.

The national award-making bodies involved include the Council for National Awards, the Technician Education Council, the Scottish Technical Education Council, the National Examinations Board for Supervisory Studies, the Business Education Council and the Scottish Business Education Council.

In addition to the associations that have a visible link with catering education, there are those that also have a direct link with working on the job in the different sectors of the industry. These include the College Caterers' Association, the Association of Domestic Management, The Tourism Society, the Association of

Marine Catering Superintendents, the Industrial Catering Association, the Civic Catering Association, the Caterers Managers' Association of Great Britain and Northern Ireland, the Food and Beverage Managers' Association, the British Association of Hotel Accountants, the Hotel Industry Marketing Group, the British Motels Federation Limited, The British Federation of Hotel, Guest House and Self-catering Associations, and the National Union of Licensed Victuallers.

The work and role of these various associations, federations and award-making bodies are now briefly described.

City and Guilds of London Institute

The involvement of the City and Guilds of London Institute in technical education has been almost as long as the existence of the first schools of cookery.

Prompted by growing public concern at the economic crisis Britain fell into in the mid-1870s Gladstone challenged the leaders of British commerce and industry, represented by the Corporation of London and the members of the City Livery Companies, to do something to reverse the decline. In particular, he put to them that the development of human resources within any economy through education (beyond the level at which the School Boards, Churches and other philanthropic organisations were then capable of providing) would enable both economic and social progress to be made.

The challenge was taken up and after a period of deliberation and negotiation the Institute was formally constituted and by 1879 it was ready to hold its first examinations — taking on from the Society of Arts, as it was then, the administration of sixteen technical subjects. In the same year the South London Technical Art School was set up at Kennington (later to be known as the City and Guilds of London Art School; in 1971 the Institute transferred its responsibility for the School to an independent charitable trust company).

In 1882 the Institute opened its Finsbury Technical College to provide comparable instruction in technical subjects. It was in many ways the prototype of present day technical colleges, but as its example was followed in other places with the gradual availability of funds from local government authorities, the need for the college diminished and it was closed in 1926.

To provide a more advanced education in the industrial application of science or the arts, the Institute established the "Central Institution". Opened in 1893 its name was changed in 1907, for the second time, to the City and Guilds College. It now exists as a constituent college of the Imperial College of Science and Technology in the University of London.

The successful and rapid development of the Institute in the years following its establishment owed much to the royal patronage which was extended to it. In 1900 it was granted a Royal Charter by Queen Victoria. Prince Philip has been President of the Institute since 1951.

City and Guilds Today

The work of the Institute has grown immensely in volume since 1900, when 15 000 entries for its examinations were recorded. The range of provision and the standard of its examinations has also developed. It has responded to a succession of Education Acts, and more recently to the implications of the Industrial Training Act of 1964, and the implementation of the recommendations of the Haslegrave Report.

The Haslegrave Report strongly recommended to Government that the Institute should undertake the servicing of the new Technician and Business Education Councils, and following their establishment in 1973, the Institute acceded to a formal request to this effect. At the same time the Institute undertook to succeed the DES in providing the administration and secretariat for a number of Joint Committees for National Certificates and Diplomas, and to operate the schemes for these awards until such time as the new Councils make alternative provision.

A similar programme of eventual discontinuation will apply to the City and Guilds schemes for Technician Certificates in the UK (they will however continue to be available overseas). The Institute will also continue to provide schemes for craft courses and Certificates and will make provision for other needs for technical education and the setting and verification of standards which cannot be met by the formal structures of TEC or BEC courses and awards.

For example, to assist in the evaluation and validation of standards of training and practical competence, the Institute has set up a Skills Testing Service which is available to industry, training centres and Industrial Training Boards requiring an impartial skills measurement facility.

Awards Policy

In September 1978 the Institute issued a Policy Statement on its Certificates, Diplomas and Other Awards. It stated that the main aims of Institute policy "are to meet the needs for:
  (a)   a progressive pattern of awards matched to career stages and related to other forms and levels of vocational preparation;
  (b)   combined certification to emphasise the essential unity of educational and industrial achievement;
  (c)   senior awards for those who attain positions of industrial, educational and social responsibility via schemes which the Institute has devised, sponsored or recognised."

The senior awards of the Institute include:
  *Licentiateship of the City and Guilds of London Institute (designatory letters LCG), conferred by the Institute on those for whom a grade of membership is an appropriate form of recognition of their achievements in education, training and employment. It corresponds in status to that of the Master Craftsman in Europe and provides a route from specific vocational preparation, via a career extension award (see Chapter 5), to wider opportunities and responsibilities in the industry. The way is already open for craftworkers in the hotel and catering industry to obtain Licentiateship. Advanced Craft level is provided in 706/3 Advanced Cookery for the Catering Industry and beyond that there is, at Career Extension level, a

Catering option in scheme 771 Organisational Studies. Other non-City and Guilds of London Institute awards are being assessed by the Institute's Advisory Committee to ascertain if they satisfy the career extension requirements of Licentiateship.

*City and Guilds of London Institute Insignia Award in Technology (designatory letters CGIA), for those who have attained or wish to progress to positions of authority and responsibility in industry, education or society. Candidates for the Insignia Award must register, present a thesis and attend an interview, as well as satisfy various criteria regarding technical training, practical experience and ability.

*The Prince Philip Medal, awarded not more than once a year in recognition of outstanding promise or achievement in the promotion, theory or practice of science or technology.

These awards are the Institute's accolades for those who follow the progressive pattern of awards and make available their expertise in key positions in industry.

Advisory Structure

For advice on the development and application of its education policy, the Institute relies on two senior committees: Policy Committee for Education and Training and the Examinations Committee.

In addition for each industry or subject an advisory committee is set up which is responsible for the courses in that subject or for that industry. Each Advisory Committee is responsible for keeping the structure of the scheme and the detailed syllabuses under constant review, ensuring that the examinations remain relevant to current industrial and educational practice, maintaining the closest possible contacts with colleges providing courses, recommending examiners for appointment by the Institute, moderating (through a confidential sub-committee) the question papers drafted year by year, and generally advising the Institute on all matters connected with the scheme.

The Catering and Food Advisory Committee has a membership of about 45, and normally meets once a year.

The Advisory Committees establish Examination Subject Committees for each examination scheme or related groups (for example Catering, Cooking, Food Service, Housekeeping and Reception). These also meet annually and are responsible for overseeing the examinations and examination standards, for keeping under review the relevance of the scheme in meeting industrial requirements and for drawing the Advisory Committee's attention to the need for syllabus revision and development. Membership comprises educational and industrial members (total about 15).

The present Advisory Committee structure dates back to 1976, when 15 such Committees were established in place of 110 Joint Advisory Committees (e.g. the Joint Advisory Committee for Hotel Keeping and Catering). This change meant that it would be possible for these Committees to meet once a year, instead of every three years as before.

The Cookery and Food Association

The connections between Herman Senn — founder of The Cookery and Food Association in 1885 — and the National Training School of Cookery and the Westminster Technical Institute were mentioned in Chapter 4. The Cookery and Food Association (CFA) is the oldest culinary association in the UK and has played a leading part throughout the years in developing craft training. Cookery examinations were devised and conducted by the Association soon after its establishment until 1968 when, to avoid duplication of effort, the CFA Craft and Domestic Cookery Examinations were merged with those of the City and Guilds of London Institute.

One of the Association's earliest activities was the promotion of culinary exhibitions and competitions. Until 1936 it organised the Salon Culinaire Internationale de Londres at which the entries compared favourably with the best exhibition work in Europe. Following the launch in 1935 of the International Hotel and Catering Exhibition — which has become known as Hotelympia — and the realisation that the CFA was carrying too great a burden running the Salon Culinaire single handed, the two events have merged. At the biennial Hotelympia Exhibitions, the CFA now collaborates with other organisations in operating the Salon Culinaire.

The CFA has enjoyed Royal patronage since its inception including that of HM Queen Alexandra, HM Queen Mary and the present Patron, HM Queen Elizabeth the Queen Mother. The Presidency of the Association is held, by tradition, by the Master of the Royal Household (currently Vice-Admiral Sir Peter Ashmore KCB MVO DSC).

Established with the purpose of promoting the science and art of cookery, the principal objects of the Association include: to assist the education of chefs and others in and connected with the catering industry or cookery: to assist in the training of young people in cookery and to honour those who distinguish themselves in the advancement of cookery.

Applications for membership are closely scrutinised by the Committee of Management to ensure that applicants possess the necessary background and/or qualifications. The grades of membership are:

Affiliate: open to those deeply interested in the art of science of cookery, but who are not professional caterers or connected with the catering industry (no voting rights, or use of designatory letters);

Associate (ACFA): for trainees or students in catering and allied subjects;

Member (MCFA): persons directly concerned or engaged in cookery, catering management or allied subjects, or in teaching any of these subjects;

Fellow (FCFA): for suitably qualified persons of standing who have been proposed and seconded by two Fellows of the Association;

Governor (GCFA): usually elected from Fellows who have rendered long and/or outstanding service to the Association. This distinction is sparingly bestowed.

In 1965 a division was formed within the CFA — the *Craft Guild of Chefs* — with the support of the Worshipful Company of Cooks of London and the Hotel and Catering Institute. The principal aims of the Guild are: to ensure that the chef takes his rightful place in the catering industry both as a craftsman and as a professional executive, to encourage its members to attain higher standards in craftsmanship and to encourage them to exercise their technical ability for the betterment of public relations both within and outside the industry.

The Junior Membership grade of the Guild is open to students and trainees who have satisfactorily completed one year's study of the City and Guilds 706/1 course or the equivalent. It is a probationary grade until satisfactory completion of the 706/2, or equivalent, with twelve months' practical catering experience when Junior Members are eligible for upgrading to Craftsman.

Craftsman II is the lower grade of full membership appropriate for young trainee apprentices and commis chefs who have completed their basic training and who are actively engaged in furthering their experience by working in well-established kitchens of good repute.

Craftsman I grade is awarded to individuals who have attained a satisfactory standard in all sections of a first-class kitchen for a period of at least four to five years.

Members of the Craft Guild are given a special membership book containing their photograph and particulars of their training and career.

The official journal of the Cookery and Food Association, launched in 1897, is called *Food & Cookery Review;* it is published every two months.

British Hotels Restaurants and Caterers Association

The antecedents of the British Hotels Restaurants and Caterers Association (BHRCA) have been mentioned at several points in the historical background of catering education.

The National Hotel-Keepers' Association was formed in 1907, following a campaign for a national body to represent the industry. Later in the year it was granted a Board of Trade certificate and became the Incorporated Hotel-Keepers Association. Three years later it merged with the Incorporated Association of Hotels and Restaurants — to form the Incorporated Hotels and Restaurants Association. In 1926 its name was changed to the Hotels and Restaurants Association of Great Britain, and in 1948 it acquired the members of the liquidated Residential Hotel Association and the British Hotels and Restaurants Association was formed.

The Caterers' Association of Great Britain — which merged with the BHRA in 1972 — has a less complex history. The first general meeting of its antecedent the Incorporated Association of Purveyors of Light Refreshments was held in December 1917 under the chairmanship of Jack Joseph of Lyons.

The BHRCA embraces every type of hotel, restaurant and catering business in its membership. At the end of 1978 the Association represented over 9300 establishments by way of direct membership and about 6500 establishments through the affiliation of local associations to the BHRCA. The Association's activities include:
- representing the views of industry to government on proposed new legislation affecting the industry, and itself lobbying government for changes in legislation;

— providing advice to members on a wide range of matters including VAT, equal pay, fire precautions, licensing laws, all legislation affecting the industry;

— through its monthly periodical *British Hotelier & Restaurateur* reporting on the Association's activities, detailing new and pending legislation, providing practical business advice, information on products and services, as well as articles of interest to its members);

— through its employment department placing trained hotel personnel, and arranging student exchanges; during the year ended April 1979 some 637 students from Britain and overseas countries were successfully placed;

— offering advice on all aspects of recruitment and training of staff, where to advertise, selection procedures, drawing up of training programmes, and courses available to employers as well as employees;

— publication of the annual *BHRCA Guide to British Hotels and Restaurants*, the official guidebook of the Association (entries in the Guide are restricted to members;

— the provision of a buyer's guide, of notices relating to hygiene, customers' property and licensing; of various staff documents, guides to legislation and stationery.

The broad lines of the Association's policy are formulated by the *National Council*. There are nine divisional committees for which elections are on a county basis: East Midlands, The Heart of England, London, Northern, Scottish, Southern, South Eastern, South Western and Wales. Any direct member of the Association can be nominated for election as a county representative, and representatives of local associations affiliated to the BHRCA are co-opted on to these committees.

The divisional committees meet five or six times a year and through their chairmen report to the Board of Management, and thus to the National Council.

There are also a number of special purpose committees. In 1979 these included the three advisory panels: Hotels, Restaurants and Catering, and Industrial Catering; as well as the Motorway Service Area Operators Committee, the Personnel and Training Committee, the Technical Education Sub-Committee and the Equipment and Supplies Committee.

Hotel, Catering and Institutional Management Association

The Hotel, Catering and Institutional Management Association (HCIMA) was formed in November 1971 as the result of a merger between the Hotel and Catering Institute and the Institutional Management Association. The history of these two professional bodies and their role in the development of catering education has been decribed in earlier chapters.

The total membership of the HCIMA at the end of November 1979 was 20 469 drawn from a comprehensive range of sectors of the industry — hotels, restaurants, industrial, educational and welfare services and including the provision of food, liquor and accommodation facilities. In the year of the merger, membership of the IMA and HCI was as follows:

	Institutional Management Association	Hotel and Catering Institute
Fellows	286	1105
Members	2940	6272
Associates	1558*	47
Affiliates	16	
Graduates		839*
Students	1301	5699

*(Note: the IMA Associate grade was similar to the HCI's graduate grade)

The three main priorities of the Hotel, Catering and Institutional Management Association are:
*to win greater recognition for professional managers in every part of the industry
*to set and maintain standards
*to help managers and potential managers develop and maintain their knowledge and abilities.
The HCIMA works towards achieving its objectives through representation and liaison with policy-making organisations and maintains a wide range of publications including *Hospitality* (monthly) and the *Mid-Month News*. The Association has twenty-six branches of which three are in Scotland, two in Wales and one in Northern Ireland.

Regular events organised for the members at regional level by the branches include social events as well as seminars, short courses and discussions on topical matters with guest speakers. At national level in addition to the national conference, which is to become a biennial event (the first HCIMA national conference was held in 1972 at King's College, Cambridge, the second in 1979 at the Norbreck Castle Hotel in Blackpool, and the third is being planned for 1981), seminars and study days are held regularly.

The Association provides a well stocked reference library for members and a wide ranging information service including advice on careers and development, on educational courses, conditions of employment, salaries, law, research, education and technical advice. Specific activities in this field have included the publication of the *Corpus of Knowledge* in 1977. The Corpus outlines the scope and range of knowledge that a competent practitioner should have. It designates areas of knowledge and skill that are relevant to professionals in the major sectors of the industry.

A new Research Register was published in January 1979, covering nearly 400 projects. The Register provides information on the title of the research, name of researcher, location of researcher, starting and completion dates, a short synopsis and contact address.

The first Salary Survey was published in July 1977 — a comprehensive examination of management jobs, salaries and conditions of employment in all sectors of the industry. The second Salary Survey was published in early 1979, the Research Register has been updated in March 1980, and the first updating of the *Corpus of Knowledge* will be completed in 1980.

From 1978 a combined Year Book and Diary has been published with information on courses and colleges, books, legal aspects, energy management, consultants to the industry, a comprehensive buyer's guide, and a list of the names and addresses of HCIMA members (Fellows, Members, Associates and Licentiates).

Aims of the HCIMA

The aims of the HCIMA reflect a combination of the former aims and orientations of the HCI and IMA. The predominant emphasis on education remains, with concern for professional standards, status and employment.

With regard to the two latter aims the Memorandum of Association states:

"To exercise supervision over and protect the interests of the members of the Association, and to secure for them such standing as may assist them in the conduct of their business or discharge of their duties, to encourage just and honourable practice in the conduct of business and to discourage malpractice" *and*

"To promote the general advancement of education, technical and otherwise, amongst members of and those connected with, and the educational and professional interest of, the Accommodation and Catering Industries . . . and to promote the appointment of qualified persons to posts of responsibility in these industries."

Of the six section committees established after the merger: National Association of School Meals Organisers (NASMO), Hotels and Restaurants, Educational Establishments, Hospitals, Teaching and Employee Food Services, only the first, NASMO, remains. NASMO has considerable autonomy and a separate identity from the Association, it elects a national chairman and committee of officers and has held its own conferences, national exhibitions and study courses.

In 1977 the HCIMA Council approved a Code of Conduct and related disciplinary procedures. The introduction of the Code gave recognition to the importance of the professional's responsibility to the consumer, his employer and himself in providing a service which can affect the health and well being of other people. The themes of the Code are firstly that the consumer has a right to be protected, secondly that members of the HCIMA must accept the social responsibilities implicit in their work, as well as their obligations to their employers, and thirdly members themselves have a right to protection on condition that they have worked to the appropriate professional standards.

A major involvement in education for the industry has been a priority pursued by the HCIMA since its inception. In the preliminary information on the new Professional Qualification agreed by the Council in December 1976 the HCIMA confirmed its intention to continue as an examining body until 1986. It also undertook to review this role in 1983 in the light of developments from the Technician Education Council and the Scottish Technical Education Council.

Grades of Membership

The HCIMA operates two classes of corporate membership and three classes of non-corporate membership. Full members are the main body of the HCIMA (8526 in November 1979) and have voting rights with the Fellows (1559 in November 1979).

There are two requirements for entry to full membership (MHCIMA). Firstly current tenure of a junior or first line management position and two years' experience at this level directly concerned with the provision of food and/or beverages or with the provision and servicing of accommodation. Secondly, successful completion of the HCIMA membership examinations or a recognised university or CNAA degree in hotel and catering studies or an HND in hotel and catering studies, or other exempt higher education qualifications.

Members can be elected to the senior grade of Fellow (FHCIMA) after ten years' full membership, or outstanding success in the profession, or on submission of an acceptable thesis, or have obtained a higher qualification.

Classes of non-corporate membership comprise licentiates, students and associates (numbers in November 1979: 3756, 6548 and 80 respectively). The licentiate grade (which entitles holders to the use of the designatory letters LHCIMA) includes two distinct categories: experienced managers whose careers are based on practical rather than academic foundations, and those who have successfully passed the membership examinations or an equivalent qualification but who have not yet had the required industrial experience for upgrading to corporate membership.

Age of entry for the first of these categories is 28, and applicants have to be in a position of executive responsibility within the industry. Relevant industrial and educational experience is assessed on a points system. To become a Licentiate member an applicant must score a minimum of 60 points of which 30 must be for experience (each year's experience scores one point; experience as a manager of one to five establishments, for example, would score an additional three points per annum). In order to upgrade to full membership, which applicants undertake to do within five years, it is necessary to score 100 points of which 40 must be for education (e.g. HCITB Instructor course scores five points, a single subject of the HCI/HCIMA Final Membership examination scores ten points).

Student membership is for those following recognised courses of study in hotel and catering subjects, for example an OND, HND, degree course, but not a craft course.

Associate membership is designed for professionals from other disciplines who are located in hotel, catering and institutional services and wish to maintain an attachment to the HCIMA. Associate members are eligible for up-grading to Fellowship after seven years.

Governing Structure

At the apex of the Association is the Council which usually meets three times a year and is ultimately responsible to members for the administration, direction and management of the affairs of the HCIMA. Council includes elected branch representatives, national representatives and, until 1980, six sectional representatives.

The Executive Committee, accountable to Council, is effectively the management committee. The Education and Development Committee, accountable to Executive, is concerned with education, careers and developing member's potential. The Board of Fellows is particularly concerned with safeguarding standards. It is accountable to Council for such matters as maintaining the standards of entry to membership, electing Members to Fellowship and advising Council on topics related to professional practice.

Joint Committees for National Diplomas in Hotel, Catering and Institutional Management

Valuable though the early work of the various examining bodies was in providing an incentive to continued study in elementary and craft subjects, there was until 1921 no comparable incentive in the higher, more professional grades of part-time education. In that year the Board of Education discussed with the Institution of Mechanical Engineers the possibility of a higher qualification approaching the standard of a degree for engineers (the standard of degrees was much lower than now, so also was the entry standard to such courses) through part-time study.

1921 is thus a notable date in the history and development of technical education for then the National Certificate scheme was launched first in mechanical engineering and then in chemistry in conjunction with the Institute of Chemistry. So well founded was it that this initial scheme has remained the essential model for all future ventures, and it was quickly extended to cover full-time schemes (Diploma courses) as well as part-time schemes (Certificate courses).

The Joint Committees have been a partnership of the relevant ministries of education for England and Wales as well as for Scotland and Northern Ireland, and the professional institutions concerned. The carrying out of these national schemes is in fact tripartite with the technical colleges as the third and far from sleeping partner.

The Joint Committees in Hotel, Catering and Institutional Management (two from 1971 — see Chapter 4) are responsible for: establishing the structure of courses, and appropriate entry qualifications; developing and approving schemes of work; maintaining standards of examination; reviewing the examination results, and awarding diplomas; approving colleges to offer the courses in consultation with the relevant education departments; and reviewing schemes.

The withdrawal of the Joint Committees will be synchronised with the introduction of TEC and SCOTEC awards from 1980.

Hotel and Catering Industry Training Board

Industrial training boards owe their origin to the Industrial Training Act, 1964. Each Board comprises representatives of employers, employees and education. Industrial training boards have now become the responsibility of the Training Services Agency, which in turn is part of the Manpower Services Commission (MSC) set up under the Employment and Training Act, 1973.

The Hotel and Catering Industry Training Board (HCITB) was established in 1966 and covers nearly all aspects of hotel and catering activity with some exceptions (e.g. government establishments, school meals and private clubs).

Under the Act, two main duties are laid down for an Industrial Training Board: it has to publish recommendations on the nature, content and length of training — including the associated further education — appropriate for occupations in its industry; and it must ensure that appropriate facilities are available for the training required. In addition it has a variety of powers enabling it to assess the standard of training, by arranging for the application of attainment and selection tests, and to undertake or assist in research, which may include research into the further education associated with training.

In addition to a grant from the MSC, the HCITB raises finance by a levy system calculated as a percentage of payroll. Having collected the levy, the Board then pays virtually all of it back to firms in the form of training grants, provided that their employees undertake training approved by the Board. A levy exemption system is operated for those firms who have reached certain standards of training, and also for those who have payrolls below a certain figure.

In the HCITB document "Five Year Plan 1979–85" the Board's specific policies and plans are outlined, including those which relate to catering education.

In the light of the influences the Board has perceived (and described in the Plan) its basic aim is "to assist the hotel and catering industry to develop and put into effect training and education relevant to, and effective for, its short and long term operations needs . . .".

In direct support of this overall intention, but within the constraints of the 1973 Employment and Training Act, the Board's specific aims include:

*to encourage companies to undertake, in consultation with their employees, sufficient training to meet their own needs, as well as those of the whole industry;

*to provide a training advisory service;

*to assist companies and the industry to plan their staffing needs and to monitor manpower trends in the industry as a whole;

*to identify changes in skills/knowledge requirements and potential shortages of key skills and to promote appropriate action;

*to contribute to the enhancement of the status of work in the hotel and catering industry, to help to attract people, particularly unemployed young people, into it;

*to conduct direct training, but only where there are needs which cannot be met elsewhere, and then progressively to a cost recovery basis.

In the Plan the Board also refers to its work in assisting the dialogue between education and industry to ensure that further educational plans do match the needs of the industry.

Since its inception the Board has provided incentives for the training of craft workers in the industry including grant aid. The scheme whereby Certificates are issued jointly with the City and Guilds of London Institute to trainees who have reached a prescribed standard of skills on the job as well as on their course has been described in Chapter 5 . The Board's work with other examining bodies has also been mentioned, and the important contribution it makes to the continuing development of individuals working at all levels in the industry has been described in Chapter 8.

Another important aspect of the Board's work has been the assistance it has given employers, colleges and students with the operation of industrial release training on sandwich courses. In 1978 it published a Code of Practice for industrial release.

Catering Teachers' Association

The Catering Teachers' Association (CTA) was formed in January 1960. It was felt that with the rapid development of catering education since the Second World War, the time had come for catering teachers to have an association of their own.

The Association has a number of aims. It seeks to foster and maintain good relationships amongst all who are engaged in teaching catering students, and between these teachers and the industry. Its members aim to help each other by the exchange of information and views. The CTA is in close liaison with other teachers' organisations. It is represented on advisory and syllabus committees of the different award-making bodies.

The CTA organises activities at a national level as well as at a regional level through its branches. These include meetings to discuss topical issues in catering education — new courses, revisions to existing courses, difficulties with existing courses; as well as seminars and conferences on topics of interest to CTA members, for example teaching techniques, industrial relations and educational visits.

The CTA publishes a newsletter regularly.

Regional Examining Bodies

These have two main aims: the object of providing standard examinations for the benefit of students attending classes in technical and other subjects within the institutions of the union's area, and otherwise to promote the objects of the institutions.

Each union is governed by a council representative of all interests, but it is in the Advisory Committees that the main work of the Union is done as a result of a real partnership between teachers from the constituent institutions, the HMIs, the Local Education Authorities' officers and the secretariat. Their work is primarily educational in the drafting of syllabuses and then, derivatively, in the assessing of examination papers. The examination scripts are marked by examiners largely drawn from the teaching staff of colleges and the results are moderated by an examinations committee.

The six Regional Examining Bodies offer examinations for operatives, craftsmen, and technicians within the terms of the revised agreement between them and the City and Guilds of London Institute concluded in 1966. They also offer examinations in commercial and other subjects as well as for some ordinary and higher national certificates. Each operates in its own territory, and all are associated with the CGLI Advisory Committees.

Where examinations in cookery corresponding to the City and Guilds of London Institute's Basic Cookery examinations are held by a Regional Examining Body, a local education authority in membership with the Regional Examining Body will normally arrange that its students will take the examinations of the Regional Body. The City and Guilds of London Institute will accept from such a local authority entries for the Basic Cookery examinations only upon the specific request of the Chief Education Officer concerned confirming that the Authority, having considered the matter, desire the candidates in question to take the examinations of the City and Guilds of London Institute.

The Institute will recognise success in the examinations of the Regional Examining Body as corresponding to success in the Institute's examination.

The six Regional Examining Bodies are:
— Northern Counties Technical Examinations Council
— Union of Educational Institutions
— Welsh Joint Education Committee

(none of which currently offer examinations in the catering field) and:
— East Midland Educational Union
— Yorkshire and Humberside Council for Further Education
— North Western Regional Advisory Council for Further Education incorporating the Union of Lancashire and Cheshire Institutes

whose courses in catering are described in Chapter 5.

Guild of Sommeliers

The Guild of Sommeliers is the craftsmen's Guild of Wine Butlers in the UK. It was set up at a meeting held in May 1953 at Vintners Hall in London, when representative wine butlers from important establishments were present. The initiative in calling the meeting had been taken by The Worshipful Company of Vintners, the Wine and Spirit Association of Great Britain and the then British Hotel and Restaurants Association.

The primary object of the Guild is to promote a wider interest in the knowledge of and the proper service of wine, and to improve the professional status of the sommelier in his craft. To this end the educational activities of the Guild are important (see Chapter 5).

There are four grades of membership of the Guild:
> *Full Member,* Class A, who must have had three years' recent experience as a sommelier and be actively engaged in his profession at the time of application. A Full Member is entitled to all the privileges of membership including election to the Council.
> *Class B Member,* one who has had less than three years' recent experience as a sommelier, or one who is directly concerned with an hotel or restaurant business or industrial catering and the service of wine therein, but is not actually serving as a full-time wine butler.
> *Associate Member,* for those engaged in the hotel and restaurant trade, the wine and spirit trade or allied trades.
> *Junior/Student* Membership for apprenticeship or learners engaged in the hotel or restaurant trade and serving wine therein.

The governing body of the Guild is the Council which is composed of eighteen elected Councillors (all Full A Members). Branches have been established throughout Great Britain, as well as in the United States of America and Malta. The Guild produces a monthly journal called the *Wine Butler*. This deals with all matters of interest to sommeliers including summaries of the lectures and reports on tastings held by the Guild's branches.

The Society of Bacchus is affiliated to the Guild. The Court of Master

Sommeliers is a body of master sommeliers within the Guild of which all master sommeliers automatically become members after gaining the Master Sommelier Diploma.

The Brewers' Society

Founded at the beginning of the twentieth century, the Brewers' Society has three classes of members: Full Members, Associate Members and Honorary Members. The subscription for Full Members is based upon the number of bulk barrels brewed during the immediately preceding financial year of the Society, or if the member is not brewing the subscription attributable to a notional 500 bulk barrels.

The Council of the Society includes representatives of the majority of the companies which belong to it. The Executive Committee includes nominees of the seven large brewery groups, as well as elected members of the Council, Members of Parliament, and a number of co-options.

The Chairman and Vice-Chairman of the Society are ex-officio members of all the committees. The Annual Report for the Society for the year ended September 1978 describes recent work of these committees, which included discussions between the Survey Committee and Government Ministers on the tied house system; the undertaking of regular statistical exercises by the Statistics Advisory Group; monitoring of wage claims, negotiations and settlements of member companies by the Employment Committee; substantial grants were made to the Medical Council on Alcoholism, the National Council on Alcoholism, the Scottish Council on Alcoholism; the Management and Hotels Committee maintained the closest liaison with the BHRCA, so that it was possible for both organisations to support the views of the other during consultation with various Government departments.

Circulars are regularly issued from the Society to members on matters of interest and concern, as well as on proposed and new legislation affecting them.

The training courses run by the Society's organisations are described in Chapter 5, and in greater detail in Chapter 8. A handbook for catering in public houses entitled *Pub Catering Operations* was recently issued through another of the Society's subsidiaries, Brewing Publications Ltd.

Local Government Training Board

The Local Government Training Board was established in 1967 by the local authority associations and the Greater London Council in co-operation with the employers' and trade union sides of the national negotiating machinery. The provisions of the 1964 Industrial Training Act, which created the statutory industrial training boards, did not embrace local government totally although some groups of authority employees were regarded as being within the scope of the industrial training boards.

The Local Government Training Board's terms of reference cover all local government occupational groups in England and Wales except teachers, uniformed police and fire employees and small numbers of staff within scope of statutory boards.

The principal aim of the Board is to increase the efficiency of local government by ensuring that sufficient training of the right quality is given to staff and employees of local authorities at all levels. The activities of the LGTB in this area are described in Chapter 8.

Wine and Spirit Education Trust

The Wine and Spirit Education Trust is an examining body, registered as a charity and approved by the Department of Education and Science. The Trust's courses are described in Chapter 5.

National Council for Home Economics Education

The National Council for Home Economics Education is an examining body. A number of the Council's courses are described in Chapter 5. Of these the Certificate in Home Economics, the Diploma in Home Economics, and the Housekeeping and Catering Certificate are recognised by the *Electrical Association for Women* for candidates entering the Association's examination for its Certificate for Demonstrators and Teachers.

Those holding a degree or diploma resulting from a minimum three years' full-time recognised course in home economics or allied subject and one year full-time employment in the field of home economics or a related area are eligible for membership of the *Association of Home Economists Ltd,* and to use the designatory letters MAHE. This grade of membership is also open to those holding a certificate resulting from a minimum two years' recognised course plus three years' appropriate experience. Fellowship of the Association (FAHE) may be offered to members by the Council of Management as recognition that they have made a substantial contribution to the Association and have, in addition, at least ten years' appropriate professional experience and a minimum of five years' continuous membership of the Association.

Royal Society of Health

The Royal Society of Health was founded in 1876 to promote the health of the people. It has been an examining body (see page 99) since 1877. There are three grades of membership in addition to the Affiliate grade mentioned in Chapter 5: Associate (AMRSH), Member (MRSH), and Fellow (FRSH). The Affiliate grade is for persons interested in promoting the objectives of the Society, but not qualified for Membership or Associateship or necessarily holding senior positions.

Royal Institute of Public Health and Hygiene

The educational courses of the Royal Institute of Public Health and Hygiene (incorporated in 1929) have been described in Chapter 5. Successful candidates in the Diploma examination in Food Hygiene are eligible, together with those with other recognised diplomas and university degrees, for membership of the Institute (MRIPHH). Fellowship of the Institute is normally restricted to registered medical practitioners. The Associate grade (no new entrants to this grade are entitled to use designatory letters) is open to persons not less than 18 years of age who have passed an examination for a certificate of the Institute or an equivalent qualification.

Council for National Academic Awards

The Council for National Academic Awards (CNAA) is the largest single degree awarding body in the United Kingdom and about one-third of all students who are studying for a degree in the UK attend CNAA courses. By 1979 more than 120 institutions of higher education were offering more than 1500 separate courses leading to awards of the Council and the number of students registered on these courses totalled nearly 120 000.

The CNAA was established by Royal Charter in 1964 as the main degree awarding body in the UK to serve the non-university sector of higher education. The object of the Council, as detailed in its Charter, is the advancement of education, learning, knowledge and the arts by means of the grant of academic awards and distinctions . . . within the United Kingdom.

It is important to appreciate that the CNAA confers awards on students who complete approved courses, but these courses are not designed or run by the CNAA. Rather they are the college's courses (and the Council's awards). The Council has no teaching staff of its own, it prescribes no particular curriculum, it conducts no examinations itself and it has very little direct contact with any of the students registered on its courses. Thus it cannot be likened to the Open University and, although it has largely replaced the University of London external system, it does not operate in the same manner, nor does it offer courses by correspondence.

The activities of the CNAA consist of:
— vetting whole institutions as suitable to offer any courses leading to CNAA awards;
— considering and, if appropriate, approving specific course proposals from particular colleges;
— registration of students on courses once approved;
— approval of assessment arrangements and of External Examiners;
— conferment of awards on students, on the recommendation of Boards of Examiners established in colleges;
— approving applications for renewal of approval of whole institutions and of individual courses after, usually, five years;
— registration of candidates for research degrees and conferment of higher doctorates and honorary degrees;
— determining policies within the Charter and Statutes;
— determining the appropriate structure of Committees to undertake its work and their composition, within the Charter and Statutes.

The Statutes make the Council responsible for "ensuring that the Degrees, Diplomas, Certificates and other academic awards and distinctions granted and conferred by the Council . . . are comparable in standards to awards granted and conferred by Universities." These awards include the Council's Certificate, the Diploma of Higher Education, Degrees, Honours Degrees, Diplomas in Professional Studies, the Postgraduate Certificate in Education, Postgraduate

Diplomas, taught Masters degree courses and research degrees (MPhil and PhD). Modes of study cover full-time, sandwich, part-time and mixed mode.

In Chapter 7 further information has been given on these awards, with an account of their role in catering education.

Structure

The supreme body is the Council — about thirty members appointed every three years by the Secretary of State for Education and Science and the Secretary of State for Scotland. Then there are Committees: Science and Technology, Arts and Social Studies, Business and Management Studies, Education, Art and Design, Research, Academic Policy, Institutions, Scotland. The seventy or so Subject Boards fall under the first five of these committees. Thus the Committee for Science and Technology has twenty-six Subject Boards which are periodically reconstituted and now annually have a review of membership. One of these Boards, first established in 1975, is the Food, Accommodation and Related Sciences Board. It consists, like the others, of about thirty members, intended to be roughly half from non-university colleges offering CNAA courses, a quarter from universities and a quarter from industry. The work covered by this Board includes catering studies, hotel and catering administration, institutional management, home economics, nutrition, dietetics, and food science. Altogether the Council has the services of about 1500 members.

Technician Education Council

The Technician Education Council (TEC) was established by the Secretary of State for Education and Science in March 1973 to be responsible for "the development of policies for schemes of technical education for persons at all levels of technician occupation in industry and elsewhere" in England, Wales and Northern Ireland. The creation of TEC had been recommended in 1969 in the Report of the Committee on Technician Courses and Examinations (the Haslegrave Report), which had also recommended the establishment of a Business Education Council (BEC) for equivalent personnel in commercial and allied fields.

The Council's tasks can be summarised as:

(a) To plan, administer and keep under review the development of a unified national system of courses for technicians. The aim will be to create a more rational, flexible and simplified range of technician courses than the present one, eliminating as far as possible unnecessary duplication of provision, without reducing the opportunities available to students and the extent to which the industry's needs are satisfied.

(b) To approve or devise programmes of study leading to its awards. As part of its service, TEC will publish standard units and programmes and provide arrangements for external assessment where these are required, but there will be full opportunity for colleges to devise and submit for approval programmes which meet the specific needs of their students and of industry, within the Council's guidelines.

(c) To initiate and encourage innovation in new areas of study (in particular to meet the changing needs of industry), in the learning situation and in assessment.

(d) To establish and control standards of performance.

(e) To confer awards on successful students. The Council makes the following awards: Certificate and Diploma, Higher Certificate and Higher Diploma.

(f) To collaborate with the Business Education Council, and other bodies in the field of technician education, in matters of common interest.

The main executive agencies of the Council are its Programme Committees. Programme Committee C4 has been appointed to be responsible for programmes in Hotel, Catering and Institutional Management, Food Technology and Cleaning Science, and has members drawn from industry, education and bodies such as the HCITB and HCIMA.

Fundamental to TEC's policies is the intention to involve colleges in all aspects of its activities, from the construction of programmes of study to the assessment of students. Colleges which prefer to do so will be able to opt for the TEC model programmes that are published in the programme guidelines or to adapt them for local use in accordance with arrangements agreed by the appropriate Programme Committee.

A Policy Statement was published in June 1974, since when a number of circulars have been issued, giving details of the phasing in of TEC Awards and guidance on policies, procedures and related matters.

Under TEC's timetable it is intended that programmes in Hotel, Catering and Institutional Management will be available from September 1980 onwards (see Chapters 4 and 6).

Scottish Technical Education Council

Scotland has developed a distinctive pattern of organisation in the field of further education, adapted to the country's industrial needs and educational resources.

In 1971 the report of a committee, under the chairmanship of Sir Edmund Hudson, appointed by the Scottish Technical Education Consultative Council, found that "the whole system of courses for technicians has become too complex and diffuse". It proposed that "the most effective way to achieve a rational and co-ordinated pattern is for responsibility for all technician courses and examinations in the technical sector in Scotland to be vested in one single policy-making organisation".

The report was welcomed by the Secretary of State for Scotland and on 1 June 1973 the Scottish Technical Education Council (SCOTEC) was established. The Council's objects include the following:

(a) to devise, prepare, organise, develop and review technician courses with respect to the technical and related sectors of employment, to join, if it thinks fit, with other bodies in providing such courses, and to investigate and consider and, if it should see fit, to give approval to such courses where devised or provided by other bodies;

(b) to take over and administer with or without modifications the courses and work carried out by the Scottish Association for National Certificates and

Diplomas and the courses and other work relating to Scotland carried out by the existing Scottish and UK Joint Committees for National Certificates and Diplomas;

(c)   to investigate, experiment with, develop and operate suitable methods of assessing standards of attainment and to undertake or commission practical research and development work relative to the general functions of the Council;

(d)   to arrange for the conduct of examinations and charge such fees in respect of the same as may be determined by the Council after consultation with the local authorities concerned;

(e)   to assess student attainment and award certificates and confer distinctions, including diplomas and other qualifications to persons regarded by the Council as having successfully completed technician level courses.

The responsibility for the development of courses is delegated to six Sector Committees each responsible for a group of disciplines. The functions of each Sector Committee with regard to the courses under its jurisdiction include:

— appointment of Course Committees to undertake the planning of courses in particular disciplines;

— approval of courses, entrance qualifications, methods of assessment and conditions of award.

In establishing the Sector and Course Committees the Council has considered carefully the appropriate balance of industrial and educational interests; as well as appointing individual members of Committees the Council has invited a wide range of organisations to nominate people to serve on the Committees.

Course Committee E4 has responsibility for developing courses in the entire field of Hotel, Catering and Institutional Management. The membership of this Committee is widely representative of both industry and education and includes a number of HCIMA nominees.

The new SCOTEC Diploma and Higher Diploma courses in Hotel, Catering and Institutional Operations/Management commence in autumn 1980, see Chapters 4 and 6. The Certificate Course in Supervision of Catering and Accommodation Services commenced in autumn 1977 (see Chapter 5).

The Council has prepared a number of statements on educational policy for the guidance of the Sector and Course Committees. In addition it has published a number of news sheets so that its plans and activities may be widely known.

National Examinations Board for Supervisory Studies

The National Examinations Board for Supervisory Studies (NEBBS) was established in June 1964 on the initiative of the Department of Education and Science, supported by all the major organisations concerned with supervisory education and training. It was charged with the task of providing examinations and national qualifications in the field of foremanship and supervisory studies. The Board is an independent autonomous body administered by the City and Guilds of London Institute.

The Board has laid down that its objectives are to stimulate and coordinate the provision of suitable courses for supervisors at all levels over the whole range of industry, trade and commerce and, by the provision and control of nationally accepted examination standards, to establish a general recognition of the cardinal need for supervisors to be properly qualified to enable them to discharge their responsibilities with maximum effectiveness.

The purposes of a national scheme of training and education for supervisors are seen as:

— to impart a sound knowledge of the principles of supervision;
— to help potential supervisors and supervisors to get the feel of applying these principles in practice.

To meet these requirements and to achieve its objectives, the Board has established a flexible structure which will assist the development of local initiative by encouraging technical colleges and industrial or commercial organisations to co-operate in devising suitable courses and examinations to meet specific needs whilst, at the same time, establishing and maintaining national standards in supervisory studies.

These courses, which are at Introductory, Certificate, or Diploma level in Supervisory Studies, have internally set and externally assessed examinations. They are fully described in Chapter 5.

Business Education Council

The establishment of the Business Education Council (BEC) in May 1974 fulfilled a recommendation of the Haslegrave Committee. BEC's role is to plan, administer and keep under review the establishment of a unified national system of non-degree courses for people whose occupations fall within the broad area of business and public administration.

To fulfil this role, BEC will devise or approve suitable courses, establish and assess standards of performance and award certificates and diplomas to students meeting these requirements.

The courses leading to BEC awards are designed to provide rungs on the ladder for those who are aiming at professional qualifications, and to provide knowledge and skills for those planning careers in business or public administration.

Scottish Business Education Council

The Scottish Business Education Council (SCOTBEC) like its sister body SCOTEC was formally established by the Secretary of State in June 1973. SCOTBEC was, in practice, substantially a continuation of the previous Scottish Council for Commercial, Administrative and Professional Education, SCCAPE.

The Hudson Committee recommended no fundamental changes either in the remit or in the centralised examining powers of the Council during the transition from SCCAPE to SCOTBEC. SCOTBEC's responsibilities include the consideration of the need for new courses, the drafting of course schemes and subject syllabuses, the preparation of examination papers (the vast majority of examinations in SCOTBEC-sponsored courses are centralised), the marking of examination papers and the award of Certificates and Diplomas in the business, administration and commerce sectors of Scottish further education.

The Council's courses in Hotel Reception are described in Chapter 5.

College Caterers' Association

The College Caterers' Association was formed in 1968 to "form a bond between college caterers throughout the UK and through this bond to promote the advancement of catering in Colleges of Education, to bring about a better understanding of the problems involved in dealing with young people, staff and administration and to help solve the problems with which Catering Officers themselves are so often faced".

The Association, which works closely with the Department of Education and Science, has organised regular conferences. The theme of the two day 1979 conference was "Student, Staff and Caterer Motivation".

Membership of the Association is open to domestic bursars, caterers and their senior assistants in all colleges, not just colleges of education.

Association of Domestic Management

The Association of Domestic Management (ADM) was formed in June 1975, taking over the assets and liabilities of the Hospital Domestic Administrators Association. The aims of the Association are:

"To do all within its powers to supply, maintain and encourage an efficient domestic service to support the medical, nursing and allied services throughout the National Health Service in their work for the healing and comfort of the sick, to provide and maintain a national code of practice to complement professional and occupational training, to take all such action as may be deemed necessary or expedient to improve standards of training amongst domestic staff within the National Health Service, Department of Health and Social Security and comparable Government service and Local Authority service and to promote co-operation by the interchange of knowledge."

The Association is the professional body for those employed in domestic services management in those services outlined in the aims, throughout the UK.

The classes of membership and designatory letters are as follows:

Licentiate (LADM), a non-corporate grade open to those holding supervisory, management and advisory grades without an approved qualification.

Student, a non-corporate grade for those following a course of study leading to an approved certificate, diploma or degree.

Associate (AADM), a corporate grade for those who have successfully completed an approved course of study (and until 1980 those who have had at least two years' managerial experience in domestic services management have been admitted to this grade).

Full members (MADM), corporate grade open to Associate members of two years' standing.

Fellow (FADM), nominated full members upon election by the Council of Management (the senior governing committee) after five years' continuous full membership and service to the Association. There is also an Honorary

Fellowship grade, for nominated non-members at the discretion of the Council.

Finally, there is a non-corporate grade of membership, *Retired,* for those previously holding one of the grades of membership, except Student, who have temporarily or permanently retired.

There are four committees reporting to the Council of Management: General Purposes and Finance, Education and Conference, Recruitment and Publicity, Management and Technical Standards.

Branches of the Association are established in Scotland, Wales, Northern Ireland and the fourteen Health regions in England.

The Tourism Society

The Tourism Society was established in 1977 to meet the needs of those employed in the tourism industry for a professional body. It is a multi-sectoral organisation concerned with the whole of tourism and with the career interests of professionals in it.

The Society's main objectives are to promote a wider understanding of the economic and social significance of tourism; to enhance the standards of professional competence of those engaged in tourism; to encourage just and honourable conduct in the practice of members' occupations, to promote an understanding and recognition of the Society by employers in tourism, and the value of the membership qualification; to promote research, scholarship, education and training in tourism; to facilitate exchange of information and ideas about tourism.

The Society is specifically intended for individuals with an involvement in tourism — in national, regional and local tourist organisations, central and local government, accommodation and catering, passenger transportation, travel agencies, tour operators, in all the many organisations providing facilities and services for tourism — as well as those engaged in consultancy, market research, public relations, journalism, education and training with an interest in tourism.

The Society's activities include the organisation of conferences, meetings and seminars as well as social functions. A bi-monthly Bulletin is published, as well as a members' handbook and important lectures. Initial funding of the Society's activities has been greatly assisted by a number of sponsoring organisations, including various hotel and catering companies.

Membership is only offered to individuals. There are three corporate grades with designatory letters: Honorary Fellow (FTS), Fellow (FTS), and Member (MTS). The detailed criteria for the different grades include current responsibilities, experience in tourism, age, professional and educational qualifications. There are two non-corporate grades of membership: Associate (AMTS) and Student.

Association of Marine Catering
Superintendents

In March 1965, the inaugural meeting of representatives of the shipping companies took place at the offices of the Shipping Federation (now the General

Council of British Shipping), and the Association of Marine Catering Superintendents (AMCS) was formed.

At that time shipowning companies had great fleets, including large passenger liners, conventional cargo liners and tankers. Many of the aims and problems of shipboard catering — purchasing, manning, personnel relations, training — were common to all those employed in the pursers and catering side of the industry and it became obvious that there was a genuine need for closer collaboration.

The objects of the Association were defined as follows:

(a)   to provide and improve efficiency within the industry by pooling members' knowledge and experience;

(b)   to hold meetings and discussion groups to achieve this end;

(c)   to encourage the raising of standards within economic limits;

(d)   to uphold and increase the status of the catering department within the industry;

(e)   to liaise with other interested associations;

(f)   to arrange practical demonstrations of new equipment and ideas from both inside and outside the industry;

(g)   to promote and encourage professional and craft training schemes.

Since 1965 the shipping industry has become much reduced in size, but with new breeds of sophisticated vessels coming into being and with these modern ships employing smaller crews, the Association regards it as even more important to continue to do all it can to uplift standards and places even greater emphasis on education and training to attract the right kind of people into the industry.

The AMCS has made a considerable contribution to the shipping industry, and continues to do so through the involvement of its members: as chairman and members of the Board of Governors of the Nautical Catering College in Liverpool, an involvement that will continue now that this college has merged with the Colquitt Technical College; as visiting lecturers; as moderators for the Merchant Navy Training Board on examinations for the Catering Officers Certificate Course (a Course Certificate is mandatory within the industry; AMCS was largely responsible for having it introduced); as members of various committees including those of the General Council of British Shipping, the Merchant Navy Training Board, the Technician Education Council, the Cookery and Food Association. In terms of numbers of members, the Association is not large and this is in line with its original intention to remain an executive association, with membership restricted to those of "superintendent status" only. (Job titles in the shipping industry vary considerably.) The present membership is about 115.

Industrial Catering Association

The Industrial Catering Association (ICA) was formed in 1937 with the object of bringing together catering managers concerned with industrial, institutional, municipal, welfare and staff catering services in the UK.

The Association has four principal aims: to enhance professional status, to promote knowledge, to define and uphold standards, to maintain a code of conduct for members.

The Association holds a conference each year: the theme of the 1979 conference was "Today's Challenge, Tomorrow's Opportunities". Regular seminars and meetings are held on a national basis, and by the branches, which number over twenty. Exhibitions are also held from time to time; the four day Food Services Exhibition in 1979 was staged at the Grosvenor House in London. The Association publishes a bi-monthly Bulletin, and, on an annual basis, both a buyers' guide and a survey on wages and food costs. An information service is available to members.

Full membership (designatory letters MICA) is open to all persons holding a managerial position in industrial, institutional, municipal, welfare and staff catering with either an approved qualification and one years' managerial experience in catering, or three years' managerial experience.

Associate Membership (AMICA) is open to caterers of supervisor status who do not qualify as full members. Student membership is open to trainees and students taking approved courses in catering management.

The most senior grade of membership is Fellow (FICA), open to a full member of five years' standing in a managerial position who has been in membership of the ICA for not less than ten years. A minimum of two years' service as an executive officer of the Association is also required.

There are two grades of affiliated membership — for companies and for individuals. The former is offered to equipment and supplies firms to the catering trade; admission decisions to this grade are made by the National Council, the senior committee. Individual affiliated membership is open to lecturers of students in catering subjects at approved colleges, or to individual persons engaged in the catering supply trades approved by the Management Committee.

In addition to the National Council and Management Committee the ICA has a number of special purpose committees, including Equipment and Supplies, Finance, Standing Orders, Education and Training.

Civic Catering Association

The Civic Catering Association (CCA) is an association of local authorities who provide and operate their own catering facilities in the various spheres of local authority activity, for example recreation and sports centres, theatres, parks, town halls, "Meals on Wheels" services, day centres.

The Association was formed in 1962 and in August 1979 had over ninety member authorities, including many of the London boroughs, plus a number of individual members.

The objects of the Association are to provide an organisation for consultation and co-operation between local authorities operating catering services, to take such action as may be necessary or advisable to develop and promote the mutual interests of these authorities; and to provide means of dissemination of information between its member authorities. The Association will, if required, carry out a survey for a member and supply a detailed report.

Each member authority appoints two representatives to the Association: one of these must be an elected member of the authority, the other an officer or person responsible for managing the catering services.

The Association holds at least two meetings or conferences each year at which members can meet and discuss their individual problems with colleagues from other authorities, as well as hear the advice of experts on specialist topics of interest.

The Catering Managers' Association of Great Britain and Northern Ireland

The Catering Managers' Association of Great Britain and Northern Ireland (CMA) was formed in 1947. It is an organisation of caterers holding managerial status in the catering trade, principally industrial catering, hotels and restaurants, college catering, government and the School Meals Service.

The CMA sets out to further the standards of good catering and hygiene, to maintain and further good relations between its members and trade suppliers, and to deal with all matters affecting the interests of its members. Other objects and aims of the Association are to promote, support or oppose legislation and other measures affecting members. Students and organised bodies are encouraged in competition by the award of scholarships, trophies, and monetary grants.

The different branch committees are responsible for arranging their own programme of events: these include demonstrations and lectures, regular meetings to discuss matters of common interest affecting the industry, and social activities.

Full membership of the Association is open to any person who holds a responsible managerial position in the catering industry, or whose qualifications are acceptable to the Council (the senior members' committee).

Student membership is open to any person undergoing an approved course of study for the industry. Honorary membership is awarded at the discretion of the Council.

Affiliated membership is open to any person or company engaged in the manufacture or supply of catering equipment, or commodities used in the catering industry, any person interested in the work of the Association, and colleges offering catering courses.

Food and Beverage Managers' Association

The Food and Beverage Managers' Association (FBMA) has three principal aims:
— to promote and develop the professionalism, effectiveness and standing of those involved in food and beverage operations within the hotel and catering industry;
— to aid, by the exchange of ideas and research results at meetings and seminars, the improvement of standards of the food and beverage product and operation;
— to foster and maintain friendly relationships and co-operation between members.

Full membership of the Association is available to all salaried management involved in or responsible for the food and beverage function on a full-time basis in the hotel and catering industry. Associate Membership is available to executive management who are deemed capable of contributing to the Association's aims. Honorary membership is available only at the discretion and invitation of the Executive Committee (the main governing committee).

British Association of Hotel Accountants

The British Association of Hotel Accountants (BAHA) was formed in 1969 as it was felt that there was a need for hotel accountants to have the opportunity to liaise more closely with each other, and with other professional and trade bodies. The aims of the Association also include: the advancement of the status, prestige and professional competence of hotel accountants, to aid and encourage the education and development of accounting personnel within the hotel industry, the support of educational projects in the hotel field and the encouragement of uniformity in British hotel accounting.

At the regular meetings of the Association (normally one a month) a wide variety of topics are discussed. There may be a predominant theme running through the year, or each meeting may be on a separate subject of interest, for example hotel crime, taxation, data processing and hotel credit. Newsletters and bulletins are sent to members on topics of special interest.

Membership of BAHA is open to hotel accountants and financial controllers (or similar) at either hotel or company level, together with members of the accountancy profession with particular interest in the hotel and catering industry. Membership is also available to certain other bodies connected with the industry and to certain colleges.

Hotel Industry Marketing Group

The Hotel Industry Marketing Group (HIMG) is a specialised group of the Institute of Marketing providing a forum for the interchange of ideas and information about hotel marketing.

One of the most important objectives of the Group is to inform and educate. Monthly business meetings are held with prominent speakers on relevant and current topics dealing with industry; established annual events include a one day seminar, and the advertising and publicity awards jointly sponsored by HIMG and the *Caterer and Hotelkeeper*, for the purpose of improving standards of marketing, advertising and publicity and updating the image of the industry. The Institute's journal *Marketing* is mailed monthly to members.

Those involved in marketing management at all levels may apply for membership of the Institute of Marketing and on entry be attached to the HIMG. Such members enjoy the use of the services provided by the Institute, which include courses, seminars, a lending and reference library and an information service.

Alternatively there is affiliate membership open to those persons involved in hotel marketing not wishing to join the Institute, or those involved in management in the industry but not necessarily in the marketing area. Affiliate members are entitled to participate in the Group's activities but not to the facilities and services available from the Institute.

There are three branches of the HIMG, based in London, Scotland and Northern England.

British Motels Federation Limited

The objects of the British Motels Federation Limited (BMF) are to promote, encourage and assist motel proprietors in improving the services and facilities available for the general public. It considers all questions affecting the interests of proprietors and their customers and issues recommended standards of accommodation and service for its members.

The Federation publishes a free Guide Map which indicates the price and facilities offered by member motels.

Membership of the Federation is open to the proprietor or manager of any motel, motor hotel, motor inn, motor lodge or similarly named residential establishment which caters particularly for the motorist in the UK. The subscription is based on the number of letting rooms of the motel. It is a condition of membership that all motels or similar establishments owned, controlled or managed by members shall comply with the minimum standards of accommodation and services determined by the Federation.

There is also an Associate grade of membership for those persons or organisations not qualifying for the main grade, who, in the opinion of the Council of Management (the governing committee), it is desirable to admit to membership.

The schedule of minimum requirements for full membership of the Federation is very detailed, covering the standard of public areas, guest accommodation, the services and facilities.

The British Federation of Hotel, Guest House and Self-catering Associations

The Federation was formed in 1916 primarily to take care of the very small family-run hotels and guest houses. When self-catering holidays became more popular, many of the Federation's members converted their hotels and guest houses into holiday flat/flatlets, hence the change of name to the present title (formerly the British Federation of Hotels and Guest House Associations). The Federation includes a number of resort associations within its membership, and extensive individual membership drawn from all parts of the country.

The Federation represents its members on several national committees including the British Tourist Authority Development and Hotels and Restaurants Committee. The Federation offers assistance and advice to its members, and has its own hoteliers insurance scheme and central purchasing authority.

National Union of Licensed Victuallers

The National Union of Licensed Victuallers was founded in 1975 to do all things necessary to protect and enhance the welfare of licensees of public houses so far as it applies to the lawful conduct of their businesses. Its objects also include: to watch over the legitimate interests of the licensed trade in the legislature and to fight all unreasonable exactions and restrictions; to advise members on all matters affecting their businesses and to act on their behalf when invited to do so.

The Union is a trade organisation. Membership is open to tenants and lessees of brewery owned public houses; owners and lessees of free houses; and directors of companies which are tenants, lessees or owners within the first two categories. Its membership comprises all such persons who are members of affiliated licensed victuallers associations or societies, regional tenant stream chairmen, and individual members who have businesses in areas where there is no affiliated association or society. Membership is restricted to bona fide holders of Justices' full on-licences for the retail sale of alcoholic liquor. The National Council, the senior committee, has the power to admit as probationary members persons proposing to enter the licensed trade as owners' lessees or tenants of public houses.

The Union is organised into six regions covering England and Wales each with a Regional Council, Executive Committee and Officers. Reporting to the National Council, which is elected biennially by the Regional Councils, is the National Executive Committee responsible for the day to day running of the Union. Various sub-committees report to the Executive Committee.

Useful Addresses

ASSOCIATION OF DOMESTIC MANAGEMENT. Mailing address: Mr Robert Morgan, Organising Secretary, 22 Larch Walk, Kennington, Ashford, Kent

ASSOCIATION OF MARINE CATERING SUPERINTENDENTS, Mailing address: 30/32 St Mary Axe, London EC3A 8ET

BRITISH ASSOCIATION OF HOTEL ACCOUNTANTS, Mailing address: Horwath and Horwath (UK) Ltd, 84 Baker Street, London W1M 1DL

BRITISH HOTELS RESTAURANTS AND CATERERS ASSOCIATION, 13 Cork Street, London W1X 2BH (Tel 01-499 6641)

BRITISH MOTELS FEDERATION LIMITED, 10 Bolton Street, Piccadilly, London W1Y 8AU (Tel 01-499 8000)

BUSINESS EDUCATION COUNCIL, 168–73 High Holborn, London WC1V 7AG (Tel 01-379 7088)

CATERING MANAGERS ASSOCIATION, 31 Sycamore Avenue, Wickersley, Rotherham S66 0NW (Tel 0742 440381)

CATERING TEACHERS ASSOCIATION, Mailing address: Bolton Technical College, Manchester Road, Bolton BL2 1ER

CITY AND GUILDS OF LONDON INSTITUTE, 76 Portland Place, London W1N 4AA (Tel 01-580 3050)

CIVIC CATERING ASSOCIATION, 3 Cornfield Terrace, Eastbourne BN21 4NA (Tel 0323 27474)

COLLEGE CATERERS' ASSOCIATION, Mailing address: c/o Mr Stuart Vass, The College of Ripon and York St John, Lord Mayor's Walk, York YO3 7EX

COOKERY AND FOOD ASSOCIATION, 1 Victoria Parade, 331 Sandycombe Road, Richmond, Surrey TW9 3NB (Tel 01-948 3870)

COUNCIL FOR NATIONAL ACADEMIC AWARDS, 344-354 Gray's Inn Road, London WC1X 8BP (Tel 01-278 4411)

FOOD AND BEVERAGE MANAGERS' ASSOCIATION, Mailing address: Mr I. A. M. Harkness, Chairman FBMA, Crest Hotels, Bridge Street, Banbury, Oxon OX16 8RQ

GUILD OF SOMMELIERS, Five Kings House, Kennet Wharf Lane, Upper Thames Street, London EC4V 3BA (Tel 01-236 4610)

HOTEL AND CATERING INDUSTRY TRAINING BOARD, P O Box 18, Ramsey House, Central Square, Wembley, Middlesex HA9 7AP (Tel 01-902 8865)

HOTEL, CATERING AND INSTITUTIONAL MANAGEMENT ASSOCIA-
TION, 191 Trinity Road, London SW17 7HN (Tel 01-672 4251)
HOTEL INDUSTRY MARKETING GROUP, Institute of Marketing, Moor
Hall, Cookham, Berkshire S16 9QH (Tel 062 85 24922)
INDUSTRIAL CATERING ASSOCIATION, 1 Victoria Parade, 331
Sandycombe Road, Richmond TW9 3NB (Tel 01-940 4464)
JOINT COMMITTEE FOR NATIONAL DIPLOMAS IN HOTEL
CATERING AND INSTITUTIONAL MANAGEMENT:

England, Wales and Northern Ireland: 46 Britannia Street, London WC1X
9RG (Tel 01-278 2468)
Scotland: Scottish Technical Education Council, 38 Queen Street, Glasgow
G1 3DY (Tel 041-204 2271)

LOCAL GOVERNMENT TRAINING BOARD, 8 The Arndale Centre, Luton
LU1 2TS (Tel 0582 21111)
NATIONAL COUNCIL FOR HOME ECONOMICS EDUCATION, 214
Middle Lane, Hornsey, London N8 7LB (Tel 01-340 4823)
NATIONAL EXAMINATIONS BOARD FOR SUPERVISORY STUDIES,
76 Portland Place, London W1N 4AA (Tel 01-580 3050)
NATIONAL UNION OF LICENSED VICTUALLERS, Boardman House, 2
Downing Street, Farnham, Surrey GU9 7NX (Tel 0252 714448)
REGIONAL EXAMINING BODIES — see Chapter 5 and for addresses of those
offering catering courses page 104. The REBs who do not currently offer such
courses are:

The Northern Counties Technical Examinations Council, 5 Grosvenor
Villas, Newcastle upon Tyne NE2 2RU (Tel 0632 813242)
Welsh Joint Education Committee, 245 Western Avenue, Cardiff CF5 2YX
(Tel 0222 561231)
West Midlands Advisory Council (incorporating the Union of Education
Institutions), Norfolk House, Smallbrook Queensway, Birmingham B5 4NB
(Tel 021-643 8924)

ROYAL INSTITUTE OF PUBLIC HEALTH AND HYGIENE, 28 Portland
Place, London W1N 4DE (Tel 01-580 2731)
ROYAL SOCIETY OF HEALTH, 13 Grosvenor Place, London SW1X 7EN
(Tel 01-235 9961)
SCOTTISH BUSINESS EDUCATION COUNCIL, 22 Great King Street,
Edinburgh RH3 6QH (Tel 031-556 4691)
SCOTTISH TECHNICAL EDUCATION COUNCIL, 38 Queen Street,
Glasgow G1 3DY (Tel 041-204 2271)
TECHNICIAN EDUCATION COUNCIL, 76 Portland Place, London W1N
4AA (Tel 01-580 3050)
THE BRITISH FEDERATION OF HOTEL, GUEST HOUSE AND SELF-
CATERING ASSOCIATIONS, Abingdon Chambers, 23 Abingdon Street,
Blackpool (Tel 0253 24241)
THE TOURISM SOCIETY, 26 Grosvenor Gardens, London SW1W 0DU (Tel
01-730 4380)
WINE AND SPIRIT EDUCATION TRUST LTD, Five Kings House, Kennet
Wharf Lane, Upper Thames Street, London EC4V 3AJ (Tel 01-236 3551/2)

Index